A Loving Deception

A Loving Deception

EUGENE COGHILL

Copyright © Eugene Coghill.

All rights reserved. No part of this book may be reproduced in any form or by any electronic or mechanical means, including information storage and retrieval systems, without permission in writing from the publisher, except by reviewers, who may quote brief passages in a review.

ISBN: 978-1-64826-995-0   (Paperback Edition)
ISBN: 978-1-64826-996-7   (Hardcover Edition)
ISBN: 978-1-64826-994-3   (E-book Edition)

Some characters and events in this book are fictitious. Any similarity to real persons, living or dead, is coincidental and not intended by the author.

Book Ordering Information

Phone Number: 347-901-4929 or 347-901-4920
Email: info@globalsummithouse.com
Global Summit House
www.globalsummithouse.com

Printed in the United States of America

Chapter 1

The black and white tabby cat, named Sylvester, was licking its paws when he heard Wanda's approaching footsteps. He lifted his head and quickly scampered out into the hallway, knocking over the bowl of milk. Wanda was startled to see him run by her so quickly, as he had seemed very lethargic over the past several weeks. Upon entering the kitchen and seeing the milk on the floor, she wondered why he didn't bother to clean up his own mess. "I don't know who you think you are but I'm not a maid to humans or animals in this house! You better learn to clean up and take out your own litter box!" She chuckled at the idea of her talking to a cat, as if he really understood what she was saying. It was early in the morning and her most favorite time of the day, when she could carve out some precious moments of solitude. It was at this hour that she could collect her thoughts and reflect on what she had to do for the day.

Rarely could she devote more than twenty minutes sitting down to a cup of coffee and savor the time for herself. She envied other housewives who would make mention of the special morning ritual and routines that made for a very tight bond in their families. That certainly was not the case for Wanda Evans and John, her husband of five years.

She glanced up at the refrigerator to see the art drawing she had saved and cherished from her seven-year-old daughter Jasmine, who was killed in a tragic accident several years ago. Even though the years had passed, she had always felt love from her daughter and at this moment, as she stared at the drawing, she smiled with contentment. Even though she had her for a short while, the memories of her had become the solid rock in her life and she knew even if only for a brief time, what unconditional love felt like.

The vivid memories of Jasmine were the one part of the union that made it all worthwhile. Jasmine was very energetic and seemed to have an endless curiosity about the world around her. Even though Wanda loved the fact her daughter was possessed with the gift of energy, she wanted it to be harnessed from time to time, especially when out in public or while in the company of a stranger. Wanda smiled, wondering just how many miles she had ran chasing Jasmine up and down the Walmart aisles when she first learned to walk, or rather run. Sadly, it was the same enthusiasm for life that eventually caused her death.

The years of heartbreak over losing her child was a turning point that would forever define her. After many months of depression, she knew she needed to rebound into life and begin to live again. She carried the memory of Jasmine and slowly with each passing day, she embraced them as an extension of her soul.

Even now at the age of thirty-five Wanda was highly attractive. As she sat there in her pink bathrobe it revealed flawless skin underneath. The years had been very kind to her, and she didn't need the makeup cream that she applied to her face religiously every morning. It was only in her mind did the crow's feet appear. And the laugh lines that she thought were a permanent blemish served to make her even more youthful looking. Her daily routine of yoga, stretching and walking had kept her girlish figure for all these years. She felt like the queen of the prom when men would whistle at her from afar and send flirtatious comments her way. She loved the attention, as it reassured her that she still had what men wanted. She didn't want to admit that occasionally she had lingering doubts and that her self-esteem sometimes was lacking. This was mostly because she longed for the attention and affection from her husband, that had somehow vanished with the passing of time. She wondered if that was the norm for married couples, until hanging out with a few of her married girlfriends seemed to prove otherwise. She didn't know what to do anymore to capture his eyes and lustful attention to her. The credit card bills certainly showed that she had tried everything, to include Brazilian waxing, and hair and nail makeovers. The closet and drawers were overflowing with sexy dresses and the drawers enclosed skimpy lingerie that would make any man pant with excitement. Of course, any normal man would, except John. Five years into her marriage with him and she was starting to feel like a widow. Funny how she let her mind drift to the thought of being a widow, thinking that perhaps it would be more comforting than being in the same bed with a man who had died emotionally a very long time ago.

It was not only that John was becoming disconnected from her, but things had gotten very intense over the past six months. First it was very subtle with him coming home later and later, and seemingly in a constant bad mood. Whenever she would ask about his day and what was wrong, she got the same sharp answer. "Nothing, and why do you always insist that something is wrong with me? Can't a guy just get some peace and quiet and be left alone? For heavens sakes, Wanda, you are getting to the point of annoying."

It was a couple of days later when he came home with alcohol on his breath and an unfamiliar perfume on his collar that Wanda blew up at him about his behavior.

"Where in the hell have you been and why did you not think enough of me to call?"

"Wanda, please do not go there. Trust me I am not in the mood." He said.

"In the mood? I bet you were in the mood after drinking so you could be with some bitch that left that perfume on you! Who is she John?"

"What are you talking about? There is no who!" John was feeling a bit nervous, and quickly he thought of what loose ends he had left untied.

"I am not stupid John. Do not play me for a fool. I can smell the alcohol and the perfume all over you. Now look me in the eye and tell me you have not been with some woman today." She stared at him hoping she was not right but knowing her instincts had not let her down before, she braced for the worst.

"Wanda, I have not been with another woman as you're thinking. The reason that you smell perfume is this. While I was at a stop in Gaithersburg, a lady was eagerly expecting a package from her son who is over in Iraq. And when I delivered it to her she was overjoyed and gave me a big hug. And as for the alcohol, yeah, I stopped and had a beer at Uno's to unwind a bit. It was a rough day and I needed to get in a light mood. There's no harm in that, OK?"

"Yeah, right." Wanda was amazed at just how good he was at lying.

The large crystal chandelier swayed and chimed from the breeze that came through the open kitchen window. Wanda loved the fresh morning air. She stood up and inhaled deeply while stretching as far as she could reach to the ceiling. She loved all the sounds that indicated the start of a brand new day. She walked over to the window and leaned close and put her nose on the screen and searched for the birds that were chirping a loud chorus. A dog barked off in the distance, and the sound seemed to echo throughout the entire quiet neighborhood.

The house was small but still warm and cozy and it had served more than the basic need of shelter. It was her idea to move into a starter home shortly before she got married. John, however, had bigger things in mind for his new bride. He never made outrageous promises to Wanda but wanted her to know that she was worthy of comfort and security. He always felt it was his responsibility to provide for her needs first and her wants second. He was happy to know that Wanda was good at managing household finances, and that he could depend on her to keep things running smoothly. That was just the way he liked it. All he wanted to do was to be able to focus on his job as a professional driver for a major trucking company.

He was well along in his career and living his dream. It still amazed him after all these years that he was actually paid to drive, which was something that not only he enjoyed, but regarded as a passion more than work. The seed of freedom and the call of the open road began for John even as a small boy. During the very hot summer days while his foster mother kept him inside not allowing him to play with other kids, he would escape his misery by pretending he was driving all over the country.

He was very intense with his imagination and, even as a child, he knew that the road meant freedom from all that he was feeling and enduring. It was his only focus to hide all the pain and loneliness that came at the hands of a foster mother that inflicted countless hours of both emotional and physical abuse.

Wanda went back to the bedroom and saw the evidence of the restless night she had, tossing and turning. The bed was a display of tossed pillows and entangled sheets and blankets that more closely represented the place where a fight took place rather than sleep. It was another night of endless thinking about her current situation. She was in her mid-thirties and in a very unhappy marriage, with no idea of how to change it or having the courage to get out of it. Very few people knew of the loneliness that she felt inside and least of all, her husband. The chill in the air seemed to make the nights even longer. She wondered as she looked at the unmade bed if other women were enduring the same turmoil or was, she the only one to have this misery at this moment.

Her life had not played out like the soap operas she had seen on TV. She longed for the day that John would come through the door with a surprise gift in his hand, selected especially for her, something that would show his adoration and appreciation for her and her love. A bouquet of flowers, a card, a small trinket of jewelry or even a ticket to get away for the weekend just the two of them. It had not always been like this or this bad. Somewhere in the passing months and years the emotional separation and loneliness grew wider and stronger. She had difficulty remembering when she was very passionate about their love. But somehow she coped, rationalizing that she had a roof over her head and some security for her. Her heart still ached at the emptiness of the house without her daughter, Jasmine. It just did not seem to be the home it once was.

She had listened to some of her girlfriends and endless struggle of making it on their own without a man. And she thought that her plight was much better than that. As she went about her domestic duties, it was becoming more and more evident that her life was revealing the emptiness within. She looked in the mirror while brushing her hair, and the woman who stared back showed very little signs of aging from the outside, but she felt very old on the inside. She knew it was vanity to think that beauty would last forever. She also knew that there were a lot of younger women who could turn John's head, and maybe even his heart. She focused on the comments from women who had mistaken her for much younger. And yes, all the men noticed her curves that seemed to fall in all the right places. This gave her some confidence.

It didn't bother her that the men wanted one thing and one thing only. As long as she got their attention, that was all that mattered. Attention from another man, even for a brief few moments for all the wrong reasons, was more attention than she was getting from John these days. She tried not to entertain the thoughts of any activity outside of their marriage, because she was first and far most a Christian and enduring a bad marriage was liken to the devotion of the Christian life. The inner voice inside her head played loudly as a cruel task master to keep her enduring the growing misery. "I knew the road was going to be difficult at times, you do not quit just because of a little adversity." The mantra would get her through the long cold and lonely nights, while tears soaked her pillow.

Returning to the kitchen she stopped and looked out the window and daydreamed for several minutes. She remembered the time her and John went on a cruise to the Caribbean, with a five night stay in the Bahamas. It was one of the best times the two of them shared, and the only time when she actually felt loved by him. One morning they both woke up in the resort hotel and decided not to do anything other than spend the day with each other in the room and make love, off and on all day. She was amazed that he could make love the entire day and be so ready for more, even later that night. Perhaps he had a deep well of passion in him that she was tapping into for the first time. John was very handsome and he kept himself in really good shape. There was no evidence that he was approaching middle age. His days of glory were long behind him but had plenty of credentials to show just how fine-tuned his body was in the days of his youth. She loved to listen to him tell the stories of the many road races he ran and how being a distance runner gave him the endurance he needed in the bedroom. She smiled when he recalled a couple of marathons he ran, and she thought how many women would love a man to go the distance under the sheets.

She had always wanted a medium sized house. However, the small house that was more like a cottage on the outskirts of Baltimore, would have to do. In spite of their differences and problems, she knew that John wanted her to do well and he was willing to sacrifice to make sure she had what she needed. But, more than a lavish lifestyle, she wanted to know that she was loved unconditionally by him. She would trade in her lifestyle for love. She knew plenty of women who were gold diggers and did not want love as much as a glamorous life. Wanda, however, thought that love would be the ticket to a great life. She thought that if you win a man's heart, then you also have his bank account.

She never asked too much of John, other than he be faithful and true. Her biggest fear was that in her greatest time of need he would desert her.

Even though she was in great health, a hidden fear was getting the news from a doctor that she had breast cancer or some other terminal illness. She knew this was irrational thinking, but more than once she was surprised about the sudden illness that had befallen one of her friends in her age group. It reminded her that she was still mortal and that death does not discriminate. She tried to push the thoughts back about whether or not John would stay with her if a life changing event such as cancer invaded her world.

After getting dressed and buttoning up her navy-blue pin striped jump suit, she quickly sat down at the computer to check her email, make notes from her calendar, and go over her to-do list. While scanning through the subject lines of the emails, she noticed one in particular that had no subject line and the senders name was Stacey. She clicked it and read the following: Hello John, it was such a pleasure to meet you the other night. You made me laugh and feel alive again. I was really impressed with your dancing and I want to thank you once again for sharing moments of comfort. We must meet again. I have your number and I will call as soon as I can. Please keep in touch. Fondly Stacey.

Wanda sat there staring at the screen in disbelief, wishing that she didn't read what she just read. She quickly read it again and in disgust deleted it. Had this confirmed what she had thought all along? Or perhaps she would give him the benefit of the doubt and let him explain himself. She was determined not to let her discovery ruin her mood or foul up her day. A few minutes later she picked up her pocket book and headed out the door, careful to set the code on the house alarm.

Chapter 2

John always enjoyed his early morning routine before clocking into work. His daily stop at the local Starbucks to browse and read USA Today was the only time he had to be reflective. It was there that he would prepare himself mentally for the day ahead. His job as a route driver for a printing company caused him to tour the greater metro tri-state area of Virginia, Maryland, and the District of Columbia. The job paid just barely enough to be respectable, but the high cost of the Greater Washington metro area would soon overcome his hourly wage. He hated the traffic but loved driving. Often, he pondered why he had not persevered and gotten a degree in criminal justice. He wanted to hone his investigation skills that he learned while working as a corporate investigator for K-Mart. His five years with the company had proven to be very rewarding, but he slacked just enough to get fired. His untimely termination is what thrust him into looking for a new job. Driving was something that came easily to him and there were plenty of driving jobs in the metro area. His first job after K-Mart, was as an independent courier. During his time as a courier he learned to navigate all over the greater metro area with efficiency and ease. He was commended on several occasions about his quickness and willingness to go anywhere and make a delivery regardless of the extra effort involved. It was his commitment and attention to detail along with superb customer service that got the attention of a customer that would routinely ask for him by name to make their deliveries. John was blushing a bit when the manager of Corporate Graphics kept badgering him about signing on as a company employee for their company. John at first resisted the idea of working for someone else and treasured the idea of being independent with choices of when he wanted to work. However, knowing that he did not have any benefits, John reasoned that the security that comes from a company sponsored benefits package would be highly desirable for his wife. So he accepted the job, a uniform, and a boss.

He pulled onto I-95 and quickly accelerated up to highway speed and flow of traffic, which was well above the posted 55mph. The white Ford Econovan had a powerful engine that was just perfect for the demands of delivering many boxes of books and documents that Corporate Graphics produced for the vast customer base in the tri-state area. It was not unusual for some of his runs to take him as far south as Richmond Virginia and as far north as Pennsylvania. While making his way to his stop, his mind drifted to other thoughts that had consumed him, mostly the pretty young lady he befriended on the second floor of the Bally's health club in Alexandria.

It was nothing that he had planned or even hoped for, but with the many visits he made to the club to work out, he found the very fit dirty blonde to have an undeniable attraction he couldn't easily shake. He was mostly shy and very awkward with women, so he found it quite surprising that this fitness instructor would see beyond his many stumbling moments and find him rather attractive also. Across the room glances and flirting conversations, they would send each other any time he was there was so obvious that even some of the patrons voiced their discontent. John did have a cover that he used to continue to have contact with her. He happened to sell a nutritional line that he wanted to promote at the club. And of course, getting the opinion of a fitness instructor as dedicated as Vicky was very valuable to him. So any time he stopped by the club he made a point to have some products on hand that he could promote to the other club members and, of course to engage in long conversations with Vicky. On one such occasion he was flirting with Vicky to the point that she was uncomfortable and she made her point known.

"John, listen it is not very professional as a company representative to flirt with your clients. People will get the very wrong impression, so why not cool it in here, OK?" She was firm, blunt and gave him a very serious look.

"You're right Vicky. I'm sorry, I didn't mean to make you feel uncomfortable. I can assure you it won't happen again. But listen, why don't you let me make it up to you over lunch or dinner sometime, outside of the club?" He had a small grin on his face that caused her to smile back. Vicky gave him a very long look and then said, "You are very sweet and I might take you up on that offer, if you promise me to behave yourself in here."

"Consider it done." He thanked her for the time they spent together and set up his next appointment for personal training.

He, sat in the van outside the club in the parking lot and reclined the seat back for a few minutes to reflect over his next move with Vicky. He didn't have the confidence to date anyone these days and it still bothered him to know that he was even contemplating having an affair. Wanda was good to him, very loyal, and it made him feel guilty to hurt her with an affair with another woman. Should he just face up to the reality of what he was feeling inside and tell her that he just did not think the marriage could continue to go on? Or let the devastating knowledge of his affair come as a shock, which would force her to abruptly end the marriage. No, Wanda deserved a lot better than that, and he thought that God would most certainly hold him accountable for the way he treated her. With that thought in mind he wondered just how did he let it get this far. Was there still time for him to turn the direction of his life around? Could he look at himself with confidence knowing that he had planned and carried out an affair with the sole purpose of breaking up their marriage. Well, something had to be done and he had better think of something quick, because tension and the silence between him and Wanda was growing.

It had been several months since they made love and often he would stay up long after she went to bed and fell asleep to ensure he did not have to share any intimacy with her. Her complaints still ringing in his ears of the fact that she did not like to have to always be the one to initiate sexual contact. It was not that the sex wasn't good, she just hated the fact that she didn't feel as if she was wanted. She knew she had some flaws in her body that could not easily be overlooked, but she could feel the passion of him every time they made love. And he never seemed disgusted with her body. Yes, he told himself on several occasions that perhaps he could seek another woman a bit more appealing and who had much more chemistry, but he also had grown used to the comfort of this woman who kept a great home and was the role model of the domestic lifestyle. He wanted to someday settle down and have a comfortable home that Wanda provided. It made sense to be practical and stop chasing every thing that had a short skirt and pretty smile. Still, his sense of adventure kept calling him to seek more and find out if he had what it took to charm the ladies that were so far out of his league. Vicky was his latest quest. So just how far would he go before his better judgement kicked in and he controlled the urges within him that should only be for Wanda his wife?

He quickly pushed the thoughts out of his mind as he got back on the road and headed to the University of Maryland campus for his next delivery. Within a few miles his mind drifted back to Vicky. He knew that something would have to be done before he went too far. He never regarded himself as a person who would cheat on his wife and was startled at this very moment that even the thought was in his mind. How could he hurt her like that? And besides did he not forget what he read in the Bible about accountability for such actions. 'God will not tolerate hypocrites regardless of who they are.' he reminded himself.

He wondered what had happened over the years to get him to this point. Was it inevitable in spite of his best efforts? He had a lot of questions about himself as a real husband now that cheating was a part of thoughts and fantasies he was not suppose to allow himself to have.

John could not bare the thought of living a lie and being very good at it. He had a conscious that would hound him with every sin he committed and a holy spirit that would most certainly remind him of his errors.

To the outside world John seemed to have it all together, yet on the inside his coping skills were breaking down more and more each day. His fast paced schedule seemed to be closing in on him with every passing moment. His gym membership at Bally's had served as a distraction and an outlet to vent his frustrations of life. However these days he craved something more to suppress the deep guilt that was consuming him. He was not known for reckless living, however every now and then he would push the envelope and live on the wild side. As a man who still had vast amounts of energy and youth, he sought to do things that would give him an adrenaline rush. Wanda was very mild and tame. John had often spoke of doing something reckless just for the fun of it. She, however was not only cautious, but her desire to see him in a more docile state meant that he would not be risking his life in some skydiving accident and thereby jeopardizing her security.

By late that afternoon, John had completed most of his stops and deliveries. He had always planned his route so that he could take advantage of the HOV lane that ran from Washington DC to Triangle, Va. It was the fastest way to Virginia around the three o'clock hour. John needed to be in Virginia by late afternoon at least twice a week, however not for business purposes. He had managed over time to find a habit that required lots of cash to fulfill. He had always told himself that it was just a little pick me up to help him get through the stress of the day. And, to be honest, that is just how it started on the day he met a pretty well dressed blonde at a Dunkin Donut's shop in Dumfries. Cindy Adams was the one pretty girl who flirted just enough with her southern accent and dazzling smile to get him to stop there every time he was in the Dumfries area. As a matter of fact, he would even make excuses to be in that area just to spend some time with her. Cindy was an office manager at the professional building that was home to lawyers and doctors and one accountant. She often took her lunch break at the Dunkin Donuts because of the close proximity to her work. Her budget only allowed for frugal fixings at Dunkin Donuts. John offered to buy her lunch every time he was in the area, as a thank you for her shared company. It was during these breaks that Cindy revealed a lot about her life and how at times she felt so overwhelmed with the responsibilities of the office. She told him that her energy sometimes lagged far behind and even the heaping cups of black coffee was not enough.

On one such visit John asked, "How do you do it Cindy? A girl like you needs her beauty rest. And you know you cannot keep up this pace for long."

She looked at him and smiled. Then she gently touched his arm and said, "Well I have a friend of mine who gives me a little something to get me through the rough spots." She grinned and then continued, "It is also responsible for my charming personality at this time of the day, when otherwise I would be ready to strangle everybody in my building."

John looked at her intensely and then smiled and said, "Ok there, cute one, what is it exactly that makes you so endearing?"

"Well, if I tell you, I need you to promise me not to tell anyone. And it maybe something that could help you out on your route. I bet it will keep you calm enough so you will not run over anybody."

"I'll have you know that I am a professional driver and I don't run over people." He smiled and began to be even more curious. "But OK, I promise and I might consider your offer."

Cindy reached into her small burgundy pocket book, took out a notepad, wrote down a phone number and then handed it to John. "Take this, call this number and tell the person who answers the phone that you are picking up for Chalice. They'll give you directions to get this order for Chalice."

"Something tells me I should not ask who Chalice is or what exactly I am picking up." He was a bit nervous but thought that he could trust this beautiful woman that had charmed him so much over the past several weeks.

"You'll be fine. It's around the corner, about two minutes from here, down that road." Cindy pointed out the large window where the road went across the large intersection and disappeared into a residential area. "Just come back here as soon as you can and we can take a drive and talk some more." Cindy smiled and flashed her eyes and slung her head back so that her long blonde hair brushed past John's face, and he could smell the sweet fragrance that made him long for her in that very instance.

"OK, anything for you darling." And with that John got in his vehicle and dialed the number.

The voice on the other end of the line was very rough and unfriendly. John was polite in carrying out Cindy's instructions. The voice told John to come to the location and someone would come out to meet him and complete the transaction. Seven minutes later, John pulled up in front of the apartment building and waited. He was careful to be mindful of his surroundings and took note of the young men who were staring at him from the sidewalk and stairs that lead up to the apartment building. It was rather obvious they had not seen this vehicle here before and knew there was a need to check it out and be sure that John was not a cop.

After about twenty minutes of trying to calm his nerves, the cell phone rang and John was instructed to drive around to the back side of the apartment building. He went to the other side of the building and parked, even more unsure of why he was there.

The back door of the apartment building swung open and out came a man walking quickly toward the van. John kept looking at him closely as he approached the vehicle. He motioned for John to roll the window down. "Yeah," John kept his comments short needing to know what this guy was up to.

"What's up, man? I was told to come meet with you and you want to do some business. Is that correct?"

"I believe so, this is for Chalice." John still was not sure of who he was. But he did not want to let this intimidating figure sense any hint of fear.

"Ok let me in and let's get this done. I got other customers to take care of and this is a freebie from the boss for Chalice." He went to the other side and quickly sat down in the front seat. He seemed a bit nervous also. "Just take this and leave a different way than you came in here. There is a small dirt road on the other side of the basketball court. Take that road and be sure no one is following you. Do not stop. You have never seen this place and I do not exist. Clear?" He looked at John with ice cold eyes that indicated that he would end this conversation by any means necessary.

John's instincts told him not to say another word and just follow the instructions. He took the small package that was handed to him and put it in his pocket. The man quickly got out of the van, did not say anything but merely pointed in the direction of the basketball court.

John drove the van out of the complex as directed. Within a few minutes he was in a neighborhood that made him even more uncomfortable than the apartment building. Knowing that a delivery van would normally not be in this neighborhood, he thought it best to quickly get out of the area and back to Dunkin Donuts to see if Cindy was still there. Upon pulling into Dunkin Donuts parking lot, he was saddened to see that she had left.

Knowing that his shift would be over in less than an hour, he decided that it was time to start making his way back to the dispatch office. He felt relieved as he got back on I-95 heading north toward Maryland. He kept thinking about the small package that was in his pants pocket and wondered exactly what it was. Of course, he had his suspicions that it probably was something he shouldn't hang onto very long.

At the Dale City rest area, John pulled in and parked his van far away from other visitors. He reached in his pocket and unwrapped the brown handkerchief to find two small vials of white powder and a vial of tiny little crystals that looked like small ice or glass chips. John felt his heart beat getting stronger and faster at the thought of using or carrying illegal drugs. What was Cindy doing with friends and connections like the man he met at the residential complex? Did she have a drug habit? Why would she introduce this to him? The questions kept coming as he stared at the contents of the vials. He heard what these drugs can do, and yet his curiosity wanted to know more.

While he was looking at the drug package, he failed to recognize the movements of the men closing in on his van with weapons drawn. In the most shocking manner he was introduced to them.

"Step out of the vehicle and put your hands on top of your head! Do it now!" The sounds coming from several police officers was quite intimidating and happened so fast that John didn't have time to process the reality of what was happening to him.

John's emotions quickly changed to sadness as he complied with the officers' orders. In less than four minutes John was handcuffed, read his rights and placed in the police car. His thoughts were erratic, and he felt like his world had just caved in. How would he explain all of this to his wife? The flashing blue lights snapped him back into the reality of the moment. How he wished he were dreaming, but clearly, he was awake and in the middle of a nightmare. As the police car sped off to the Prince William County Detention Center, John began to feel a deep remorse.

Chapter 3

Wanda found it difficult to concentrate as she stared at the screen on her desk top computer. Her mind kept drifting back to the email that she had opened regarding Stacey. She wondered what led John to this need and desire, for another woman. The doubts kept creeping into her mind as to whether she had been a good wife and, most importantly, the kind of woman John could confide in. She was supportive of his career changes and thought she was giving him everything that he needed and wanted. She heard him tell her countless times that she was everything that he ever needed. Was she living a lie with this man or was there something she lacked?

The small marketing firm that she worked for had always been supportive of her family needs over the years. She was granted extended maternity leave due to the birth of her daughter, at a time when the company needed every person in order to launch a major marketing campaign for Pepsi. She felt nervous asking for the extension, although she had the support of the medical staff and plenty of documentation to warrant it. There were times when she had to rush out of the office in a hurry to head off to the emergency room or to the school because of some unexpected crisis. When the death of Jasmine had all but emotionally crippled her, the company offered counseling and more support that she thought any company would do. She wondered if the firm would be gracious to support marriage counseling and perhaps a vacation to get away to try to repair the damaged relationship with her husband. She looked up from her desk to see the floor supervisor Jackie Canton staring at her.

"Wanda, is there anything I can help you with? You seem a bit distracted." She asked.

"I'm fine. How are you Jackie? I was thinking of the best way to draft this proposal to the Pepsi executive for the project." She had to seem focused even if it meant not telling the entire truth.

"Well if there is anybody who can write a dead-on proposal, it's certainly you. That's why we put you on this project team after seeing the way you handled the Anderson team last year. We're counting on you, to get us through the front door."

"Well thank you for your trust in my skills. I will do my best." Wanda said.

"Yes, we are more than confident that you will. Take a break if you need to get some creative ideas in that head of yours. Go ahead, it is beautiful outside."

"I think I shall do just that, Jackie."

Minutes later, Wanda was striding through the glass doors with her pocketbook in hand. She'd take the next half an hour to clear her mind. She enjoyed going to the small picnic area located in the courtyard where she could see the huge buildings that were connected together by a long glass corridor. On many occasions she would glance up there to see office romances that were forbidden in the work area come to life. As a matter of fact she was wondering just how many wives and husbands were interacting up in that corridor with other people they were not legally bound to.

While she tried to hold back the thoughts of the email, still it nagged a bit and came pounding to the forefront. Panic usually never controlled her emotions, however with each passing minute she was thinking of what she would do if John left her for another woman. Her job could barely pay for the little extras that she wanted and needed. It certainly could not sustain her survival. Wanda could not see a different life other than being married to John. She would just have to find a way to work out the issues that were hindering their relationship and use some new found faith in God to see it through. Faith was something she used to be very strong with but with the passing of time, it all seemed like a fading memory. Yes, she believed in God, yes, she believed in the Bible. She had many doubts after the death of Jasmine. She was very much aware of the many doctrines and principles to live her life by. She had faith for others, but now she seemed to lack it for her own life. Perhaps God would listen to her requests and pleadings to not have her endure the embarrassment of a divorce or other hardships that had plagued so many of her close friends.

Upon returning to her small desk, the blinking red light on her phone indicated a caller was on hold and waiting. Perhaps another client she was following up on had called back for more marketing statistics or some other detail of the business. To be really good on the phone with a client meant that she needed to clear her head of any negative thoughts and focus on the task at hand. She took a deep breath and pushed the talk button and gave her salutation, "Wanda Evans speaking how may I help you?" A few seconds later and she heard the following: "Mrs. Wanda Evans Hello. My name is Sgt. Anderson from the Prince William County Police Department. The reason I am calling is to inform you that your husband John has been arrested and detained. It is necessary for you to come to our precinct so we can go over the details and arrange for his release. These are very serious charges your husband is facing, so it is urgent that we meet with you. Again my name is Sgt. Anderson with the Prince William County police department. Do you know our location and how to get here?"

Frozen in silence and fear, Wanda sat back in her chair and let the words ring in her head some more. 'No, it must be a mistake, because John is out driving and making deliveries. He would not be in Virginia.' She thought of every possible reason not to believe what she was hearing.

Again, the voice on the other end cut in, "Mrs. Evans I know that this is a lot to take in at this time. However, we do need you to come as soon as you can. Do you need directions?"

"No. I know where it is, thank you. I will be leaving here in about five minutes and get there as soon as possible. Is John alright? What is going to happen to him?"

"Yes ma'am, he is just fine, perhaps a bit nervous, but he will be ok. We will give you all the details when you arrive. Please drive carefully and try to remain calm. You do not want to drive on your emotions. We will see you in a bit."

She thanked him and hung up. Sitting in her chair she suddenly started shivering from the shock that was setting in. She knew she had to get herself together and find the courage to face whatever was ahead. She tried to contain her thoughts but yet they nagged at her. 'What could he have possibly done that would land him in jail?'

She was weak and lightheaded as she quietly gathered her belongings and walked to the personnel office to request to be excused for the rest of the day. It was just way too embarrassing to explain the details of why she needed to leave urgently, and she did not want to lie and say that it was something wrong at home.

"Ms. Parks I am so sorry to have to ask this of you, but it is necessary for me to take the rest of the day off. A real emergency is developing and to tell you the truth I am just too ashamed to tell you the details. But I promise you I will call back in a couple of hours when things have settled down a bit. I am so sorry."

"Wanda, we try to be very understanding here and more than family friendly. All we ask in return is honesty and the truth. Listen, I can see you are quite upset so I am going to grant your request. But this comes at a really bad time. As you know the firm is depending on you to land that account. How will you make things happen if you are gone so much?"

"I was hoping to talk to the supervisor about doing some work from home or perhaps she will let me come in and do a few all-nighters until the project is complete. I do want to stay on this account because I know just how important it is. My life just seems to be falling apart at the worst time . . . and . . ." Her tears began to flow as she sat down in the small chair next to the desk.

Ms. Parks quickly gave her some tissues and got up came around and gently hugged her. "I don't know what is going on, but when you feel better, please come and talk to me. We can work something out because you are one of the best employees we have here and we don't want to lose you. Take the rest of the day off and update me later. You also have my home phone. Feel free to call me there too. You have time on the books that you can use so don't worry about that."

She was sobbing more freely now and her tears unstoppable as she slowly conveyed her sincere gratitude.

"Thank you so much and I will call you as soon as I can."

The sky had darkened with rain clouds coming in from the west. And she knew that the traffic on the beltway would not be forgiving this late in the afternoon. With any rain the drive would soon become a nightmare. Normally she would want to race to the police department, however this time she felt that the delay of traffic would be what she needed to get her mind, emotions and faith ready for whatever lied ahead.. As she steered the car into the heavy traffic, Wanda began to pray.

While John sat in the interrogation room, he thought of all the times he had seen Cindy and what could she have done to cause this turn of events for him. How could he possible keep his affair a secret from Wanda? He would be forced now to explain why he was in Virginia and why he was in a well-known drug community.

The door of the interrogation room swung open and a small, well dressed investigator stepped inside and kindly smiled at John. He had a large folder that obviously was the paper trail, of evidence the state had against John. John's heart sunk a bit deeper at the thought of trying to muster a defense against drug trafficking and possession.

"Hi John. My name is SGT, Bill Martin. I am here to explain to you why you were brought in and what is going to be happening from here on out." He stared at John to see his reaction. It's well known that the interrogation of suspects can be very emotional and they need to be observed closely for signs of distress. Interestingly enough the distress the suspect feels is the tool the interrogator uses to obtain pertinent information as well as confessions.

"John, do you know what charges you are facing and just how serious this is?"

"Yes, sir, I do."

"I understand that you have been read your rights and been given the opportunity to speak with a lawyer, is that correct?"

"Yes, sir."

"Do you wish to speak to me and make a statement at this time, John?"

John looked down at the table while clasping his hands in frustration. He could not lie his way out of this trouble he was in, and yet he knew the consequences would be devastating to him personally and his entire family. Nonetheless this was the time to begin to put things in order that led up to these events. "What if I want to have a lawyer here at some point while talking to you?"

"If at any time you wish you can speak to a lawyer, we will allow you to do that. It is your right. Do you wish to proceed?" The SGT had an instinct from conducting so many previous interviews and interrogations that John was about to 'lawyer up'.

John began to stutter a bit and then more clearly said, "I think I should have the advice of a lawyer because this is way more than I am prepared to deal with. I don't want to say something that I shouldn't."

"OK, if that is the way you want it. But you can be sure we will get the truth. And I can assure you that the more you cooperate with us, especially now, the more we can do for you later on. You think about that."

The interrogator stood up and went to the other side of the room and opened the door very slowly, leaving John to want his freedom even more. He turned back to John and said, "The more you cooperate, the more we can put on the table, including dropping some of these charges. You are way too young to give away your best years, if not all the years of your life to prison." Not that John was going to do any real lengthy prison sentence, but the investigator knew that under pressure some client's fear of the unknown was just enough to get them to reveal all that they otherwise would not tell.

Chapter 4

The four story building could be seen from about a half mile away as Wanda sat at the traffic light on Route 1 south. The knots in her stomach almost made her vomit as the fear crept up inside her. This was a bit more than she was ready for. What had he done? She thought back over the past couple of years and all the events that she had stood beside him. Her mind flashed back to the day they stood in the small living room of the local Justice of Peace and promised to love each other and support each other in sickness and health, for better or worse. Maybe this would be a test of their marriage. But could it survive this?

She pulled into the parking lot and was very careful to park at the far end of the parking lot so that she could have the time to compose herself as she walked slowly to the precinct. Perhaps this would be quick and she could get out of there before anybody sees her body signs that indicate shock and the possibility that she might faint.

The automatic doors swung open and she stepped into the brightly lit lobby. It was well decorated and did not at all resemble a police department. The huge lobby had comfortable couches and seats, where no doubt lawyers and clients had strategized for hours. There was a directory that had large bold white letters against a black background. She searched for the police help desk, and across the other side of the room her eyes found a well dressed uniformed police officer sitting behind a desk with computer screen protruding over the front side.

He looked up and found Wanda to be quite attractive, well dressed and wondered why she was here. Thinking that she might be a lawyer, he smiled and asked, "How can I help you ma'am?"

Wanda was a bit startled smiled back and said, "Where do they take people who have been arrested? My husband was recently taken here." She then felt horrible and a bit ashamed that she had to admit a relationship to someone that was arrested.

"What is your husband's name?" The desk officer leaned in closer to the computer to input data.

"John Evans." She reached into her pocketbook to get the note with the name of the officer who called her at the office. "Oh, I got a call from Sgt. Anderson, who told me he was brought here."

"Ok, ma'am, I have it here. I will have SGT Anderson come out and meet with you." Pointing to the chairs in the lobby, "Please have a seat over there and he will be out shortly."

"Thank you." Wanda sat down and did all she could to hold back the tears and her fears.

Her telephone rang and it startled her. While trying to shake off the chill she was feeling, she saw the number of her close friend and longtime confidant, Sandy. She knew Sandy cared and would be very supportive of her during this crisis. It was that knowledge that put her at ease just a bit. The few minutes of talking to her was enough to keep her calm and face whatever was on the other side of the door marked "Criminal Investigations Division".

Another ten minutes passed before SGT Anderson opened the door and strode toward her. "Hello I'm SGT Anderson, the gentlemen who spoke with you on the phone earlier. How are you doing?"

"Hi, I'm Wanda I think I am ok." She could feel her stomach tighten and the knots starting to form. "Is John ok? Can I see him?"

"Yes, he is doing fine, I can assure you. You can see him as soon as I get some more information." The officer directed her back to his office, where a series of forms and yet more questions awaited her. The office was small and the desk seemed to be overflowing with ongoing investigations. He motioned for her to sit down, while he took off his jacket and loosened his tie.

Wanda recalled many police shows and episodes of "CSI" and still could not comprehend that this was her reality. She thought of how different this was, from the cozy warm couch and blanket she had been accustomed to. Experiencing crime and justice on the television screen with a remote control was nothing like this.

"Can I get you anything? We have coffee, soda and a few snacks in the break room."

"No thank you, that is very kind." Wanda tried to smile but her obvious fears kept her lips frozen.

"Wanda, I have to be honest with you here. Your husband is facing some very serious charges. They include, drug possession, drug trafficking, and using narcotics." He read the details of the charges and then put the stack of papers back in the folder and waited for her response.

Wanda's head begin to spin as she heard the allegations against her husband. "No, no, sir there must be a terrible mistake. John has never been involved in anything that has to do with drugs." She sounded adamant about John's innocence.

"Wanda, I honestly wish I could say that it was not so, but the evidence is overwhelming that we have on him. I cannot go over any more details at this time because the investigation is still on going. But know that we will do all that we can to help him help himself. The more he cooperates with us now, the better it will be for him later. And that is where you come in. I need you to speak to him and convince him to cooperate so that any defense he puts together can be seen as favorable. Are you up to that? He has been read his rights and he has agreed to talk to us regarding this, and he wanted you to be here. He is deeply sorry he has let you down in a big way."

The shock was still apparent, and Wanda was rendered speechless.

"Are you alright, Wanda? I know this is a lot to take in right now. We do not have to do this right now if you don't feel up to it."

"Yes, I will . . . I need to know what is going on and why." She began to feel cold.

Chapter 5

The investigation was moving along at a fast pace, and SGT Anderson needed to get all the facts from John before the final formal charges were filed. He hated to admit it but actually, he needed and wanted Wanda's help in getting a confession from John. However due to spousal conversation privileges any conversation between husband and wife would be rejected in court. So it would be necessary to get information or a confession by other means. He briefed Wanda of what she could expect with the investigation. Thinking that Wanda would be very reluctant because of the husband-wife relationship, he was a bit surprised when Wanda agreed to get John to open up and talk. While whatever facts John would reveal may be to help with the investigation, for her it meant getting the answers she had longed to hear over the past couple of years. Perhaps it would put the pieces in place of why their relationship had become so broken and unfulfilling.

It was then that the officer interjected and briefed her that what she was proposing was not in protocol with these types of investigations. "Mrs. Evans, we have a unique situation here and while I can appreciate your wanting to help us, honestly it is illegal for us to allow you to question him on our behalf. It seems as if your husband is and has been involved in something much larger than any of us could imagine. I cannot speak on this investigation any further. I am sure you understand."

Wanda was frozen as she looked at Sgt. Andersen. "Can I see him now?" The tone of her voice indicated that her patients and cooperation was limited.

"Yes, of course. Right, this way."

The small interrogation room was sterile and had two uncomfortable wooden chairs with a large metal table bolted to the floor. When John was brought in wearing handcuffs and shackles, the escorting officer secured his leg shackles to the table. When the officer turned to leave the room with John's hands still handcuffed, Sgt. Anderson asked that they be removed. "John, we are going to let you visit with your wife for 20 minutes. Be sure not to try anything. You know we will be watching you." Sgt. Anderson pointed to the security camera overhead in the corner and to the two-way mirror directly in front of John.

When Wanda came into the room, John was moved by the beauty she possessed. It made him feel even more ashamed to know that she would have to be put through all of this because of his careless and reckless lifestyle. She smiled at him, mostly to mask her own fears and to show some strength for his sake.

"Baby, it is so good to see you. I am glad you came, but I am so sorry . . ." John was finding it difficult to complete the sentence as his grief and regret was now showing. "Oh, Wanda I don't know what I can say to you about all of this. . . . .I'm a total failure and disappointment to you."

Wanda looked at him and sat down in the other chair close beside him. She leaned on him and hugged him around the neck. "Shush, hey it is OK, I am here now . . . it's alright baby, and we will get through this." She spoke those words, not even knowing if she could. She needed so many answers to so many questions.

She looked at him, reached into her pocketbook and pulled out a small napkin to wipe the tears from her eyes and then his. "John, please darling, whatever you have done, I don't care how bad it is, I need you to tell me everything so that we can figure out a way to help you. You have to do that for me...for us. Ok?"

The sound of her voice caused John to hurt and ache inside. His mind began to recall all the events that had led to this. Truly now was the beginning of the day of reckoning. He knew he was worthy of any amount of justice that was going to be handed out. It was difficult to reveal all that had transpired in his life over the past year that had led to this moment.

But Wanda deserved to know why the last year of their marriage had been so turbulent and volatile.

He looked at her and could clearly see the hurt and pain that he caused her. He knew about the nights she had spent in bed softly crying, especially when he would open the bedroom door coming home after sneaking out to meet a late-night fling. He suspected she was aware that something was wrong when the 2 a.m. phone calls would always result in him leaving for a "rush delivery" to a customer.

"I wish there was an easy way to explain all of this but there isn't. I don't even know where to start." He had a deep sadness in his eyes that Wanda had never seen before.

"Start with the truth, John that is all you have to do. . . . It is all we have." She looked at him and knew this was the most difficult thing he would have to tell her. The answers she had been needing and all the questions of his behavior had come down to this. She searched his face and saw only despair. It hurt her deeply to see him this way.

John leaned in close to her and took both of her hands into his. He took a deep breath and began to tell her the events that had begun so long ago.

The many twists and turns in John's life were easily smoothed over and covered up by his charm and outgoing personality. When Wanda first met him years ago, he was larger than life. He always found a way to make her laugh and his quick wit and endless humor she found irresistible. The attention and spotlight was what he craved the most. She didn't mind allowing him the pleasure of all the attention he would seek because she knew that his early childhood had plagued him with enough horror. As a boy John was extremely shy and timid. It was hard to detect if he would grow into the man capable of both private moments of seclusion, and the stage commanding performance of a public speaker. His previous careers had prepared him well for the latter. The delivery job gave him the perfect balance of the quiet solitude that he needed to soothe his soul and the perfect atmosphere and circumstances to bring out his thirst for adventure not to mention the art of flirting. Flirting had landed him with many female contacts and sexual exploits over the past few years. And though his wife was very loyal, faithful and held steadfast devotion to him, he never seemed to have that thought in the forefront of his mind as he slid his body between the sheets of the women he met along the way. The guilt was almost unbearable at first but with time and practice he managed to suppress the feelings. As a matter of fact, it had been many months since he felt even slightly uncomfortable being with another woman other than Wanda.

With the next few minutes of confession, it was clear that he did not know how much he needed the soul cleansing session for all the things he had done. He hated for her to have to hear it first hand from him like this. His eyes became moist with tears and his lips seem to tremble a bit as he slowly began to speak.

"Baby, I do not even know where or how to begin. You deserve the truth about all of this. But it is so hard for me to hurt you with all I am about to tell you. Let me say right from the beginning that you had nothing to do with this. This is totally my fault and I bear total responsibility. I take the full blame here and I do not want you not even for one-second to think you are the cause of any of this."

Her heart ached even more to see him lament in such pain. She did not show any emotions, but stared blankly into the face of a man she now was beginning to doubt if she even knew.

"I am in serious trouble here. I have done some things that I am not very proud of. To tell you the truth I am not sure if there is much forgiveness for all of this. You are here because of my unfaithfulness to you. You are here because I have tried a thousand ways to cover it up and hide from it and seek to drown out the guilt with . . . drugs and alcohol."

Wanda grimaced at hearing drugs coming from the man who sat in front of her still holding her hands. He continued while searching her eyes and seeing the pain that was so evident. "I know what you must be thinking. 'How in the world could I ever get myself involved this deep in something that can destroy our marriage?' Well, to tell you the truth I don't know. It just happened. That must sound like a very lame excuse right now."

Wanda closed her eyes, took a deep breath, opened them again, and whispered, "When did this all begin and what is her name?"

"Her name is Cindy, but there have been others. This began a couple years ago when you started volunteering more at the church with the leadership group. I hate myself for saying this, but I was feeling very lonely and left out when you started spending time there. I know it is not an excuse, but just maybe it can help you understand."

It was in that moment and the way John said 'understand' that caused the anger to swell up inside her and she could not maintain control. "Understand! You bastard! You expect me to understand! How could you do this to me . . . to us?" She stood up and backed away from him out of sheer disgust. She put her face in her hands and began to shake her head in disbelief.

John became irritated with her reaction and began to show his own frustration.

"Listen, Wanda, true I am guilty of a lot of things, but please do not act as though you don't contribute to the stress of this marriage. You do not know how I have been feeling and you certainly are not in tune with what is going on inside of me. As a matter of fact, when was the last time you tried to talk to me instead of at me like I am a child!"

"Don't try to blame any of this on me! I did not make you have a drug habit and I most certainly did not make you cheat on me with some whore you met on the street! I have been lonely too John. But did I go and see another man or drown out guilt with drugs and alcohol? No. And believe me I have had plenty of opportunities, but my loyalty was to you . . . you bastard!"

"It happened, OK, this is where we are now. And this moment and situation right now is what we need to deal with."

Wanda looked at him while trying to wipe the tears that were streaking down her face. Her heart was feeling so many different emotions at the same time it was hard to determine which one was strongest. From anger, hate, and rage, to pity, love, despair and to utter shock and disbelief. One thing was becoming very clear . . . that life would never be the same knowing what John had done and was capable of doing. The more she looked at him the more he seemed unrecognizable. Was this the same man who five years earlier had walked down the aisle and read his own vows of loyalty and devotion with God as his witness? What had happened and how did he become the man she now saw in total disgust?

She had been visibly strong to the rest of the world and to her family. She had endured a lot of hardship in her personal life with no help, other than a few family members and church leaders. This new crisis was very embarrassing to speak about to anyone but the thought of enduring this alone seemed unbearable. She was near a breakdown. She was afraid for her life and for the future of her marriage.

The most agonizing thoughts of the moment for her was how had life come to this. She had often heard of the many untold stories of couples who were broadsided by some major event that had been going on for decades. She thought she was smarter than the rest of the world and thought that her keen sense of discernment was a failsafe to this type of thing. She had thought the only type of major personal crisis that would have pushed her to the brink would have been a severe or perhaps terminal illness. This left her so unprepared and caught way off guard.

"Were you taken by surprise by all of this, or was it something in the making for many years?" She was searching his face for the many unanswered questions.

"I really wish I could tell you that I had a good answer. But the truth is that even I am shocked that it has come to this. It was never supposed to happen and I do not know if I ever saw it coming." He shook his head in amazement.

Wanda's thought drifted to the detective who was waiting out in the other room listening to all of this. She knew that getting John to talk about all the details of what had happened would be what she needed to hear but that it would also give the police enough to make a solid case against him that could put him away for a very long time. The thought of that made her whole-body shiver and then she screamed, "Why! Oh my god why? Why me John? Why hurt me like this? What have I done to deserve this?" She felt her legs getting weak, and in an instant, she hit the floor.

John lunged for her to break her fall but just a second late, because of his shackled legs and could not prevent her from hitting her head on the grey concrete floor. He yelled out for help, and moments later the detective rushed into the room and leaned over Wanda calling her name for a response. There was none. He pulled out his phone and dialed 911, quickly gave the dispatcher on the other end details and location. About two minutes later, the sirens of emergency crews pierced the quiet hallways of the precinct. Wanda's vital signs were checked and her pulse was steady. She was still in a state of shock but had regained consciousness.

John stood back along the far wall in a state of disbelief of seeing his wife in this condition. It cut him deep in the heart knowing that he had delivered this blow to her. He knew he loved her and as the EMT crew began putting her on the stretcher, he made it known.

"Baby, please I am so sorry, so sorry. I love you so much and I did not want to hurt you. I never wanted to hurt you, Wanda."

The crew quickly cleared the room, hurried down the hall, and out the door to the awaiting ambulance. They decided to take Wanda to the hospital with the hope of releasing her within the hour.

Detective Anderson walked over to John and asked him to sit back down in the chair. Even though John's wife was on the way to the hospital, the matter at hand was still urgent.

The detective sat down and pulled up his chair very close to John so that he was facing him and almost had his knees touching him. The very thought of this man so close to him provided the fuel to intensely interrogate, dig deep, draw out the facts, and then withdraw a bit. It was a tried and proven method that had been used many years to get under the skin of those who thought they would never disclose the crimes they had been brought in for. Slowly he began to speak.

"John, look at me, please just look at me. I know what you must be feeling and thinking right now. Let me be honest with you, I do have compassion and am very empathetic to your current situation. I know you are scared and do not have a clue when all of this is going to end or how it may turn out for you. I am not here to judge you or lecture you on the anything you might have done. I am simply here to get the facts and give you the opportunity that nobody else will at this stage of the game. I am offering you the chance to tell your side of the story before the district attorney tells it for you. Are you with me so far and do you understand?"

John lowered his head into both palms of his hands and closed his eyes tightly.

"Yes, I understand."

SGT Anderson continued, "Do you believe that I am here to help you, help yourself regardless of how bad it is?"

"I hear you saying that but to be honest I do not fully believe it." John stared hard and deep into the eyes of the detective, and it was clear that fear was his biggest emotion. "How are you helping me when the things that I have to tell you are going to put me in prison for a long time?" John was restraining emotions that were welling up inside of him.

"John the realities of getting a long or short sentence is directly tied to your willingness to come clean about all the details and whether or not we have to spend man hours and resources to dig up the truth. I am talking about the truth that you can tell me today, right here and now in this room." The detective looked at John for a brief moment, then slowly pushed his chair back away from John and stood up. He opened up a briefcase and pulled out a yellow legal pad and pen and placed them on the table near John. "Ok, John, here is the bottom line. I am going out that door and I will be back in here in ten minutes. When I get back, I am going to ask you one question. With the answering of that one question, you will set in motion the course of your fate. I am warning you that I am the only friend you have right now. Trust me when I tell you that if someone other than me comes through that door, all bets are off and there is nothing that I or anyone else can do for you. I hope you understand."

Sgt. Anderson, slowly walked toward the door and turned and looked sympathetically at John. When the door closed, John dropped his head to his knees and began to rock back and forth, knowing that fate truly was in his hands.

Even though she was conscious and feeling a little bit better, the headache Wanda was feeling made her long for sleep. She could feel some pain in her right elbow where she had collapsed and hit the floor. The ride to the hospital was less than seven minutes and she could barely hear the sirens as the ambulance sped north up Route 1 to Potomac Hospital. It had been a long time since she had been down in Prince William County and was amazed at just how much the sprawling community had grown. The only recognizable buildings to her along this stretch of highway was Walgreens and Nissan car dealership that had been recently renovated. Her thoughts turned to John and she wondered if he realized what his deeds had done to her.

Her phone rang again and it was her friend Sandy. In less than two minutes Wanda explained everything that had happened at the police station and she reassured her that they were only taking her to the hospital for precaution. She said she would call back again just as soon as she was released and able to get back to the station. Detective Anderson had called the hospital and told them that he would send a police cruiser over to pick up Wanda when they released her, so she could come back to the station and pick up her car.

The brief ten minutes that John sat alone in the interrogation room seemed like an eternity. He stared at the grey blank wall in front of him and thought of how this would impact his family and inner circle of friends who had respect for him. He wished that he had options that did not require him going to prison for a long period of time. He wondered how he could have misjudged the character of Cindy so badly. Why did she set him up? Would ratting her out help his chances of leniency? Knowing that there was no way out for him now, he thought about what Detective Anderson had said minutes earlier when he left the room. Maybe, if he came clean and told everything some leniency could be granted. He struggled to get his thoughts in order and recall all the events that had brought him to this moment.

When the door opened, John was jolted from his thoughts and a tidal wave of fear swelled up inside of him. It was at this moment that he knew his moment of reckoning had arrived. It was all too painfully clear to him now, that when he left this interrogation room that his life would be changed forever.

The detective pulled up the chair close to him and leaned forward to read the expression on John's face. There was a determination on his face that John had not seen before.

"From this moment forward you shape your destiny. Now, do you want to tell me everything that got you to this moment? We are going to start with the truth John. Nothing else."

John could barely breath as he uttered the word, "Yes." And with that, the detective slid his chair back, reached into his briefcase and pulled out Miranda documents for John to sign, after having them read to him. With uncharacteristic gentleness, the detective pulled out a digital recorder, placed it on the table and slid it slowly in front of John. After an agonizing twenty minutes, all of the details were recorded.

Strangely, even though his confession was complete, John did not feel the rush of relief that he thought his confession would bring. Instead, he thought of the shame that he had brought to himself, to his family and church, and above all, to Wanda.

Chapter 6

She was released from the hospital and after picking up her car at the precinct, Wanda went back home to face a very long night. Eventually she took two sleeping pills, a small glass of wine and drifted off to sleep. The crushing headache she felt early the next morning was the indicator of just how much of an emotional crisis this ordeal was. Wanda lay in bed with the visions of the previous day's events consuming her mind. She wanted more time to consider what her options were and figure out how to prepare for what lay ahead. She rolled over to see the time on the bed side clock and realized that she had to function and go to work. She wanted to be anywhere besides work, facing people who were well-meaning but could not begin to fathom the magnitude of her crisis. When she sat up in the bed her head felt like it suddenly weighed fifty pounds. She was aware that a crisis that was so draining on emotions can also have a dramatic impact on body and health. She was not as fit as she would like to be but did take strides to do the basics like eat better and do some moderate exercise as her busy schedule would allow. The brief solace she found in the long, hot shower also allowed the moments she needed to face her emotions in tears.

After her shower, she picked out some bright colored clothing in an effort to brighten her mood. She stared into the large mirror and saw a woman who was struggling to hold it all together and put on a good face. She also wondered how long she could keep it up. Her inner strength had served her well during times of distress, like the time her mother died and she was thrust into the role of taking over her mother's estate and administration of the will. It was a task she was not prepared for and the learning curve of the legal details was at times overwhelming, but she pushed ahead with fierce determination to complete the task.

She flinched and was startled by the abrupt ringing of the telephone. Her nervousness intensified when she read the caller ID. It was Ms. Parks from personnel. At that moment she realized that she forgot to call her and give her an update. It was time to give her the details regardless of how embarrassing it may be. She answered the phone slowly and cautiously. "Ms. Parks, Hello. How are you? I first want to apologize and say how sorry I am for not getting back with you yesterday. I was overwhelmed with all that is going on in my family right now."

"Wanda, I called to check on you and find out how things are with you. We are worried. Now, I talked with Ted about giving you some extended time off. We can list it under your accrued personal days. Don't worry, you can still work on the account from home. Just call in and give him some updates and briefs on the clients. Will that work for you?"

"Oh, my God, Ms. Parks! You don't know how much I appreciate this! Yes, that will be fine and tell Ted I will call him in a couple of days to go over the client list and prioritize the ones we can close soon."

"Great! And please, if there is anything we can do to help you get through this, please give us a call. We are all here for you."

"Yes, I deeply appreciate it and I will be in touch. Thank you for the call, Bye."

She let out a huge sigh of relief after hanging up the phone. With the flexibility to work from home, for several weeks if necessary, she could focus on the endless barrage of things to do and phone calls to make while John was locked up. She didn't know where to begin or exactly what to do, but she did know a few friends who she thought would be helpful with this type of situation.

Andy Johnson was one such friend who Wanda had kept over the years, in fact many years past their on-again-off again fling they had while she was in college. He had often wondered why she would marry anyone other than him and he begged her to give him a chance at the life she deserved. But Wanda seemed to want a bigger chunk of life than what

Andy's security job could afford. Over the years however they remained very close and Andy was a constant friend in her life and had proven that he would do just about anything for her in a vain attempt to win her heart again or, better still, to get her to leave her husband. She decided to give him a call to see what advice he could give her, hoping that he would not press her for too many details.

She was a bit surprised that she actually could not remember the number that she had dialed so many times at two and three in the morning even when she was half drunk at a college party. After finding the number, she went to the living room, sat down on the couch and got her planner and a pen.

The sexiness in Andy's voice brought back memories of long ago passion. It was no surprise that he still sounded very youthful even though he was older than she was.

"Well hello baby, this is a very pleasant surprise! What have you been up too? His voice elevated with excitement.

"Oh my goodness! It has been a long time. It is so good to hear your voice. So how is the handsome one doing these days?"

"Mostly missing you and wondering why I still have a hole in my heart that you left there. But other than that I am doing just fine." He was mostly probing to see where her feelings stood with him after all this time.

"Andy come on now, you know you can be a bit dramatic at times."

"Dramatic, are you kidding me, Wanda? Girl, you do not know just how I feel about you and you probably never will."

"Ok, Andy maybe things could have been a little different between us, but now is not the time to look backward. I did not call you for that."

"Ok, so what did you call me for?" His curiosity seemed to be barely contained. "And please say that you still think about me often as I do you."

Wanda hated how Andy would press her to reveal feelings and thoughts she had about him. She knew he was a bit insecure and needed to be reassured of her love from time to time when they were dating, and it seemed that over the years it only intensified. "Andy, you know that I love you and nothing will ever change that. Of course, I think of you often. Don't you know that by now?"

There was a few seconds of silence as Andy pondered if Wanda really was happy with her current life and had somehow managed to block him out of it.

"Yes, I think I do. What's on your mind? You seem a little disconnected and distant." He said.

Wanda could feel the knot in her stomach growing with each breath as she began to tell him. "Andy listen to me, I need you to calm down and listen to what I have to say. If you can offer any advice or help, that would be great. My husband John got arrested on drug charges. He is in jail in Prince William County and I do not know what to do right now."

"Oh, my goodness, Wanda! I have to tell you, I am a bit shocked. I cannot imagine what you must be going through. Try not to worry too much. I will make some phone calls and get back to you. Does he have a lawyer?"

"I don't think so. Most likely he will go with the public defender. We do not have a lot of money." She said.

"Wanda, how are you taking all of this? You know I will try my best to be there for you if you need me for anything."

"Yes I know you will. I am just taking this one day at a time, but I must say I am deeply hurt by this. I have never had to deal with crap like this before."

Andy was elated that she confided in him and wondered if there was anyone else she felt just as confident in. "Have you told anyone else? Who knows about this?"

"No. No one else."

"Ok, we will try to figure something out and see how to get through this. How is John holding up?" Not that he cared but it was a way of showing some small empathy and to gage Wanda's feelings toward her husband. Andy had figured that the statistics were in his favor of their marriage breaking up and then he would have a chance to renew his ties to her. Three to five years was not too long to wait and he did not feel any shame for secretly wanting Wanda and John to divorce.

The faint softness in Wanda's voice spoke volumes of what she was feeling. "To be honest, I do not know what he is feeling and not too sure how this is effecting him. All I know is that I can barely hold up to all of this." Her weeping began again and Andy was deeply moved.

"I understand. I am not going to let you go through this all alone and shoulder the burden by yourself. Keep in touch and if there is anything

I can do or anything that you need, let me know. I will call or stop by to check on you this week."

"Thank you. That is very sweet. I would love that. Goodbye."

She hung up the phone and thought of the conversation and wondered if he really was that sweet or was there something else, he truly wanted. For now she would take any real help she could get. This was so overwhelming that it really didn't matter, as long as he could deliver on his promises.

This crisis in her life meant many decisions and actions in her life would be life changing for her and John. The thought of divorce lingered in the back of her mind, but she quickly diverted to anything else so that it would not nag her constantly.

Chapter 7

The Sunday morning services at Mount Zion Baptist Church under normal circumstances would be a welcome relief to the hectic week Wanda would have to face. However, this morning came with little emotion or enthusiasm to stand up in the church and sing, clap or even acknowledge her presence to other people. She had driven into the parking lot, put her head back on the head rest, closed her eyes and silently prayed for something, anything to make her feel better. A few moments later she looked at the bible laying on the passenger seat and wondered if perhaps some scripture would find the meaning of this experience in her life. After flipping through the Old Testament and into the New she landed on a very familiar verse: That stated "We live by faith and not by sight."

"How interesting." she thought. Moments later she strode into the church, still in search of some real answers for the events in her life. And like a dim light growing brighter, her thoughts turned to Andy. She tried to fight the movie playing over in her mind about how he could be a nice diversion to all she was feeling and that spending some real quality time talking to an old friend would allow her to become more creative in finding solutions to how she should move forward.

After an hour of songs, praising, clapping, and watching deacons pray long prayers as if to beg God to hear them, the service came to a close. Wanda often questioned her own spiritual commitment these days, as she had not felt the closeness of God in a very long time. The one thing that she was sure of was her knowledge of God and that he was totally in charge, even if she did not have the clear answers she was looking for.

She sat in the parking lot pondering how to spend the rest of her day. Usually Sunday's was a family day when her and John would try to catch up on missed chores around the house that week. Now that he was in jail Wanda had to come up with new ways to fill in the time. She tried to push back the creeping thoughts of loneliness, however the images of crawling into a big bed for another night of no comfort were causing her to mind to drift in different directions. She picked up her cell phone and called Andy.

"Hello!" The voice on the other end of the line was soothing and pleasant to hear.

"Andy, hi, it's me, Wanda. I hope I did not catch you at a bad time."

"No, not at all. How are you holding up?"

"I am ok, I suppose." Wanda said.

"Well now that does not sound like a woman who is at all sure of her mood. Tell me what is going on."

"I am sorry. I know I sound a little depressed, but this is all a bit much for me to handle and I sort of feel abandoned to bear it all."

"Wanda I told you that you do not have to do this alone and that you could count on me to be there for you. What you need right now is a way to reduce some stress, so why don't you come over to my place and relax for a while, have a glass of wine to clear your head. Maybe even watch a movie to get you laughing again. I bet you have not laughed out loud since this whole thing began."

"Ok, that sounds really nice, and yes you are right I have not laughed in a while."

During the ten-minute drive over to Andy's house, Wanda reflected back on all the good times that they had. Andy was kind, considerate and often would surprise her with gifts and gestures that would make her laugh. She also thought of the deep passion that they used to share. Just the thought of his gentle caress and tenderness moved her in ways she did not want to resist.

Pulling up into the drive way she felt a little nervous, because she was not accustomed to going over to another man's house, alone. However she pushed her uncomfortable feelings aside, glanced in the mirror over her visor and put her lipstick on. She wanted to be sure she looked perfect and thought of the outfit she was wearing and hoped that the form fitting skirt would reveal enough of her legs to entice Andy. He was a leg, thigh and booty kind of guy! She was very confident that her physical assets would keep his attention on her for a long time. She smiled at the thought of unique compliments that he would most likely give her that were long overdue from John.

She walked up the narrow walkway, rang the doorbell, took a deep breath, stepped back and waited for the door to open. A smile consumed her face when she saw him, he smiled back and was elated to see her beauty. Without much thought or hesitation, the next moment they were embraced for a long time, neither wanting to let go of the other.

"It is so good to see you." She said.

"It is so good to see you, Wanda. It has been way too long, you look gorgeous. I have missed your smile for all these years." Andy squeezed her even tighter as he relived the passionate moments of their past relationship.

"Come on in, make yourself comfortable, feel right at home. Wanda you know you are always welcome here. Have a seat and let me take that jacket. You look fabulous."

"Well it looks like you have been taking very good care of yourself also, Andy. I see you have gotten a bit buffed out over the last few years. Those big arms of yours felt really good holding and hugging me. Are you still working out and going to the gym?"

"Not as much as I used to. Seems like life sort of catches up with you, but I do find myself jogging and speed walking. Just trying to push back the middle age in me."

Wanda blushed a smile. "From where I am sitting I do not see any middle age in you anywhere."

"Well thank you Wanda that is very kind of you. Listen, can I get you anything . . . wait forget that. Let me get you something to drink. I will be right back." He quickly spun around and dashed into the kitchen and opened the refrigerator to get the bottle of wine that was half chilled. Moments later he reappeared in the living room with two glasses, a bottle of White Zinfandel and sat down beside her.

"Here take this, it will help you relax a bit. Listen, while you are here with me you do not have to have any worries. Clear your mind and let the world that you just left stay outside."

"Andy you know that is easier said than done."

"I know, but that is why we are here." He then moved his face close to her and whispered the same thought, "That is why we are here." His lips brushed against hers ever so slightly as to send a quiver down her spine. She groaned just slightly. When he did it a second time, it was with a sense of urgency to beckon the passion that was waiting to consume them both.

Wanda took a deep breath and then thought of a way to delay this moment even if for a few minutes. "I like your place Andy. My God, you were never this classy when we were together. Has some other woman upgraded your decorating skills, or did she decorate this place perhaps when she moved in?" Wanda was probing for some details of his life since they broke up and pondered if another woman held his heart. She looked the room over to find details and clues of a woman's touch. She knew Andy was not sophisticated and that he often said he did not need fancy décor in his private living space. He prided himself on being a very simple man and did not need much to keep him happy. In a way, she liked that about him.

"Well when you spend a lot of time talking to other folks, you pick up a few tips here and there. You kind of implement them for yourself and see how things work out. You know me, I never was a handy man. But here is my secret . . . I let other women decorate my place." The laughter in his voice still showed the boy that was quite animated when he thought he had a well placed punch line.

"Ahh! I see, is that how that works?" The smile on Wanda's face seemed to indicate her total amusement with Andy. Especially now that he seemed to want a bit more out of life than he had several years ago. Back then he only wanted to live for the moment or maybe the next, but beyond that was a burden he did not dare take on. Funny now after all these years, Wanda had come to realize that was exactly what had drawn her to him and sadly, what had torn them apart. She continued, "I must say they did a great job, and it makes me wonder if you have a great taste in women. And speaking of women, have many women have you had over here decorating your place?"

"What kind of question is that? My God, you must think I am a gigolo or something. Look it was just a few friends from time to time when I threw a party. They gave me some decorating ideas to liven the place up."

"Ok, if you say so."

"Hey, what kinds of music do you like these days? Are you still into Jazz?" Andy had always found Wanda to be very passionate about music. Often when they were dating, he would hear very loud jazz blasting when he stood just outside her apartment door and wondered why the neighbors never seemed to complain. Wanda had mentioned how she loved to get up late at night when there was hardly any traffic on the highway and cruise for about 60 miles listening to the latest Boney James CD.

"You know me, I cannot be without my Jazz."

"I got a new album I would like to try out on you. Tell me what you think." In a flash he got up, turned the stereo on and inserted the cd. He turned around and look back at her and said, "Anything you want to do or need just let me know, I just want you to be comfortable, OK?"

"Andy, your company is all I need really. I am just fine being here with you. Now come here and sit down, you need to relax. Do I make you nervous?"

"No I am not nervous, I am hospitable!" He sat down next to her and put his arm around her and drew her close to him. "Well if my company is all that you need, then my company is what you will get, as much of it as you want."

He then ran his fingers through her hair and leaned in and kissed her on the cheek. He took his time and smelled her hair and griped her face with his hands and kissed her. Slowly at first and then with ever deepening passion.

Wanda felt the temptation and deep longing to be held and loved. And equally as strong were the thoughts of resistance. Her mind was locked in turmoil between letting her body be touched and caressed and pampered to by a man who was so good at it, and her moral convictions of righteousness and obedience to God. It gave her much frustration that at times made her a bit angry and resentful.

"You know I really shouldn't be here with you." she said.

"Oh, and why is that?" Andy seemed a bit puzzled.

"Well you know that I am married. Even though that jerk of a husband got into a world of trouble and I do not know what is going to happen with us, I cannot abandon him and cheat on him."

"Nobody is asking you to cheat on him. I will not put you in a bad situation and I most certainly do not want to make your life complicated."

Laughing out loud at the last remark of a "complicated" life, Wanda then blurted out. "Are you serious? Do you really think that somehow my life could be even more complicated than this right now? Trust me when I tell you that I have had real practice at having complications in my life. Now if I were only good at handling it, I would be alright."

"I don't have all the answers to that but I can be here for you and help you try to figure it all out. Would that be OK?"

She looked at him and saw the boyish charm that attracted her to him so many years ago. She felt the rush of passion sweep over her. She leaned in closer to his face and said, "Yes I think that is exactly what I need, and at this moment I need . . . The kiss was long and deep and the moans were the only sounds that revealed her inhibitions slipping away. It did not take very long for the two bodies to become entangled in the satin sheets that adorned Andy's bed. Their love making was long, ravenous and deeply fulfilling for both of them. And what surprised Wanda the most was that it felt very natural, even right. She could not seem to find any guilt or shame to keep her from making love to Andy again and again, until the night found the morning.

Chapter 8

John found the jail environment to be far more intimidating than he had imagined. He knew some inmates had far more serious charges and wondered if perhaps their behavior reflected the crimes they had committed. The place was loud and the noise relentless. He was shocked to see grown men screaming as loud as possible just to irritate the correction officers and anyone else who was in the dorm. Having seen countless television shows about people in lock down, he was still surprised that the Prince William County jail had a few surprises. He would have preferred to be in a private cell to have some seclusion. And in his mind the added privacy would be a small temporary haven from the explosive events that were bound to happen in general populations. Although he did not feel directly threatened, he knew that his safety would be maintained in part by skillfully avoiding direct eye contact and saying very little. Still in the back of his mind he wondered what he would do if the pressure of another inmate grew beyond evasive measures. He had not been in an actual fight since grade school. And as he recalled, in that incident he was on the losing end and had to be rescued by other classmates and the teacher.

One tactic that John thought should work well in his favor was to stay physically in the near vicinity of the guards. His thinking was that by staying close to guards not only could he engage some friendly conversation with sensible people, but also if an altercation were to go down he stood a better chance of staying out of bodily harm and it would be good to have an officer witness his actions if an aggressor should provoke an attack.

While he thought that manipulating other people was relatively easy on the outside, it proved to be absolutely worthless in this environment. The guards rarely said anything other than to give the rigid commands needed to make the institution work and function efficiently. He sensed the coldness in them most of the time and had to believe that they regarded the inmates as faceless subjects. He tried to put himself in their shoes briefly and wondered what it would be like to have to monitor and control the likes of him, and hundreds of others that are far worse.

The routine of the jail is what he found to be the most fascinating. He wondered how having such a rigid lifestyle could be productive to having calm inmates. The coldness of this place made him long for the life at home where he was catered to by a loving woman, who cared for his every need. In jail however he was just another number who had been arrested for doing something horrible. In reality it meant that no one cared, his status meant nothing, his willingness to cooperate meant nothing. His only purpose there was to be held until the courts made a resolution of his case, and if that resolution did not go in his favor, then the jail would serve as a permanent holding place. He let his mind drift a bit and wondered how many of those orange jump suits were there for rape or murder. To amuse himself and pass the time away, he would try to guess what each inmate he encountered was in for. Having to tread lightly, and not make much contact with the inmates, he played this mental game to himself with much amusement. But after learning about a man three cells over, who from all appearance looked like he had once been a well-dressed and highly successful businessman, who had been arrested for the brutal slaying of several of his family members, John quickly dismissed the thought of matching people to their crimes. After all he thought, no one would have ever thought of him as someone who would ever get involved with drugs.

The jail provided more than enough time to reflect on what brought him here. But he made a conscious decision not to dwell on it too much. John thought his energy should be directed toward his upcoming arraignment and subsequent trial. He knew that his chances of getting a great defense attorney on the state budget was slim at best. Yet he could not see too many options at hand due to his personal finances that were just above bankruptcy. Of course there was no guarantee that even with a lot of money to get the best attorney possible that he would get a better defense. But the thought of a serious charge in the hands of a less than enthusiastic state appointed defense attorney, made him feel extremely uncomfortable and a bit nervous. He wanted to know exactly what he was up against and what the worst-case scenario could be.

It has been said that there is no typical day in the life of an inmate. And John would soon experience that first hand. The tensions of the inmates would fluctuate for no apparent reason. It did not take anything rational to set someone off, and more often than not it was just a way to get attention to break up the mundane existence of life behind bars. Even though John did all he could to avoid brewing conflicts, it was inevitable that he would cross paths with some inmates that wanted drama to go to a whole new level. That occasion came on a Wednesday afternoon just as lunch was being served in the chow hall. The inmates were filing along in line holding there trays in front of them for the helping of mystery meat and god knows what else, when an argument broke out between one inmate and the line server. Apparently the inmate thought the server had short changed him on the amount of serving he was allotted. In a flash the server and inmate were exchanging fists and just as quickly other inmates joined in. John got caught in the middle of the pushing and shoving and a few fists landed on his left jaw from an unknown assailant.

Moments later he was trying to pick himself up off the floor where several other inmates had taken cover. The chaos brought guards in from every side with batons in hand. They immediately began barking orders and landing blows.

"Line up against the wall with your hands in the air, now!" One guard shouted while at the same time drawing back on his baton to emphasize what would happen next if he did not get immediate compliance.

Several guards were entangled with the two primary inmates who began the fighting on the serving line. They were pulled apart and put into full restraints and led away, presumably to the segregated section. That was where they housed anyone who caused trouble and did not follow the rules. Landing in the hole was not just a threat, it literally added time to the sentence for anyone who wound up there.

That was something that John thought was very cruel and unfair. But he quickly realized that the old rules of fairness were and forever would be outside of the gates to the jail.

It took several minutes to restore order to the chow hall, but the guards were very thorough in frisking every inmate and returning them one by one to their cell. When John's turn to be frisked came he attempted to reason with the guard. "Officer I do not understand why we all have to go on lock down because only two people started this and I saw the whole thing. Would you like to hear the truth about how it all went down?"

"Shut up! One more word and you just bought yourself a week in the hole. Do you hear me? Now put your hands on that wall where I can see them and don't move!"

The humiliation of the moment, almost was unbearable and he knew without a doubt that he needed to lay low for however long it was going to take to appear in front of a judge. He could only hope that his defense attorney was as eager for his freedom as he was.

A couple of days passed before John was finally able to have a visit with his defense attorney. Upon first seeing the young man, neatly dressed in a dark gray pin striped suit with a bright red tie, John felt a bit uneasy as he was hoping to have gotten someone who looked like they had been in the game of life for a while. This young defense attorney looked like he just finished his SAT's about six months ago. "My god they sent me a high school senior". John hope this lawyer could not read his lips. If he was to trust his life and future outcome of his case to a defense attorney perhaps it was a good idea to believe that the lawyer was indeed experienced both in and out of the court room, and that he did not get legal counsel from his other beer drinking colleagues about the case he was currently working on.

Visitation in the jail seemed more like the likings of a caged animal being observed by people at a zoo. When his defense attorney arrived, it was obvious that he had not been inside of a jail to visit with inmates much. The awkward way he approached the viewing window and picked up the phone was a dead giveaway that he was not comfortable in this setting.

"Hello, John my name is Jesse Watkins. I have been assigned your case and will be handling your defense. How are you holding up in here?"

"Well I guess I am doing as best I can, considering the current circumstances. Did you actually seek out my case or was it the next thing in line and you got the draw?"

"Believe it or not John sometimes it works both ways, however another attorney was to handle your case but a sudden death in the family took him out of town, and he will not be back in time for your arraignment, which has been set for next Thursday morning at ten o clock."

"Well now that is where I come in and the exact reason I am here. We have to lay the ground work of your defense and you need to be well prepared for what the state is going to prepare against you."

"Well now that is where I come in and the exact reason I am here. We have to lay the ground work of your defense and you need to be well prepared for the state is going to prepare against you."

John stared through the glass window as to look past Jesse, and lowered the phone from his face. Jesse turned briefly to see what had his attention, and found nothing.

Tapping on the glass to get John's attention, he spoke softly. "What is it John?"

"Look I know I am in some deep hot water with these charges. I need you to level with me because I do not want any surprises. What is the worst case scenario and outcome I could be looking at." The sharp frown on John's face told of the fear that he was feeling inside. His eyes searched Jesse's face for any sign of anything less than what he feared. "And what specifically are they charging me with?"

"They are charging you with possession of cocaine, and you are looking at two to five years jail time."

John closed his eyes and shook his head violently at the thought of five years behind bars. The short time he had been incarcerated was already beginning to take its toll, and he could not see how he would endure five years. "Ok, so how do we handle this to give me any hope."

"There is always hope, John. I specialize in hope and I am going to give you the best defense possible. I just need the truth from you on all matters regarding this case, OK?"

John nodded in agreement and looked intently at him, then said. "Alright, I will lay it all on the line for you, just please do whatever it takes to get the best results. I know it is a long shot to think I will get only probation but I hope that is a possibility."

"Like I said before John, there is always hope."

The deep southern accent amused and startled John a bit as he listened to the lawyer give a brief strategy of his case.

Thirty minutes later he was back in his tiny cell and his mind drifted to Wanda, and the quietness of the home she had made very comfortable for him. He wondered what her life would be like if he were vacant for two years. Would the marriage survive? Could they both rebuild and start life over after he got out? He knew she was a very strong woman, but realized that she did not deserve what may lie ahead. Nobody did.

Chapter 9

Wanda was sitting at her office desk when her cell phone rang in her purse. She quickly opened it to see Andy's number on the screen. She was reluctant to take personal calls on the job but decided it must be important for him to call at this hour in the afternoon. In a hushed whispered voice, she answered. "Hello Andy, listen I hate to be so abrupt, but I cannot talk long I am at work, can I call you after five when I get out of work?"

"Ok, that will be fine, I forgot that you might be at work. Please be sure to call me, I miss you."

"OK I will talk to you then, bye." She hung up wondering why he thought it so important to call her at work. It was something that nagged in the back of her mind the rest of the day.

The strain of John's incarceration was starting to take its toll in small but noticeable ways. The long sleepless nights and midnight headaches had her feeling very run down during the day. She thought it would be a good idea perhaps to go to the gym and try to work off some of the stress so that she would be tired enough for a great night of sleep.

Twenty minutes later she strode into the Planet Fitness facility where the energy level was high and she could sense the male eyes searching up and down her body, when she walked past the free weights to get on the elliptical machine. While some women did not welcome the additional attention to their bodies, Wanda for one craved it. She needed to feel good about herself and the approving eyes of the men and even some of the women was just the ego boost that she needed.

She connected her ear phones to her cell phone and placed it on the cradle on the machine and began a vigorous cardio workout. Within minutes small beads of sweat formed on her forehead. The music pulsing in her head took her mind and imagination to a time when nothing but the joy of childhood and good memories brought laughter to her soul. Thirty minutes flew by virtually unnoticed and then she slowly took the five-minute cool down and looked at the total calories burned on the machine. While she did not really love the fact she needed to do some weights, today she wanted to be sure she did a complete workout, and that is not complete without the dreaded weights. She smiled knowing that with the burned calories she could treat herself to a well-deserved snack or treat, and lately chocolate mint ice cream was her guilty pleasure of choice.

Just as she was putting the key into the ignition her cell phone rang and seeing the caller Id made her a bit nervous. It was Andy. She hit the answer button and hesitated for a brief second. "Hello Andy."

"Hi, Wanda wanted to follow up and see how your day is going, and I also wanted to apologize for calling you at work. I did not mean to alarm you."

"Oh it's ok, and thank you so much for your care and concern. I think I am holding up for another day."

"I see, well to tell you the truth Wanda I do not see how you could be holding your self together at all."

"Andy I am a big girl and I have been through hard times before, and with the help of friends and my church and spiritual family I shall get through this also."

"Ok, great I am so glad to hear that. So what can I do right now, right this minute that will put a smile on your face?"

Wanda smiled and thought this was the perfect opportunity to get her sweet indulgence absolutely free. "Well since you want to be a real sweetheart, why not meet me at Friendly's and treat me to mint chocolate chip ice cream."

"Great consider it done. I can be there is 15 minutes, and I am going to bring a big appetite also."

Wanda was smiling and thinking just how easy he was to maneuver and manipulate. "Ok, I will see you there, bye."

Ten minutes later she parked her Honda near the sidewalk close to the front door of Friendly's. Glancing in the mirror she pulled out her glossy red lipstick and applied it sparingly. She ran her fingers through her hair and tossed it to back while combing through it. This was surprisingly one of those moments when she was getting a bit self conscious about her looks even though she knew that the man inside adored her and had always wanted her body. Even still she could not quite shake the uneasy feeling of wondering what the other customers in the restaurant would think upon their first look at her.

She strode through the door and quickly spotted Andy located in the back booth on the left. He was wearing a beige knit sweater over a blue dress shirt and red tie. He looked strikingly handsome and confident. That was something she admired about him over the years and found it very comforting at this time in her life.

Andy looked up and saw her coming and quickly got up and a big smile came to his face. He reached out with open arms to give her a hug, when she quickly said. "I just got finished at the gym and I have not taken a shower yet." She was just a bit embarrassed and wondered if any noticeable order was coming off of her.

"Girl give me a hug and be quiet."

They hugged for a few seconds and then sat down opposite each other. The table menus were neatly placed in front of both of them by the smiling waitress who was quick to take their drink order.

Andy looked at Wanda briefly to assess her mood, and then smiled and placed his hand over hers across the table. "OK, my dear. So, how was your day?"

"Well not bad, you know work was work. Nothing changes there. I have not been sleeping well the last few nights so I decided to go to the gym and work out in hope of working out the stress and getting tired enough to sleep like a rock tonight. At least I hope so. That is the plan."

"Yes, I think a good night's sleep will do you good. As I recall you are a very different person when you have not rested." Andy was grinning as he recalled the countless mornings he woke up beside her, just to found out that she was already up and in a really bad mood. It was in those early moments that she would flat out tell him, "This would be a good time for you to get some more sleep instead of talking to me right now or for the next hour or so."

"Andy, you know me too well."

"As I should. Isn't that a good thing?"

"Yes it is sweetie, yes it is."

Looking down at the menu Andy pointed out some of his favorite dishes he had tried before. "So what can I treat you to besides ice cream?"

"Well let's take a look at the menu and see. As I recall they have a tuna melt that is very good, I think I shall have that with some fries." Wanda was mindful that even though she had just burned off over 500 calories, she still should eat sensible.

She sat back and looked at Andy and smiled. He was even more handsome now than ever. She could tell that he had taken good care of himself over the years and for a guy who considered himself as an aging baby boomer, he had most of his generation beat hands down.

Even though she hated to admit it, she always felt very comfortable in his presence. Andy had a way of making her feel like she was the only woman in the world, even though she suspected that for sure there were several others that he had wooed to the same level of comfort that she felt.

"So tell me Andy, what would you do in my shoes about John?" She could not believe that she asked the question so straightforward. She valued his logic and unemotional approach to thinking about life. Many times while they were together, Andy would make a point to emphasize the bad choices that can be made when they are emotionally based.

"Well Wanda I must admit that this is a tough situation even for me to think about if I were in your situation. But I guess it gets down to the truth and a whole lot of honesty about your relationship with him and do you have enough love to get through this. The bottom line is only your heart can give you guidance in that area."

Wanda's eyes trailed off and stared toward the back wall that had beautiful pictures of cars from the 50's era. "To be honest all I feel is a lot of hurt and pain and anger. I feel lost and alone."

"I have known you for a very long time, and I have seen you in bad situations before. I have known you to be a very strong woman who was able to take on the world. And you did it well. But baby, you were not meant to be this strong or take on this burden. I feel it is unfair and not just, and Lord forgive me because I am trying to respect your marriage, but John was acting very selfishly when he decided to put drugs before you. Remember Wanda, that HE chose to make drugs more important than you."

"Ok, OK I know all of that, but what do I do about it?" The tears began to slowly well up and her speech became broken. She reached for the napkin to wipe her face. "I love him, but I do not think I can fix this. And how am I going to live without him for several years if he gets convicted?"

Andy got up and slid in the booth beside her and put his arm around her and pulled her close to him. With his other hand he took her napkin and wiped the tears that were flowing freely down her face. "Sweetheart that is why I am here. I am going to love you through it. You will not be alone. Will you let me do that?"

She put her head on his shoulder and wept. She nodded yes and said, "I am sorry for this, I just . . . I just . . ."

"Hey it is OK, you do not have to explain a thing. Just know that I am here for you and I promise to be here for you on the other side of this, OK? Now the first thing I want you to do right now, and I need you to trust me on this, is get you home for a good night sleep. A good night sleep can be good medicine for you at a time like this. And personally, I do not think you should be alone because you will be lying in bed all night thinking and racking your brain. So why don't you come over to my place. I will fix you a hot bubble bath and you can take all the time you need to just sit and relax and I will make you a nice drink to calm your nerves. How does that sound?"

"There is a part of me that says I shouldn't, but you are right if I go home I will not get any sleep. It will be another night of tossing and turning. Ok, lets go before I change my mind."

"Wanda, sweetheart I will not take advantage of you at such a vulnerable time in your life. I have slept on my couch before and I can do it again tonight or as many nights as it takes until you are better."

She looked at him for a moment and wondered if she could resist him. "Aww, that is so sweet and kind of you. You may be on your couch far longer than you want to be."

They ate and chatted about any and everything. After eating they spent another 15 minutes talking and laughing about some old memories they had made from long ago.

She smiled at him and then nudged him and slid out of the seat slinging her purse and started walking toward the front door.

Andy paid for the check and after a brief stop at the men's room he walked Wanda out to her car. The ten minute drive to his house at this time of evening was pleasant by comparison to the usual rush hour grind that was common in the metro area. Wanda had often expressed her desire to move to another part of the country where rush hour consisted of nothing more than a couple of large farm tractors and combines taking up a two lane country road. But for now this is where her life, career and uncertain marriage were playing out.

Upon coming inside the house Andy was quick to point out that the place was not as clean as he would like, and that over the weekend, it would sure to be done and crossed off of his To Do list.

"Believe me Andy if your house was a total mess I would tell you. It looks just fine. Besides you are guy, it will never look like a woman lives here. And you are not that talented in cleaning. I have seen the way you clean."

"Oh, really! So what exactly are you saying about my cleaning?"

"Well, let's just say that you get the basics but skip over the details and that is just fine. Most people are not anal like me, or compulsive. You have never heard me complain about your place, now have you?"

Andy thought she was going to give a couple tips to improve his domestic skills, but instead she plopped down on the couch and picked up the remote. "Is there anything good on TV tonight that you want to watch? I see you found the remote."

"Well I was thinking of finding something good on the movie channels. I want to watch a good movie to escape reality for a while. I find myself in the same boring routine of coming home and watching the news, which repeats itself for two hours."

"Oh my god, yes I know exactly what you mean. As a matter of fact if you have watched even a half hour of news, you already know what the next couple of hours of news will be. But feel free find whatever you want, and I will make us some popcorn, and something that you are going to love."

Wanda recalled the last time she was over at his house before they had broken up and the long night of passionate love making that followed. Somehow she would have to get better at resisting him, because after all her emotions would only complicate things if she were involved in an affair, regardless of how bad she wanted to justify it, it was still wrong.

While Andy was mixing up the intoxicating drinks and making popcorn, he found himself humming and singing out loud, very elated to have her with him all night again. Even though he had replayed their last encounter over and over in his mind, it was always like the first time he had met her when he was in her presence. He never could quite forgive himself for letting their relationship falter and fade. He was a bit immature then and he knew it. Besides he just felt like a committed relationship was something that required too much work, and work was something he was trying to do less and less. But now he was a more responsible person and needed to prove to himself that he could do the work necessary to grow a committed relationship. He was getting older and could sense that his youth would give in to practical living. And while it was a long time coming, he was ready. His only regret was that now that he was ready to trade in his playboy ways to the committed life, the woman he really wanted to commit to was now married. And worse yet she was sitting on his couch, needing his comfort and support as a friend. He had played that role to other women so often until they took for granted that all he ever wanted was to be a big brother to them. It made him frustrated, because he thought that if God wanted him to have a sister or sisters he would have gave him some.

Coming back into the living room, Andy put the bowl of popcorn down in front of Wanda and a large salt shaker.

"You know you should not be eating a lot of salt. Are you still keeping your blood pressure under control and taking your medication?" Wanda inquired.

"Yes as a matter of fact I am. It took a while for the doctor to find the right combination but after about two years and up to four medications, yes, it is well under control."

"Good, because I know you. You have a habit of not taking your pills daily and thinking that just because you feel fine, that you are fine. I would not want anything to happen to you, so do not be stubborn. You are not getting any younger and you need to take care of yourself." Andy plopped down beside her and handed her a drink. "Here take this, it is one of my favorite special creations just for you. I think you are going to love it. Tell me what you think."

Wanda looked at him for a moment and tried to hold back the thoughts of date rape and the many cautions that went with it. Surely Andy would not drug her and then take advantage of her. No, no. He just was not the type to do that. She took a sip and savored the taste, knowing that it was as delicious as it was powerful. "Wow that is pretty strong. Do I dare ask what this is?"

"Well you can ask, but that does not mean that I am going to tell you." Andy was smiling while looking at the bewilderment on Wanda's face. "But listen sweetheart just to put your mind at ease I did not put anything in here but love juice."

"Love juice? What exactly is that?" Wanda picked up the glass and stared at it and then turned to Andy.

"Wanda I am going to ask you to trust me and know that it is all good, and you know I would never make anything to harm you."

"Well to tell you the truth Andy it is not the harming I am concerned about, it is the non consensual sex."

"Wanda please, don't go there. I should not have to say anymore. We are both grown adults and we are both smart people. So I would appreciate it if you would give me the benefit of the doubt." Andy seemed to be a bit frustrated and angry that Wanda would think so negatively about him.

"Ok, I am sorry, I apologize I should not have said that. And you are right you have never been out of line or disrespectful toward me ever."

"Ok, great, now we are here, I want you to relax and enjoy the evening. Watch whatever you want and let me help you with those shoes." He kneeled down beside her and slowly untied the shoe strings to her sneakers that housed delicate feet. "Now doesn't that feel better?" Andy slowly and gently rubbed and massaged her feet for a few minutes.

"Wow! You are good, and I think I will bring my tired feet to you more often for treatment like this."

Andy smiled. "Yes, you can bring them here as often as you wish, no charge."

"I am a little bit surprised at you. How did you learn how to pamper a girl like this? Who has been teaching you all this stuff? You were not the pampering kind when we were together. So tell me, what happened? What changed in you?"

"Changed, what changed? Nothing has changed. Wanda you seem to be so independent. You did not strike me as the kind of person who wanted much attention and pampering so I didn't. As a matter of fact it hardly ever crossed my mind with you."

"What girl does not want to be pampered?"

"Well sweetheart all you had to do was make your request known, and I would have certainly done it. But I am willing to make up for lost time, tonight."

"Are you really, Well I tell you what Andy, I will let you make up for all that time."

"Ok great! Consider it done, and it begins with this bath, and some. . . ."

Wanda put her fingers to his lips. "Shss no don't tell me what you are going to do. Just surprise me, ok, just simply surprise me."

"Very well." Andy said. He then hurried off toward the bathroom.

The few minutes she was left to herself gave her time to reflect about the times when John used to be far more romantic than he had been in recent years. She had wondered if the daily strain of marriage just took its toll or was there something else going on. As a vibrant woman full of sexual passion, she knew that if it was suppressed too long she would end up resentful and bitter of any other woman who was in a healthy relationship. She heard the water running in the bathtub and wondered just what exactly Andy had in mind. Whatever it was she most certainly needed his tender touch and caress. She needed to be loved and appreciated in any small way. And she was open to even the smallest gestures of romance.

Her thoughts drifted to John. She knew he detested the way drugs wrecked lives and destroyed families. Which was why she found it so hard to believe that he could be involved in the charges that were brought against him. What went wrong, and how did he get so far off track that he could not find his way back? The thoughts came rushing over her, and she had to concentrate hard not to panic.

From the bathroom Andy's voice could faintly be heard. "I will be with you in a minute and help you get some stress off of you."

"Alright, thank you." Wanda turned toward the bathroom down the hall and noticed that the lights were very dim and actually flickering. The thoughts of a warm relaxing and soothing bath was something that she anticipated, especially since her arms and neck were a bit sore from the workout at the gym. She lifted weights moderately to bring some much needed tone back to her arms. While for the most part she kept her repetitions high and the weights low, however today she put on more weights than she had been used to. And now that it was late evening, the soreness began to show up.

She jumped in shock as she felt the cool touch of Andy's hand on the back of her neck. He slowly with his fingers gently massaged her neck muscles and then let his hands fan out to her delicate shoulders and down to her arms. She moaned at the tenderness of his touch, which made her long for so much more. Whispering into her ear, he said, "Come let me take care of you, now just close your eyes and promise me you will not slap me."

The smile she gave him was all he needed to see to understand just how much she approved. "Ok, I think I am going to like this."

"No, you are going to love this!"

He unbuttoned her blouse and helped her slip out of it. Underneath was a pink sports bra that accented her near perfect breast. With slow precision he unfastened and discarded the bra on the floor. Taking both hands he continued to massage the front of her while standing in back of the couch bending over at the waist. When he brushed against her nipples with his fingers, he stared at her face to get an expression. When nothing appeared he slowly and methodically began making small circles around the nipples and then slowly rolling them between his thumb and index finger. She heaved her whole body in response, slowly at first and then the passion crept up with a force Andy did not expect.

Wanda took both arms and extended them high over Andy's head and grabbed his head with both hands and with directed purpose pulled him over her shoulder and pressed his head against her begging breast.

The awkward position had Andy's body weight slowly taking his whole body upside down and he slid down on to the couch in a crumpled mess beside her. Wanda laughed out loud when he came over the edge and was awestruck at the position of his head. Andy could not restrain his body from the fall into her lap face first. With his face buried between her legs and his mouth aligned perfectly at her vagina, Wanda even surprised herself when she pulled down her yoga pants and panties forcefully and then took his head and mouth and pressed it against her opening. She held his head in position with the tightening of her thighs to ensure compliance with her need for immediate pleasure and gratification that only his tongue could give. Andy tried to yell out "Wan. . ." It was at that very second with his mouth wide open that Wanda pulled his head firmly in place with his mouth over her vagina. He obliged her the pleasures she wanted and they both worked up a level of passion that had lied dormant for so many years.

Minutes later Andy was struggling to get his pants off while hoping on one foot to the bedroom with Wanda in tow. "Well I guess your bath will have to wait for a while." Andy said.

"You do not hear me complaining do you?" Wanda smiled.

The love making was ferocious and sweet and delicate all at the same time. Wanda threw caution to the wind while lying in his arms. She looked at him and rubbed her hands along his long lean body that was still pulsating with the energy of the intense sexual passion they shared.

Chapter 10

Wanda still lying still with her eyes closed could hear the deep breathing of Andy sleeping beside her. She wanted to feel the warmth of his naked body next to her for a few more minutes before jumping in the shower. The memories of long ago seemed to drag on as the sun grew brighter in the room. The digital alarm clock read 0732, which meant the morning would be fast and furious before checking into the office. The thoughts came very slow at first and then the rush of everything that she had been feeling on and off about her renewed encounters with Andy, came pouring in. She could not deny that she was a Christian and that there was accountability for her relationship with him. And then the fact that she had not been a good witness and the scriptures came pouring in relentlessly to remind her that she was not accustomed to the same sinful acts that the rest of the American culture deemed as normal. She could not be politically correct and still represent Jesus Christ. Of course she knew that. But why did her human side justify her every thought of Andy? And why did she seemed to have a right to do so, after what John had put her through?

She agonized over how much she needed wanted and deserved to have the physical love of a man to make the unbearable, bearable. Perhaps she would just delay for a bit longer before breaking off the physical relationship with Andy, or maybe it would dissolve on its own. But for now she was too weak to say no to the passion she so desperately needed, and wanted to hang on as long as the justifications in her mind would allow. Yes the guilt was there, but surprisingly not as strong as she thought it would be. She took only a little comfort in knowing that she did actually feel some guilt, knowing that the Holy Spirit was still very much a part of her. Without a doubt sooner or later she would have to listen and obey, but for the moment she needed to dull her senses enough to make love to the man beside her one more time in the morning passion that was always a favorite between them.

Twenty five minutes later the twisted bodies lay panting on the bed that was looking like a war zone. Panting for breath Andy said, "Girl I don't know what happens to you in the morning when you wake up and want to make love like that, but I sure love it! Trust me when I tell you that I feel sorry for everybody who thinks drinking a cup of coffee is the way to get energized in the morning. For me just give me a double helping of Wanda, caffeinated!" His laughter was loud and he leaned over on her in uncontrollable outbursts. "Whew girl I am telling you it don't get no better than this."

"You are so crazy" Wanda picked up the pillow and flung I at him just to see him duck as the pillow sailed past the lamp desk barely missing it and landing on the floor.

"Yes I know I'm good, and getting better all the time." She took full glory of the proud moment to praise her sexual conquest.

"All I know Wanda is that you and that body can be very addicting."

Wanda looked at him and smiled. "Good, then I have you just how I want you, totally addicted to every inch of me. And trust me this is one addiction you will not break so easily." She took her finger and brushed it across his lips and then leaned in and kissed him with a deep hunger than only he could satisfy.

Minutes later the shower stalled steamed from the hot shower she took. And during those stolen moments of peace, quiet and solitude, Wanda slowly let her thoughts get organized for the day ahead. She would call the office and let them know she would be running a few minutes late as she had an appointment with legal counsel regarding John. She needed to know what his chances were of beating the charge or what he would be facing in prison time. It was the kind of information that would change and shape all of her decisions going forward.

She never liked to think too far ahead as life always had a way of undoing all of her plans. But with the prospect of living without John for several years she needed a game plan for survival. His income was the stabilizing factor, that she had grown used to. A comfortable lifestyle was something she had taken for granted, knowing that his job as a driver was relatively secure and that his long time with the company was the catalyst for the 401K and stocks he had acquired with the company. Now all of that seemed not to matter since his arrest. Also the thought of him ever getting a job again was something that shook her to the very core. If he was convicted, he would carry a felony conviction for the rest of his life and that meant, he was not going to see the prestige of the jobs he once had.

It was at this moment that she realized she needed Andy far more than she wanted him. It was very embarrassing for her to ever ask for help or get money from anyone, but the truth was that sooner or later the bills would be piling up and deadlines would come and go, and not enough money in their checking account to cover it all. The mortgage was the biggest concern that was only a week away, followed by a car payment the following week.

She felt a little stir of anger from not taking control of their finances earlier in the marriage, for not saving more of her own money for situations just like this. She had heard the stories of other women who were married and let their husbands control them financially as a way of keeping them in very abusive relationships. She swore it would not happen to her and yet here she was now in a situation just as bad, and in much the same despair as the women she thought were too weak to manage their affairs. Truly she had to think of a way to take control of this before it got way too bad. But how? And who could she trust to understand what she was facing and be willing to give her sound advice.

As the water from the shower streamed down her back, she closed her eyes and visualized herself relaxing from the head down, letting the stress and tension drain into the bathtub along with the suds. In that moment a few people came across her mind to consider confiding in. One was a lifelong friend named Angie, who had been married, divorced and everything in between to include some alternative lifestyle choices that both shocked and intrigued Wanda. She would call her later and just get a feel for how she would approach this. Angie had been in serious financial trouble during her divorce and on more than one occasion she came close to losing everything, and even repossessions hunted her down. Wanda was amazed at how strong she was and managed to bounce back even stronger than before. Even though the two were close, Wanda never told her how she admired her courage and strength during those difficult times. She really wanted to ask her just how she kept it all together and seemed to have such a calm spirit even when all hell was breaking loose all around her. Yes, this would be a good time to look into her soul and see just how she did the impossible when things were at their worst.

There were times when the adventure side of Wanda would lose all sense of reason and things practical, such as bringing a change of clothing to go back to in the office in. She had thought her stay at Planet Fitness would bring her back into the same routine of going home, taking a shower then neatly preparing for the next day of work, and finishing up her domestic duties of house cleaning and perhaps dinner. Last night seemed to take a life of its own, and now here she was less than an hour from the start of work without any clothes.

With her hair still wet and a large beige towel wrapped around her, she stepped into the hallway and called out for Andy. "Andy, I have a serious problem honey!"

Andy called out from the bedroom, while putting on his boxer briefs. "Now just what kind of problem could you have at this moment?"

"Well it seems my dear that I do not have any clothes!"

Andy could be heard laughing out loud. "From my point of view that is not a problem at all, as a matter of fact I feel very fortunate that you don't have clothes on!" Andy was at the other end of the hallway looking at her.

"Stop it Andy, I am serious I do not have any clothes for work. I came over here last night from the gym, and I did not bring a change of clothes. I got to get some clothes for work. Would it be possible for you to buy me something simple to hold me over for the day. Just a blouse, skirt, and bra and maybe and accessory or two? Please please! I promise I will pay you back when I get paid on Friday."

The lump in Andy's throat grew at the thought of putting out more money for people in need. Over the past several weeks he had been stretched very thin, helping a lot of his 'friends'. Just happen that all of his friends were women, most of which he had a history with. And the fact that he felt needed even though their relationship was far from mutual, was enough to keep them in his life on some level. But he hated the phone calls that only came when one of his 'friends' had a most urgent financial need. He looked at Wanda and wondered if she too would fall in this category. But for now he was sure she was in genuine need, and after all the night of passion they shared came by impulse and that was what put her in this predicament.

"Ok, not a problem don't sweat it."

"Great, now listen we don't have much time because I have to get to work by nine. Follow me to Kohl's over by the mall. I will get a few things get it paid for and be on my way. You are a sweetheart and thank you so much for getting me out of a tight jam. And don't worry I promise to have clothes with me next time I come over here."

"Wow, that's too bad! I kind of like it when you don't have clothes to wear."

"My, God you are impossible! Hurry up and finish getting dressed we have to get going."

"Umm! Could you tell me what you are going to wear in the mean time?"

"I am sure you have a pair of sweats I could use. Get going please! I cannot be late, I probably should have went home last night anyway, but I stayed because. . . well never mind! Just hurry please."

Ten minutes later they were speeding toward the merge onto I-270. Wanda knew that traffic at this time of morning would be very heavy and that rush hour could care less about her work schedule. With that in mind, she began the precision driving that is best suited for race car drivers, with her weaving in between cars and taking every opportunity possible to pass. She watched the rear-view mirror to see if Andy would follow her every move. He did. The stop at Kohl's was frantic as she hurried about picking out a skirt and blouse that was semi color coordinated. Without even second guessing her size she found herself minutes later in the checkout line hoping that the cashier was quick and efficient. "Listen," Wanda began, "I need a really big favor. I am running late for work and I needed to buy these clothes because I did not have anything to wear. Would it be OK if I could change in the dressing room? I will only be a couple of minutes."

"Yes, sure I understand, it is back in the left-hand corner of the store." The cashier smiled and handed her the bags after processing Andy's credit card. While he was signing the receipt Wanda quickly hurried to the back of the store.

Andy waited outside by her car until she came out. Minutes later she appeared at the front door and was looking in her purse for car keys.

"Wow! You look fabulous!" Andy's eyes lit up at the sight of Wanda and the way she filled out the just tight enough skirt, with curves that most certainly would get her far more attention than he would be comfortable with.

With a brief kiss and a hug Wanda told him she would call him later and again thanked him for his help. Andy stood there as she backed up and sped through the parking lot to exit the mall. Shaking his head in disbelief he smiled, got in his car and with careful control and mindful that a parking lot was dangerous to other cars and pedestrians, he proceeded much slower.

Wanda stepped into the office feeling a little uneasy and nervous from her night spent with Andy. And to make matter even worse, her job, she had heard rumors about upcoming layoffs and wondered if she would survive these rounds of cuts. She was a great worker but the downturn in the economy had force the company to make some drastic changes, and a reduction in force was the first of cost cutting measures they had proposed. Corporate restructuring was something she feared, because she had seen firsthand several long-term associates with more valuable skill sets become suddenly expendable. Over the years she had committed herself to retraining and going back to school and had thought about getting an advanced degree but chose not she when she got married. Looking back on those decisions now that John was in jail, she wondered if the sacrifices she had made on his behalf to be a good wife to him was worth it. Even though John's predicament was much different now, in her mind it seemed very clear that he still got the better end of the deal. After all he was given the time and freedom to advance his career. She had always stood by him regardless of what goals he had set and challenged him to do more. Would she now pay the price for self-sacrifice with the many days of loneliness that would come if he were convicted and incarcerated?

She was a well-groomed neatly dressed professional virtually all the time, but this morning she did not feel or look at her best, and wondered if other people in the office would notice. The thoughts in her mind would not allow her to concentrate on work. She was needing to plan for some time off and use her vacation time for the upcoming trial for John.

It made her upset to think she would have to spend her vacation time in a courtroom instead of the Virgin Islands, that she had planned with John just a few weeks before.

The door to Mrs. Parks office was open. Mrs. Parks the personnel director, always kept her door open as much as possible to reflect the open-door policy in the company and the open lines of communication between management and associates. Wanda knocked lightly on the door hoping that openness and understanding would rule the day when she asked for the time off.

"Hello Wanda, how are you? Please come on in. It's good to see you."

Closing the door behind her Wanda took a deep breath. "Thank you, Mrs. Parks, I seem to be hanging on. Listen the reason I needed to see you is to ask about using some of my vacation time for a personal matter that has come up. I just wanted to know how much time I have on the books. I am not sure as of yet the exact time or days I will need but will keep you updated." The lump in her throat grew as she explained that her husband had been recently charged and incarcerated and awaiting trial.

Mrs. Parks listened with great attention and seemed to be very empathetic. "Oh my God, Wanda I cannot imagine what that must be like for you. Listen, I will talk with your department head and see if we can get someone to fill in for you the week of the trial. I would hate for you to have to use your vacation time for this. Just keep me posted about the time you will be needing off and we will do everything we can to free you up, OK?"

Wanda smiled and thanked her, just before tearing up. "I am sorry, I just have been . . ."

"Oh sweetheart I know you been through a lot, here." . . . she offered her the tissues from her desk drawer. Why don't you take the day off and we will see you Monday? It will give you a bit more time to get yourself together. Don't worry about the office, your accounts are in good order and we have a temp that needs something to do, so we will train her at your desk. I want you to take care of yourself. Is there anything else we can do for you?"

"No, but I so deeply appreciate your understanding, and I will be in touch."

Wanda turned to open the door and leave when Mrs. Parks said, "Wanda, do not hesitate to call the company Life Resource Line, if you need someone to talk to at any time. They have some excellent counselors and I have called them myself when I was going through my divorce. We all need some help from time to time, remember you are only human."

Wanda breathed a little sigh of relief when she stepped out of the office and walked to her car. Knowing that she could take the rest of the day off, she wanted to prepare for the visit to see John on Saturday.

Chapter 11

For John jail life was different than what he had imagined and most certainly different than what was portrayed in the movies. And even though there were times he welcomed the solitude, his jail cell was small, and very noisy. The other inmates were very loud and there seemed to be a constant clanking of the bars. The bright lights were overwhelming especially when he wanted to go to sleep. At home he had grown accustom to daytime naps, but this was not an option here. The food was barely edible, and he tried not to think about what could have been put in his food before it reached his cell.

The correctional officers seemed very hard and cold toward all of the inmates. John reasoned within himself that having to go to work every day in this type of environment could do that to a person who had otherwise lots of compassion and sympathy. What came as quite a surprise to John was how many young inmates were around him. They also seemed to be the ones who were loud boisterous and seemed to have the most infractions. It appeared they had a lot to prove and would get in fights with other inmates just to show their status to their peers and anyone else who challenged the power struggle that was never ending. John just wanted to keep a low profile and get out of this place as soon as possible. He knew that if convicted on the charges he could be in jail for a very long time. That thought kept nagging at him and even though he tried to push it out of his mind, the thought of being in this type of environment finally hit him. He felt a deep sense of fear and dread. He did not have many legal connections on the outside, and good sound advice was hard to come by inside. All of the jail house lawyers who boasted of legal expertise, had not done much to advance the simplest cases of far lesser charges.

He knew that Wanda would try to find a decent lawyer, but she was already overwhelmed with all of this. He hated that he put her in this hard position to overcome. He wondered what kind of man he would be after spending several years in a prison. He had heard dozens of stories of how prison life can drastically change a person. He had never thought of jail or prison as a "correctional facility" as nobody's behavior had ever been corrected by being locked up for an extended period of time. He chuckled to think that he may become his own test case. His mind kept drifting back to Wanda, with him wondering how she was holding up under the strain and stress. Visitation hours were from noon to three pm on Saturdays, and thought surely, he would see her soon. He could only hope that her anger had subsided, although he knew it would be unreasonable to think that she would forgive him any time soon even if she was a Christian.

He reflected back on all the ways that Wanda had made an extra effort to make the small house a home. During his off time and when he would finally make his way home, he spent a lot of time alone to himself on the computer or reading. Wanda wanted to make a separate room that was both cozy and warm for the both of them to spend much needed alone time together. She wanted him to have his own space to relax and do the things he enjoyed. Having his own man cave would put him where she wanted him the most, home. She surprised him like no other with a 47-inch flat screen tv, that was waiting for him one weekend when he came back from work. She had it installed along with theatre quality surround sound. What a startling contrast compared to his 6X9 cell that he now occupied.

Several days had gone by before he heard from his public defense attorney. At his brief arraignment he pleaded not guilty. He knew it was very risky to have an unskilled public defender to handle his case, but he could not afford anyone else. While he did his best to keep the bills paid at home, he never had anything set aside extra in savings for a rainy day or times such as this. The thoughts circulated through his mind how people with lots of money and means had much better defenses and better outcomes in front of a judge or jury.

Chapter 12

Wanda absolutely hated the fact that she was now the sole bread winner of their household due to John's incarceration. She wondered how long it would be before the struggle to keep a roof over her head and food on the table would take its toll. Andy had offered to help her from time to time, especially when John's paycheck did not seem to be enough to make ends meet. But she forced herself to deny him, because she did not want to be obligated for sexual favors in return. Andy had never implied that sexual bribery was in his thoughts but the two of them had a history and a very steamy romance before and it would not take much of a spark or even an excuse to rekindle it again. Furthermore, she did not want to put herself in a position to be dependent upon him to bail her out every time she was in trouble or financial need.

The Saturday morning visit to the jail was very trying on her emotions. Every time she showed up, the tight security and entrance processing made her feel like she was an inmate. Saturday traffic was horrendous and these visits were putting a strain on her nerves and then there was the additional cost of gas for the round trip from Maryland to Virginia. She was a nervous wreck and nearly in tears every time she picked up the phone in the visitor's room to talk with John. On one such visit she broke down in tears and dropped the phone and put her head down on the small window ledge and cried uncontrollably for several minutes. It crushed John's heart to see her fall apart, knowing that he alone was the cause. He took the receiver from his ear and tapped on the window begging her to pick up the phone and continue. It seemed like an hour before she picked up the phone and then looked at him with tear stained eyes and slowly said, "John I do not know how much more of this I can take. I do not know if I can do this anymore. I hate that you put me in this situation. I can barely keep it together. I am falling behind on the mortgage, I have missed a car payment. They are about to cancel my insurance. This is just awful, and I have never had to do this before. I have never lived like this before, John! How could you do this to me? What am I supposed to do and how am I going to survive?"

Her words cut deep into John's heart as she lashed out at him over and over again for his selfish act. He was so lost to find words to console her, knowing that he was powerless to really do anything meaningful to help her while in lockup. He shook his head at her showing utter despair. "I just do not know what I can do, and baby I am so sorry I got you into this."

"I do not know if our marriage will survive this John. I think there has been too much hurt and pain to heal. Things will never be the same between us.... never!" Shaking her head she got up from the small chair, looked at the man she thought she knew and slowly kissed her hand and placed it to the glass. "I have to save myself now John, you left me no choice. Goodbye." And just like that she turned and picked up her pace as the emotions swept over her and she quickly disappeared from John's sight. He almost collapsed as the realization of his marriage dissolving finally hit home.

Surprisingly she felt numb while driving back home from the jail. The drive home was even more intensifying with nagging thoughts of Andy in her mind. She knew she would have to tell him that this could not continue, and that it was wrong, and that they both needed to repent. The real agony came from knowing that she would not be able to see him on a regular basis as before. But in her mind she wanted some small justification to continue to see him some more. The guilt and shame began to creep up on her, but she knew that was part of the sin that she had committed. She was glad to have the rest of the day off. She needed to rest and clean the house and do anything to get her mind off of the things that had been plaguing her lately.

Arriving back at home, Wanda sifted through the mail that was in her mail box. She seemed a bit nervous as she flipped through the envelopes, noting the bills were the ones with the little windows. In her mind she was sorting out which ones could be paid at the last minute and even go past due for a week or so until her paycheck was deposited into her checking account. She was not ready to feel the mounting pressures of the bill collectors. The two hours she spent in the house made her feel very lonely and a bit depressed. She forged ahead with cleaning and vacuuming and dusting just to fight off the urge to climb into bed and cry the rest of the afternoon. She was very glad to have the rest of the day off but did not know exactly what to do with herself. After finishing cleaning in the kitchen, she plopped down on the couch and looked at the envelopes and the bills contained therein. And then her mind began to wonder. She had no doubt that the word of God was true. Countless times she had seen the word of God and select scriptures unfold before her very eyes. She knew deep down in her heart that God would not make an exception or excuse her sin. She recalled too many times how her sins had played out with just punishment. What she feared the most about this was that she had read somewhere in the scriptures that sexual sin, in particular fornication and adultery was sinning against your own body. Which meant in her mind that some kind of physical ailment, and she had always thought that the countless illness and diseases that plagued people such as cancer and other life-threatening diseases, could have been the direct result of sin. She was reminded of the words of Jesus to someone in the Bible, in reference to a healing he had done, in which he had told the person, 'go and sin no more unless something worse should happen.' She did not want to think about the adultery act was listed in the top ten of God's commandments, and that it demanded a just punishment of death. It took a moment for her to get her head around that thought. She could just imagine the rocks being hurled at her if she was in the middle east and had been caught in the act of adultery.

Hoping perhaps that Andy did not want anything more and would not pursue the sexual aspect of their relationship or try to rekindle a romantic bonding, she would let time go by and hopefully this whole thing would subside. She did not want a confrontation with him and hated confronting him directly with all of this. She did not know what his spiritual status was as a Christian. But hoped that he had the decency to understand that what they had engaged in was very wrong.

The uneasiness kept growing inside of her, she tried to push it back, but the thought was there. That small still voice that was nagging at her with the truth that she could not deny. As a matter of fact the more she tried to push it out of her head the louder it grew, "You shall not commit adultery." That was immediately followed up with, "Fornicators and adulterers, God will judge." and "Your sin will surely find you out."

She knew that the guilt that she felt was going to drive her to reconciliation and repentance over her act, well at least she hoped that it would.

Chapter 13

It was not always clear for Wanda, but there were times when she knew that some advice from a trusted friend could be very valuable. That friend was Angie Wilkerson, who had a lot of wisdom and inner strength that got her through some very tough times. Wanda suspected that Angie perhaps thought that something was not right in their marriage. She appreciated her discretion in not vocalizing it. She still felt a little bit shamed and embarrassed to have to confirm what Angie most likely already knew. So it was a natural act for Wanda to call her and get some insight into her growing predicament. The butterflies only grew stronger with each press of the button on her cell phone, and when the familiar voice of Angie said hello on the other end, there was a moment of silence.

"Angie, how are you girl?"

"Wanda, it is so nice to hear your voice. I was just thinking about you just the other day."

"Wow, thinking about me, that is so sweet of you. It is nice to know that someone is thinking of me these days. Angie, I know it has been a while and I am so sorry and apologize for not contacting you sooner and keeping in touch more."

Angie listened intently, hoping that she could break down the emotional barriers that hinder honest conversation.

"I wish I could tell you that I was caught up with a thriving career and very busy with work and an activity filled family life. But the truth is, my life seems to be..." The long pause was painful as she struggled for words. "exploding out of control and I don't know what to do to gain it back." She fought the tears to no avail and was a bit angry that she could not be stronger in this moment. 'Damn, why did John do this?'

"Wanda, honey, what's going on? What's wrong?" Angie's mind began to speculate but thought that if Wanda found the courage to call her, she would most certainly open up.

"Everything," The sobs were heavy, and her breathing was forced and labored. "Angie you just do not know how much I need to hear something that I can believe right now, from someone I can trust and believe in." She thought about that for a moment and then continued. "I was supposed to be able to trust and believe in my husband, but he . . .he betrayed me Angie."

This time the silence was deafening even though brief.

"Oh, Wanda honey I am so sorry to hear that. What is happening between you to?"

"I thought I would never find myself on a phone explaining to someone that my husband cheated on me and got arrested for drug distribution and he is in jail at this moment facing some serious prison time. No this cannot be my life; it must be something I saw on television or a movie somewhere. Right?" She took a paper towel and wiped her eyes and sat down on the couch feeling very drained. The thought of getting up again made her feel even more tired.

"Oh, my God, Oh my God! I do not need to ask how you are holding up, and I know you are doing everything in your power to pretend you are strong. But honey you do not have to be strong for things like this. As a matter of fact, a famous person once said, 'take my yoke, because my burden is light'."

"Angie, please do not take this the wrong way, and I know you mean well. But I just do not feel any power from God right now, as a matter of fact I do not feel him anywhere near me. All I feel is hurt anger and confusion and despair, and I am not sure any bible verses are going to fix that." She could feel the anger at the edge of her tongue. She knew it was not fair to be angry at God, but the truth is she was.

She prayed many years ago for a husband and family and thought that John was the answer to that prayer. Of course, she had to also admit that she literally picked John up from a night club and got him drunk and then seduced him to have sex with her several hours later. Truly she had not read the part of the Bible that gives wisdom on how to choose a good mate or what qualities a husband and man of God should have. She was lonely and wanted the attention of a man, and she was used to getting what she wanted, and John was another victim of her strong and demanding ways. Now at this moment in her life, she wondered why God did not stop her from making such a grave mistake. Her anger with God was because of his loving grace that would not intervene against her will. Pretty much what God had said was, "have it your way."

"Wanda I am not going to pretend that I have all the right answers and all the wisdom from God to give you. But I do know this, he intimately knows your situation and not one detail has slipped by him, and he is willing to hear all the things you want to tell me, and trust me when I tell you that he can do far more for you in his silence that I can with a thousand words. Does that make any sense to you, sweetheart?" She hoped that it was not too offensive, and that Wanda would know she had her best interest at heart. The silence continued.

"I am just so drained and do not know where to begin to put all the pieces back together again. There is going to be a trial and a lot of ugly things are going to come out that I may not want to hear, and I am so scared of that. I am scared that I do not know the man I married." Her voice began to rise as the panic set in. "What will my life be like if and when he goes to prison?"

"Listen Wanda those are the details that will unfold in time. In the mean time you need to think about your immediate survival, and the day to day routine that you need to keep. Does your job know what is going on?"

"They do not know the full details, but I am going to talk with personnel again and plan some time off for the trial when it comes up." Her tone was more moderate, and she seemed to be gaining control of her emotions.

"Can I ask you something Wanda?" Angie was a bit reluctant to push further but felt the need to. "Have you and John ever sought any help before things got to this point?"

"What does that matter now? It is way too late to do any good." Wanda felt a little bit of resentment for Angie asking such a question.

"Please do not get me wrong, Wanda there is usually a reason for these things to pop up without the other person ever knowing. And sometimes the warning signs are visible and just ignored, and at other times people need help to see them and recognize what they are, regardless of how uncomfortable it is. I remember you telling me several months ago that you had a strange feeling that things just were not right with John. Do you remember that?"

"Yes, I do and apparently I was right. But I do not know if any kind of intervention would have prevented this." Some despair could be heard as her voice trailed off.

"That might be true, but a little education can go a long way in preparing you for the possibilities, and this is the kind of thing that you are going to need some help dealing with regardless of John. Does that make any sense, and are you willing to consider that when you feel ready?"

Again, there was a long silence on the phone while the terrible pain came crashing back in on Wanda's heart. And in a strange way so did the thoughts of Andy. Why was she thinking of him at this moment? Why did she feel the need to be close to him while this crisis in her life played out? "You know Angie, you are right. I am going to need some time to process this, but yes, I will get some help. And thanks for caring and I know you are only trying to help."

"Am I pushing too hard?"

"No, it's just me, I am feeling a bit unglued, and I suppose that is normal. I am sorry if I seem to put you off. I don't mean to."

"It's OK, you just hang in there and know that I am here for you. I think we should get together soon and talk some more, as I think you could use a friendly distraction in your life right now."

Distraction! That was exactly what Andy was becoming. And maybe she did need some more distraction. "I am sure I will take you up on that, and thanks again for listening. Take care, OK?"

When the call disconnected, Wanda stared at the phone and could feel the urge to call Andy. In some strange way she wanted a reason not to call him, but with each passing second the sensation grew and grew. Shaking her head, she wondered what reason she would give for calling him, after giving him the cold shoulder hours before. Her thoughts just could not keep from reliving the passion of years ago and the hours of laughter and silly craziness that he brought to her life. She had to admit that in some strange way she needed it to feel alive. Andy made her feel alive in a lot of ways and feeling sexually alive was when he was at his best, and he most certainly knew how to bring out passion in her that she had needed to feel. The moral conflict did not seem to be as intense as before and she did not give it much thought as she wanted to feel numb to any hint of condemnation for wanting to give in to her most basic human need and wants.

The trembling of her hands became faster with each pressing of the key on the phone. Her mind was about to go blank when his voice came over the other end of the line.

"Is this the lovely and talented Wanda calling me?"

"OH, I am both lovely and talented! Of course, I am." Her smile broke out into a hefty laugh. "I have many talents to my credit."

"Yes, I am quite aware of your many talents, and I think together we can expand on them a bit."

"Umm Andy I know what talents you have on your mind and maybe I am not thinking about that." She smiled knowing that she was exactly thinking about that, as her memories of the past passion between him and her flooded her mind.

She wondered what advice Angie would give if she knew the thoughts she had toward Andy or the most recent night of passion they had shared. Well, it really did not matter, because no one could possibly understand the history and the overwhelming attraction she had to him. And she recalled that Andy was very sweet and kind to her, when he was not in bed with her, which was rare.

"Wanda, the fact that you said, 'you are not thinking about that', tells me that you are. Am I right?"

The long pause was not the answer she wanted to give, but the truth of the matter is she did not know what to do, about Andy. Yes, she wanted him, and still in the back of her mind she knew that what she wanted was not what she needed.

"I suppose so but, I also really want your support and try to be understanding if my emotions go all over the place. I am lonely, confused, and do not know how I should be acting on this."

"Acting!" His voice rose on the other end. "Wanda are you kidding me? Girl you have been put through hell, having your life go upside down with the most shocking news any person could receive. There is no script for this, and you are not supposed to know how to deal with this, because in the ideal world, you are not supposed to be subjected to this. To be honest with you Wanda, if this were happening to me, I would not know how to deal with this either."

"What am I going to do Andy if he goes to prison?" The fear began to creep back in and made her weak with anxiety.

"You will survive, and life will go on. That I can promise you and you will find yourself to be a lot stronger than you are at this very moment. And I will be holding you up every step of the way."

Andy could hear the faint sound of sniffles on the other end. The thought of her crying tore at his heart.

"Right now, Andy what I really need is someone to hold me!" Her voice trailed off as the sobs began to get louder.

"OK, I understand sweetheart I will be right over. You hang in there, I will be over and hold you as long as you like, as long as necessary for you to feel better. Are you OK with that?"

"Yes, please I would love that very much."

"Ok, baby I am there."

Chapter 14

John stared at the grey ceiling that seemed to have fresh paint, from his bunk bed. The tiny cell was more like an echo chamber as every sound in the surrounding cells and the entire block was amplified through the cinder blocked walls that had no insulation.

He slowly replayed over and over again in his mind the events that got him arrested. The unanswered questions were relentless. Why did Cindy send him on that errand to pick up? Was she setting him up and why? How did the cops know to search his vehicle and him at the rest area? Did she follow him and call the cops? What was going on with her and her associates?

He knew that the police had a good solid case against him and that it would be in his best interest to at least hear what plea bargain options were available. The only consuming thought for him was to get the smallest prison term possible. Perhaps the county wanted a conviction on the most serious of charges so they could brag about the stepped up efforts to stem the tide of drugs in the area. He could only hope that they were not going to use his case as the one to set an example or to send a message. He needed to know the reality of what his lawyer could do, and if his case was a learning curve for him. An experienced lawyer was what he needed. Not some guy who is still admiring the gavel every time the judge demanded order in the court room.

Under the circumstances he would not have much choice other than to rely on Jesse to bring about the best result possible. Right now he just wanted the process to move as quick as possible.

Three weeks passed by before he met with his lawyer Jesse, who seemed even less sure about his case than the first meeting. "John I am going to be straight with you, some times these cases can get reduced to a simple possession for the first time offender and then you are looking at fines, probation, and some community service and most likely some kind of drug intervention program. That probably sound very good to you right now. However here is the problem. The new District Attorney transferred to this jurisdiction for the specific purpose of waging war on the drug culture that got out of hand here in the county. Without a doubt she is wanting to make a statement and make a name for herself as the DA you do not want to mess with. I do not know much about her, but I do know she is tough and all the judges and cops seem to love her already.

I heard just last month she won a conviction on a otherwise minor marijuana charge, and got the judge to hand down the maximum sentence on a first offender. She has a reputation for getting max sentences on nearly all her convictions. Her name is Judy Kimal, and I am afraid that is who we have to play ball with in the courtroom."

John's heart almost stopped after hearing that his case was most certainly going to be a case that Judy would want to make a hard example of. "Ok so what do we do? Is there anyway we not get her to prosecute? Or at least put the thought of some leniency on the table? My goodness I made a bad choice and terrible mistake. I am not hung up or a part of the drug culture and this was not me working for someone else.." John rapped the phone receiver against the glass several times while pointing at Jesse. He then screamed into the receiver. "You pull my record and you will see that I am clean with no issues with the law. Just traffic violations way back in the 80's. That has to count for something! How is it that she can get a judge to throw the book at me when there are addicts and heavy pushers walking around the streets, with no fear of being stopped?" The glaring anger in his face steamed up the glass.

A few seconds passed before Jesse, spoke. "John I am going to meet with her and go over your case in great detail and put you in the best light possible. But I got to tell you that before she is going to even consider anything in your favor, she is going to want some detailed cooperation and information. Because in her mind, she is going to start with you and shake you hard so that you drop some names, places and contacts, and then she will begin to shake them hard until she gets to the top. That is the way this works John. So if I were you I would strongly consider helping yourself out here with the only shot you got. Now I will be back in touch with you by the end of the week and we will set up a meeting with her. You be prepared to save yourself, OK?"

"I told you I do not really know much about . ."

Jesse raised his hand and spoke into the receiver. "John you need to level with me about how and who got you to the cocaine, because I know it was not served up at the Dumfries Dunkin Donut shop! You had better have those answers for me, because you do not want Judy to force those answers from you. Because if she does it, then she has no reason to deal with you. You see the whole idea is for me to have the bargaining chips so that I can give her a little something and then she can give me a little something that will help you. Think about it long and hard John, this whole thing is in your hands now. You want to get back to your life as soon as you can, now is the time to make that happen. I will see you soon."

John was still stunned as he watched Jesse close his briefcase, and calmly get up and walk out past the guard without even looking back.

Chapter 15

John was escorted back to his cell on a Friday afternoon and stayed in solitary confinement until Sunday morning. The jail house routine was in full swing, as most inmates were on there best behavior to ensure that their visitation privileges would not be denied. It was the weekends that he dreaded the most because without the frequent visits from Wanda his loneliness seemed to increase. The only thing he could look forward to was Sundays. It was the one day of the week that seemed tolerable and even civil.

The inmates filed into the small but brightly lit chapel, which had inspirational posters plastered on every wall. It had become known by most as the most positive room in the entire facility. Just about every Sunday John saw inmates filing into it with uplifted spirits and smiles that were so rare in the jail. One inmate caught his attention. Inmate Robert Miles was known for his very mild manner and pleasant attitude. However, that had not made him so notorious in the jail. It was the hideous crimes that he had done that had put him there, which made the local newspapers several years earlier. He had been convicted on two counts of rape and murder, of a mother and her teenage daughter. Whenever John saw him, he had a hard time believing that this same individual was responsible for such awful crimes.

Staring at the Bible, Robert was holding, he wondered how God could possibly help his situation. Yes, he had faith and of course he knew that God will not excuse sin or the consequences that come from unwise choices. However, in this instance perhaps he did not need God to get his circumstances changed on the outside but rather to get his heart condition changed on the inside. He had heard time and time again how some people really do have to hit rock bottom before getting to the point and realizing that their lives are messed up beyond repair and that they don't have the ability to fix it. He thought that yes, this time the man in the mirror was he who had hit rock bottom.

Even though he had read many parts of the Bible before and found it to be enlightening, he was skeptical about the changes that some people claimed to have as a result of reading it and having an experience with God. He did not want an experience he wanted a complete makeover.

However, it was Robert who prompted John to attend the Sunday services in the first place. Several weeks earlier they had spoken about John's incarceration and John had opened up to him about how he thought his life had hit rock bottom. Robert listened closely to him during those moments and encouraged him to seek God for his help. John was a little bit defiant, thinking that God was just a crutch for those who could not put their lives together on their own. To which Robert replied, "That is the best crutch to have in a situation like we are in." It was something in their conversation that Robert said that got John's attention.

"You know John, all of us come into this world with a strike against us and a fatal disease. And what is interesting about that is that not only does it affect our bodies as far as death is concerned, but for the whole time we are here it affects our minds, our emotions, our ability to think, the choices we make and our capacity for living. This may sound oversimplified John, but all of your problems, all of my problems and every inmate that is in here, one thing put us here: sin. That sin made us make bad choices, it caused us to act on those choices and here we are with the end results. Now I know you think that is too simple of an explanation, but I think if you took the time to look back over your life, look back over the events that got you here, you will see exactly what I am talking about and would probably agree."

John stared at him and wondered if at one time he had been a preacher, but quickly dismissed it in light of the crimes he had committed.

"Sin" said John. "That does sound way to simple if you ask me."

"Well to tell you the truth we are simple people and it does not take much to get us sidetracked."

John was a bit skeptical of people who had religious fervor while incarcerated. Countless times he had heard of inmates who had a Jesus experience, while they were in, just to have a devilish incarnation within a few months if not weeks after they got out. He could not help but wonder if this was the case with Robert.

Robert sensed the doubt that John was feeling and gave him an offer he could not easily refuse.

"John tell me, what do you know about God? Or do you know anything about God at all?"

"Well I know about as much as anyone else could know. I believe he exists, and I know he has a son named Jesus Christ who could or could not be one and the same. And he intervenes in the affairs of man. What is there for me to know exactly?"

"Do you know me, John?" Robert looked at him with an expressionless face and stare.

"Well I know your name, and I have heard some things that you have done. Other than that, I guess I do not know much about you."

"Isn't that interesting John? I am standing right here in front of you, talking to you and looking you in the eye, and you don't know me. That is exactly why I asked do you know who God is and what you know of him. All the stuff you have heard about me John has been handed down to you from someone else. But here I am in front of you and you still do not know me. Could that be because you have not asked the right questions? Have not dug deep to find out who I am? It's not that I would not tell you who I am."

"Ok, what's your point, Robert?" Feeling a bit agitated and thinking of leaving, John stared at him with a uneasy feeling coming over him. Just who was this Robert Miles and had he been some kind of con artist that was playing his game on him?

"John, I think you need to find out who God is for yourself."

"Ok, and how do I best do that?"

"Well lucky for us is that God has revealed himself to us in many ways that we can understand. He uses nature, like all of his creation to reveal his power and detail of intricate watch and care over us all. He uses other people to reveal and speak to us, and uses his written word, the Bible. Any combination of those works really well. I would encourage you to read God's word first. It is pure, and it does not have an agenda. And it is intended to give you a big picture overview of God, his earth and creation, all the people on it, what his plans are, how we got this way and exactly what he is going to do about it. And most important, what our outlook looks like in the future. And when you read it, you are going to discover a lot about yourself that you did not know and a whole bunch about God that you probably never knew. John there is a concept I want you to understand right now before you pick up a Bible to read it. That concept is called born again. You may have heard of it."

"Being born again . . . yes I may have heard of it from time to time."

"Have you ever heard people say from time to time how they wish they could do life over, or if they knew then what they know now things would be different?"

"Yes as a matter of fact I have been telling myself that from the moment the gates and bars closed in behind me. Of course, I am way too late for that now, and from the looks of things, seeing how you are in here with me for a very long time, it's much too late for you too."

Robert smiled at him and then broke out in laughter.

"What's so funny?" John was at the edge of defensiveness, thinking that any moment he would have to brawl just to move on with the rest of the day, and be sure that Robert would not bother him again. This was not like jail in the movies, far worse, by living with high anxiety and fear from guys like Robert.

"You can get a do over in your life John. Literally a do over. You can be born again and redo your life over. But it has nothing to do with going back in your mother's womb, it has everything to do with having a new mind and emotional outlook, and different perspective on life and those around you and this world in general. That is what being born again is all about. Now John I will be the first to tell you that your mother has nothing to do with you being born again, that is something that only God can do for you. After all he made you the first time. He is the only one who can give you a new mind and make over from the inside out. Once you get a good understanding of that concept John, this world, even this jail will never be the same to you. And neither will the people around you.

Now I am going to be going to the chapel from time to time, I do not get the chance to go every Sunday, because I tend to rest and read a lot. But you are welcome and invited to go, I think you will learn some things you never knew."

John stared at him for a moment, wondering how this same guy who killed two people seemed so at peace with himself while doing a long sentence. Or was he the ultimate swindler who had a lot of people fooled in hopes of getting released early, just to go back to perhaps killing again. He could not resist the urge to confront him on the matter.

"I am not sure if I buy what you are saying. I mean how is it that a two-time murderer like you can become a Jesus freak and start talking all this God talk. Why did you not do that before you killed people?" There he said it and was waiting for the devil to reveal himself in Robert Miles, surely there was a dormant demon that would surface any moment now.

Robert looked at him and smiled, which made him even more uneasy.

"John, there is hope and redemption and forgiveness for any and everybody regardless of who we are or what we have done. Did you know that one of God's best men was an adulterer and a murderer! His name was David the king of Israel. It is a very fascinating story and I hope you get the chance to read it. You see we humans think of justice and mercy and forgiveness on our terms. That is not the deal with God. Because if the truth be told, if God were to give me what I justly deserve . . . poof!! I would be a pile of smoking ash right here where I stand, in a split second, faster than I can blink. And so it is with you . . .John."

"Well the fact that I am in here tells me I am getting what I deserve and maybe even a bit more." John's voice trailed off as he thought about the upcoming trial and most likely a sentence that would have him seeing the gray dull paint of the jail for many months to come. "Well, Robert all I can say is that I hope this works out well for you. For now, you seem to be coping pretty good. Is that because you have given up hope from the outside?"

"John these walls do not contain my spirit, or my hope. Even if I die in here, trust me when I tell you that I am already a free man." Robert pointed to his head and then to his heart. "You see the freedom that I found in Jesus Christ no one can make me a prisoner to sin again, except me. When you find that for yourself John, you are a free man indeed."

"Yeah, I think I have heard that before. I hope I get to that point sooner or later."

"John you can be free in seconds, it begins with your acknowledgment of Jesus as the only savior that can forgive you of your sins and believing that He is the only Son of God who was specifically sent here to earth to demonstrate the life we are to live and to die and pay the punishment and penalty for our sins. It begins with that understanding in your heart. You see John everybody that is on the outside of these walls is in some prison and they might not even know it. People out there judge people like us and look down on us for our crimes and sins. The bottom line is, they are guilty of different sins and stand just as guilty before Almighty God as you and I.

Chapter 16

The next time Andy saw Wanda, the passion between them was uncontrollable and stronger than ever. The two of them began spending increasingly more and more time together. Andy was staying over about three nights a week at her place and the rest of the time, Wanda was waking up in his bed at his place. Their love making was a consistent theme and activity that became more and more regular, and for Wanda it came with even less guilt. Wanda conveyed her fears of not being able to pay all the bills and that she feared her life would come crashing down and had visions of her being homeless and living in her car.

"Wanda I will never see you homeless or living in your car. As a matter of fact, I will do whatever it takes to make sure that you have some stability in your life. You can move in here with me, or I can help you financially to keep above water. Just let me help you get through this. Let me be whatever you need me to be for you right now."

A few weeks later Wanda woke up, feeling very nauseated and weak. She knew she had been stressing lately about the legal proceedings with John and the bills that were piling up with no end in sight. As her morning routine began to take shape she just could not seem to muster the energy to function. She had not felt this bad ever and she was a bit frighten when she went to the bathroom just to throw up what little breakfast she had eaten. Her mind reasoned better safe than sorry and decided to driver herself to the local urgent care for a quick check up.

Twenty minutes later she strode through the automatic doors of the Urgent care facility feeling even weaker than before. She filled out the admin forms and sat in the waiting room for about seven minutes when a nurse called her name and directed her toward the exam room.

An hour later Wanda walked out of the medical lab with sheer shock and disbelief on her face. That awful feeling she had been feeling was the early stages of a pregnancy, that was verified by a medical exam. Another life changing event was at hand, with no answers in sight of what to do about it.

In the wee hours of the following morning Wanda was lying in bed staring at the wall as she could not sleep. Her mind was preoccupied with the proposal that Andy had offered her, about being all that she needed him to be, and his pledge of financial support. She was pleasantly surprised after she got the courage to tell him of her pregnancy, that he was still committed to being what she needed him to be, even if that meant taking on the new role of father. He was very calm, however she was scared and felt that deep down in her heart this was just not the thing she should be doing. However, as she reflected back over her circumstances, she did not see another way out. She tried to reason that if she hid the pregnancy long enough and the baby when it was born, that perhaps she could divorce John and get him out of her life before it all came out. She was still having a hard time believing that she had allow herself to get so involved with Andy to the point that they now shared a child.

Furthermore, she knew she was not ready at all for a pregnancy. Her finances were a wreck and her emotions were even worse. The upcoming trial for John, had put additional stress and strain on her that she had never endured before. She could not imagine just how this would all turn out.

With three more hours of restlessness, Wanda glanced over at the clock just as the alarm went off, wishing she could grab ten more minutes of sleep. She reached up and hit the snooze button and curled up in a tight ball underneath the sheets. It was during these moments in the early morning hours when she started to feel the subtle aging process. And that was just the beginning of things that were to plague her before getting out of bed. Over the next ten weeks the pressure at work was mounting up, as she was assigned to multitask several projects. She had always welcomed the challenge of that, however with her personal life a total wreck now, it was starting to become obvious, that her ability to focus on the job was diminished.

Most of her other associates at work knew that she was going through stress, and they had also sensed that something big and major had taken place in her life to produced that. Ever so often the quiet whispers could be heard in the bathroom and in the break room, concerning Wanda's increasing weight. The speculations flourished that it could be from stress, however a couple of keen associates did notice that the weight was centered in her belly area, and some of them wondered if a possible pregnancy was to blame.

She actually found it quite surprising that anyone would care at all about her being pregnant. For the past several years most people in the office seemed to stick to themselves and have their own little social groups, which did not include Wanda. That was probably because she was prominently rising through the ranks of the marketing firm. Moreover, she was being promoted past other well credentialed candidates, with more experience. Her sometimes blind ambition drove her to obtain responsibilities that required her to function at her best all the time to make up for the lack of confidence that lied just beneath the surface. She never let on that she did not feel qualified or fully confident of the most recent position of Senior Marketing Director. However, she managed to land several good contracts within her first two months on the job and that impressed the Vice President and President so much that they routinely went to her for ideas to move the company forward regarding fresh cutting-edge marketing campaigns. She did not want to ever let anyone down who had bet on her skill set. Somehow, she would have to figure out a way to balance the crisis in her life with the career goals that she imposed upon herself. Keeping that in mind, maybe Andy's proposal would be just the thing to give her the breathing room and allow for some fancy manipulation as needed. Strange how now she was not as reluctant as before to going through with something that might wreck several lives, including her own.

In her mind she somehow knew that in the middle of the deception, the greater good was to protect John from the awful truth.

The fear and uncertainty inside her grew at the thought of bringing a child into the world, and then having to hide and deny its very existence.

She wondered what kind of dad Andy would be and if his fathering skills would be better than John's.

She did not expect or even ask Andy to go with her to the many routine doctor visits and the upcoming prenatal care appointments but was very glad and somewhat comforted when he offered. The thing she hated the most about the doctor visits, was the endless round of questioning about her pregnancy. She especially grew uneasy anytime the conversation turned to the father of the child. Anticipating that someone would ask about the father, she did not go to her primary care doctor, because obviously the whole staff knew she was married to John. The public health clinic seemed like the likely place since it was routine to see young mothers with missing in action dads, both known and unknown.

She had scheduled her appointment for one in the afternoon, and Andy had taken off the rest of the day to go with her. After the appointment Andy wanted to take her to his apartment to show her the small baby room he had put together and wanted her input for decorations. He always loved her taste in style and realized that even though he was getting better at living the domesticated lifestyle, his bachelor ways were evident throughout his home. He loved her sense of warmth and knew she would make any place comfortable for the new arrival.

She thought of the much-needed time off from work she would be taking throughout her pregnancy. The company was very good at allowing the flexibility that most associates needed for personal time, and she could only hope that the good will would continue during her maternity leave and on days like today when she would have to steal the rest of the afternoon to devote to herself and the small child that was growing inside of her. The brief phone call with Mrs. Parks in personnel was polite and she was relieved when her mind was put at ease. Mrs. Parks was well acquainted with the demands of other pregnant women who worked with the firm. Wanda convinced her that she could handle the work load and still juggle all of her other responsibilities. Mrs. Parks however cautioned her to focus as needed on getting her personal life and affairs in order so that when she could come back to work full time, she would be in a position to devote her full attention to the firm. The professional decor Wanda understood and certainly was gracious that Mrs. Parks gave her the benefit of the doubt, because of her past work performance. Only a small tinge of doubt swept through her mind when she hung up the phone but realized that part of her work motto was that she gave her best performance under pressure.

While looking through her closet she thought of the new line of maternity clothing she would soon be wearing. Even though she loved her flattering figure she hated the physical changes that a pregnancy would do to her body. More importantly she wondered if she would ever get her body back to its original shape after the baby was born. She had heard of the endless struggle some mothers had getting back into shape. Andy suggested that she get all of her maternity clothing from the local Salvation Army thrift store. His thinking was 'why pay full price for new clothing that you will only be wearing for a couple of months, and it might only be a once in a lifetime event.' She did not argue with his logic in that regard and heeded his advice. So, in addition to helping him set up a baby room in his apartment, they would also pick out some much-needed maternity outfits. The thought of trying to make sexy out of maternity clothes was a stylish challenge she would learn to overcome. Somehow, she had the feeling she was going to have to learn a whole new way of living, even if it meant, leading a double life to all that knew her.

She was in the bathroom putting on her make up when the telephone rang. She let it ring until the voice mail picked up on the loud speaker and could hear Andy's voice. "Hi, it's me I just wanted to touch base with you, and make sure that all is well and that we are still on for this afternoon." She quickly walked into the bedroom and picked up the receiver.

"Hello, Andy. I am home. I was in the bathroom putting on some make up. How are you?"

"I am good, I am very good. I called to see if everything is good for this afternoon. I was hoping we could start selecting some stuff to piece together a baby room for our future son or daughter." To hear him say it like that made her a bit nervous. "Our future son or daughter? So what do you want Andy?"

"You know me Wanda, I am not a hard man to please. It really does not matter to me as long as the baby is healthy, and strong. Whatever you deliver I will take."

Wanda smiled at the thought of him trying to change a diaper and asking for directions. "Well that is good to know, very good to know. Are you sure we are going to be able to pull this off? I mean this sounds so far-fetched Andy that I am just a bit concerned. We have a lot to lose if this does not go over well. We both could end up in jail."

"Wanda we are going to be just fine. We just have to stick with the plan. Remember when the baby is born when you come home from the hospital, he or she comes to me and we begin from there. You can do this Wanda, but I need you to stay focused. Can you do that?"

Wanda loved how he was reassuring even when he did not have all the answers to some of life's biggest problems. "Yes, I think I can."

"Wanda this is not trial and error time, I need you to come through. You got enough on your mind and you need to take one issue at a time. Speaking of time, what is going on with John?"

"I am not sure yet. I think they are going to set a trial date soon and he said he would let me know."

"Are you up for handling that?" Andy was hoping that she would have a degree of certainty of the relationship falling apart and subsequent divorce.

"Well I don't have a choice, do I?" Wanda remarked.

"No, I guess you don't. Well listen I will be over about two o'clock to pick you up. Is that ok?"

"That will be fine."

"Alright I will see you then. Take care."

"Bye, Andy."

Wanda hung up the phone and sat down on the side of the bed thinking about her situation. No doubt the people at the church may have noticed her weight gain and she needed some way to explain that if and when the questions started coming. She knew sooner or later that the rumors would begin to spread and that she would have to address this head on before the story unraveled and took a direction she did not want. The only person she could depend on in this delicate situation was her friend Angie.

She wanted to arrange a meeting to go over the details. Angie was a very sweet person and she hated having to lie to her. Of course, even the truth would hurt Angie just as bad. She glanced over at the alarm clock on the nightstand and realized she had a couple of hours before Andy was to show up. She decided to give Angie a call and set up a quick lunch date. With each press of the number keys her anxiety grew.

"Wanda." came the voice on the other end. "What a pleasant surprise. I have been thinking about you and praying for you. How are you?"

The thought of Angie actually praying for her made it even more difficult to have to lie to her about the pregnancy.

"Well I am good, so much better than the last time we talked. As a matter of fact, I have some news to share with you and that is why I called. Could we set up a lunch date perhaps? What are you doing right now?"

"Wow you got some news! Do tell girl, do tell." The excitement in Angie's voice was so odd to Wanda. She had always viewed her as a very calm and controlled person who had been through so much that wisdom seemed to be her strongest point.

"I would like to see you in private if you don't mind."

"Ok, sure Wanda that is no problem. What did you have in mind?"

"I can meet you at Dunkin Donuts in about twenty minutes. How about that?"

"That will be just fine. Is this good news?"

"Yes, as a matter of fact it is." Wanda's voice trailed off at the thought of the deception and lie that she was going to tell a friend.

"OK great well I will see you in a bit, bye."

Twenty minutes Wanda pulled into the small parking lot of the local Dunkin Donuts. It was located in a tiny strip mall right off a busy highway. It always seemed to be full and she liked that because the noise and distractions she found to be rather comforting in a situation like this. Her mind drifted to the thoughts of whether or not John had done this in the past with his personal trainer friend that he had been seeing for some time.

She was keenly aware of her changing body and was hoping that the small developing baby bump would not show too much through the white blouse. She glanced in her rear-view mirror while putting on more lipstick. Quickly she got out of the car and stepped inside the noisy donut shop and could see Angie seated in a corner booth in the back.

Angie looked up and smiled and began waving her arms beckoning her toward the table. Wanda approached and sat down in front of her.

Angie was beaming. "You look wonderful girl! What have you been doing? You have this glow about you that I have not seen in a long time."

The glow, it was always the pregnancy glow that was a dead giveaway. And Wanda sensed that Angie would discover that shortly.

Angie went on and on about her appearance. "Wanda you look so healthy and your skin is so youthful looking. I have not seen you look like this in such a long time. With all the stress you are going through, how is it that you look like a young teenage girl?"

"Oh, just stop Angie I have not done anything different. But I do have some good news to report that might explain my glow."

Angie looked carefully at her and listened closely.

"My glow is because we are welcoming a new member of the family!"

Angie looked stunned and muted her response. "Oh wow! You're pregnant?! Oh, my goodness when did this happen?"

Wanda stared down at the table unable to maintain a joyous smile because of the lie she was creating. "Well apparently just before John got locked up. And I did not know about it until a couple weeks ago when I went to the doctor for a checkup."

Angie looked at her. "Is that what you both want? How does John feel about that? Does he know?"

Wanda was feeling a bit of shame as she spoke. "No, I have not told him yet to be honest, because he has a lot on his mind to deal with right now, and news like this just might be too much for him to handle. I will tell him, and I am sure he is going to want to know. But I am not sure of how he is going to take this news."

When Angie heard that she quickly went from joy to deep concern for her friend who was in water way over her head. "Wanda, you have to tell him. You cannot keep something like this a secret or hid from him. Are you prepared for this? I mean he is in jail and he might be in for a while after sentencing and trial. Are you prepared to raise this child by yourself for an indefinite period of time, maybe five to seven years? Are you prepared for that Wanda?"

"I have thought about all of this Angie, believe me. I have racked my brains for the past several weeks. I will most likely deal with all of that when the time comes. I know I am going to need a lot of help. I am going to need a lot of good folks around me as I work my way through this. I will get through this somehow." Her voice trailed off at the thought of Andy having custody of the child.

"You know I am here for you Wanda and willing to help anyway I can. Just tell me what you need me to do. I just hope you are not into something over your head. Are you sure you had no idea?"

"Well to be honest with you I am not so sure. But none of that matters now, because the fact is the baby is here and I have to deal with it. However, I think it will be something good for the both of us. This baby that I am carrying may even bring us closer together. It gives us something to focus on besides each other when he gets out. Also, this can give him a reason to stay strong while he is locked up. It will give him something to look forward to on the outside. Don't you think?" She was hoping that Angie could see and agree with her logical thinking. Angie nodded slowly. Wanda began feeling very bad about deceiving Angie, who genuinely cared a lot about her and had her best interest at heart. She thought it best not to have much contact or conversation with her throughout the pregnancy. She did not know how things were going to play out, so just knowing that she was someone she could talk to if needed would be good enough. She decided to end their meeting abruptly.

"Well Angie I want to thank you so much for meeting with me on such short notice. I hate to leave so quickly, but I got a bunch of errands to run today and I want to get a lot done at home in preparation for my little bundle of joy." She pointed at her swelling belly. "I wanted to share the good news with you, and you will be hearing from me over the next several months, but please understand I will be so busy that I might not have much time to socialize and chat as before. So forgive me if you do not hear from me as often. If there is anything that I need I will be sure to give you a call. I am sorry to have to leave this instant, but I do have another appointment."

"Ok, Wanda well thanks for sharing and I am so happy for you and wish you all the best. Keep strong and let God give you wisdom and guidance throughout all of this. I will be praying for you and John. Don't be a stranger. Stop by the church anytime, you know you have a big spiritual family that loves you."

"Thank you so much, I needed to hear that. Oh and one more thing; would you mind if we keep this just between me and you? Because I just do not feel like sharing it with the rest of the world right now." Wanda thought about what she said, realizing that as her stomach grew bigger and bigger over the upcoming months, her secret would be hard to hide."

"Oh, that is no problem at all Wanda, I totally understand. I know this is a very personal matter and that is the way it should be."

"Oh, thank you, I am so glad that you understand."

With a big hug and brief smile Wanda stepped out and headed back to her car.

Chapter 17

During the short drive back home, Wanda turned up the radio in her car and let her mind drift off to the sounds of the country music that was blasting out of the speakers. She felt joyful that she was going to be a mother even if it was not under the ideal of circumstances. She envisioned the hours of playing and loving her newborn. She thought that perhaps having a new child would be the catalyst to help her actually begin a new life. Of course, the other half of that equation she wondered just who the man would be to be there to help raise it. The more she thought about this the more she leaned toward the prospect of Andy. Andy was at least available and financially able to support them both for a while if needed.

She wanted to envision where her life would be in the next few years and hoped that a family of some kind was intact. She had grown more and more uncertain of John. His incarceration gave her a lot of time to think about their entire marriage and if it was at all fulfilling to either one of them. She knew deep down in her heart that he was a rather decent guy but just could not get past the fact that he had not grown up or matured enough to know that she needed so much more from him. She even questioned why she married him in the first place. Was it her deep sense of longing to belong to someone or was it the impulse of hearing him say he would take care of her for the rest of her life and would never leave her side?

She thought of just how strange that statement was now, especially since he did abandon her with his current incarceration, and he most certainly was not in a position to take care of her. Moreover, his time away from her was indefinite and he had no power to make any decisions about her otherwise. It was all in the courts power.

She pulled up in the driveway and parked. Once inside she quickly made sure the place was tidy and expected that Andy would be carefully scrutinizing the environment that the newborn would call home for a short while before staying with him.

Twenty minutes later the doorbell rang and she opened the door to see the ever so handsome Andy standing there looking more well-dressed than she had seen him in a very long time. She could not help but wonder who was dressing him these days, because when they were together his fashion style was just awful.

"Well hello Mr. Handsome! It is not every day a great looking and well-dressed guy is standing at my front door. Come in, and tell me how is it that you seemed to have found a fashion sense that I could not get you to do when we were together?"

"Well it is nothing special really, I just consult the mannequins and they give me the latest fashion news and trends." He was smiling from ear to ear.

Wanda stared and him and by the frown on her face she was perplexed by his answer. "Um, excuse me?"

"My dear you see dressing well is not all that difficult and it does not require a fashion magazine." He seemed so sure of himself.

"Is this the same Andy who used to show up with plaids and stripes and colors from the Crayola collection?" Wanda moved in closer to him and rubbed his cashmere sweater.

"Who would dress like that?" Andy smiled while embracing her and then gently kissed her.

"I am glad you came; I think this will be a very fun and exciting shopping trip for the three of us." She placed his hand on her stomach and held it in place.

"I see, I just hope that your fashion sense can carry over to decorating a room for the little one there." Andy stared at the stomach as if he could literally see the baby.

"I am thinking we will make a fine team together." She grabbed his hand and clasped her fingers into his and led him to the kitchen.

Once in the kitchen she offered him something to drink and quickly cleaned up the counter. "Ok my love perhaps we should get going you know how the traffic can be around the mall in the afternoon, and I do not want to waste all of the day in baby stores. As a matter of fact I was wanting to spend the rest of it with you, just the two of us. What do you say to that?"

"I think that sounds great, and let the adventure begin."

The shopping mall was busy as expected for the afternoon in an around the metro area. Most of the time when ever Wanda would go shopping, she would choose very early on Saturday mornings, when the Friday night hangover crowds were usually still in bed sleeping off a hangover. Of course, the Saturday morning shopping trips was a catalyst for an argument between her and John as he just did not seem to want to participate an any domestic activities and especially anything that involved spending money. He made it a point to remind Wanda time and time again of just hard he had to work to earn the money that she was willing to spend in a matter of minutes.

Andy on the other hand was much different. He was not rich but did not see money as something never to part with. Instead he saw it as a tool to enhance his life and the lives of others around him. He was very generous, as a matter of fact sometimes too generous to the female friends he had befriended over the years. That was a sore spot with Wanda, but soon realized that was just the way he was and that he was equally liberal with her as well.

The brightly lit Baby R Us store was the first stop, and as they strode hand in hand into the store, Wanda was giggling about how she could never imagine feeling happy about going into a baby store. She mumbled about ridiculous prices for items that will have a short shelf life as the baby will outgrow everything in the first two years so fast that several trips to the same store will be in order. She marveled at all of the variety of items that were available for babies.

"Man, I cannot imagine a child with all of this stuff." She seemed like a kid in a candy store literally running up and down the aisles, dragging

Andy along with her. Andy did his best to curb her enthusiasm, mostly because he was just a bit embarrassed.

"My dear Wanda, I know you are very excited about all of this, but let's keep in mind that we do not exactly know if we are shopping for a girl or a boy, and that there is a lot that has to be done before we finalize the room." He had hoped he did not do the equivalent of throwing water on her.

Wanda looked at him and then gave a big sigh. "Alright I know you are right. But isn't this a lot of fun?" She looked up at him with pleading eyes.

Andy could not help but laugh at her child like behavior. "Yes, this is fun. And it is even more fun watching you. I am not sure now who exactly is the child here, you or the little one in your stomach."

"Well, at least there should be one adult among us here, and it's ok if you are not up to the job, my dear!" She started laughing out loud and poked him in the stomach.

"I am going to tickle you until you take that back!" He grabbed her and pulled her into him and began tickling her until she was literally gasping for air and trying to break away from his embrace. There public antics got the attention of most of the shoppers nearby at the check-out counter.

They were quite playful and were acting like teenagers who had just fell in love, and to some degree they had. The next several hours they were darting in and out of different stores to put together the list of items that they for sure would want to decorate the room of the baby that was just months away. It fast became apparent that they both enjoyed the prospect of starting a new family together even if it was under distressed circumstances.

Later that evening they had dinner at a local restaurant near the Potomac Mills Mall in Woodbridge, Va. Wanda sat through her meal and ate very little and seemed a bit distant.

Andy thought perhaps she was tired because of the hectic pace they endured shopping all afternoon. "Seems like the mall got the best of you." He was smiling.

"It is rare to see me drained of energy from shopping, which is one of my favorite past times. I have to admit I have been feeling a lot more tired lately, and I think it is because of our growing bundle of joy here."

"Is there anything else that has you so reflective? You have not eaten much at all. Were you not hungry?"

"I seem to eat in spells these days and not very much at all." She looked very sad as she said it.

Andy did not want to push but sensed that something was troubling her within. He wondered if it had something to do with the pregnancy and all the circumstances surrounding it.

"If something was truly bothering you, you would tell me, right? You do know that you can talk to me and we can work through any issues. None of this is easy for you, but do not think for a moment that you have to share the emotional burden alone, because I am here to help you with that." He looked at her and tried to read her facial expressions.

Wanda sat back in her chair and looked at him intently for several seconds. "What if this is all wrong and it backfires on both of us? What then?" Her conscious had put the morality of her adulterous affair front and center again as she was most certain it would.

Andy shook his head thinking, 'here we go again.' "Wanda, I told you before that this is the only way to have any kind of outcome that will spare you the nightmare you are thinking about right now. Now I need to know are you committed to this or not. We are not in a game here that you can recall or ask for time out. There are no do overs or play reviews. You and me, we have to dictate the outcome and execute the plans to get the results we want. I thought we were clear on that." The tension and frustration in his voice, startled her.

"Yes, Andy but this is wrong on so many levels. Can we really live with ourselves through all of this? And if we get away with this to some degree, what does that say about the kind of people we are? I know you and I may not be on the same spiritual ground, but this is way out of bounds for any decent human being." She looked away from him, knowing that what she said may have wounded him a little.

Andy finished drinking his water and slowly leaned over to her. "So, what are you saying? What is your plan? If you have something so different and so effective, let's here it."

He stared at her with an unnerving glare she had never seen in him before. It frightened her just a little. "I don't know!" She felt helpless to offer anything remotely like a solution.

"Well you listen to me young lady. Since you don't know, I do, and I say we stick with the plan and I do not want to hear about anything else except how we move forward and what great progress that baby is making. I am dead serious, Wanda. Enough of the self-pity and all that crap, we have to stand up and fight to make this happen. Now I know this may not jive with your religious convictions, but you are way past that now. And I refuse to let you shipwreck the lives involved here. As far as I am concerned this is case closed. Are you with me or not?"

She looked at him and wished this moment could go away. "I will be glad when we are on the other side of all this and life gets back to normal." Of course, for her nothing would be normal again, as this was her new reality. It could never go back to being normal.

Chapter 18

The loneliness engulfed him like a thick fog. His spells of doubt were far more frequent now than when he first found himself behind the thick bars of the Prince William County Detention Center. He had a hard time understanding how other inmates seemed to have a rather pleasant social life inside of this hostile environment. His own observation as well as some comments from other guards, mentioned how each inmate has his own way of coping, and that he would have to soon develop his.

Psychological evaluations were court ordered to those inmates, who the system thought to be a danger to themselves or others. John was reminded that if such an order was in place for him, that it would not look good at his trial. An incident free incarceration was the only record that had a chance to stand before the tough judges these days.

His lawyer Jesse visited more often these days to go over even more strategies he had conceived somewhere. John had lost a lot of hope and faith in the legal system and even more in his lawyer, however he welcomed the company as it was a break from the boring routine of the jail life. He would accept anything that would invade his loneliness. The meetings with his lawyer served more as a social break than legal counsel. The most recent visit found John in a happier than ever mood. So much so that the lawyer's curiosity was peaked.

"You seem so much different today John. I don't think I have seen you this joyful the entire time we have known each other. What's your explanation for this new found joy?"

"Well to tell you the truth it really does not have a whole lot to do with me, it is more like a person I just recently met a few weeks back." John was anxious to tell his conversion story, however, was unsure of how it would be accepted.

"I don't quite follow you John, elaborate."

"Well it has taken me a long time to get to this point frankly. And as strange as this may sound, this whole situation, to include my incarceration maybe my biggest blessing in disguise. Now I know what I have to say may sound strange but trust me when I tell you that this whole thing could really be the turning point in my life that I have been looking for." John sat back and smiled the whole while looking at him. Jesse seemed to be amused that John was enjoying himself so much.

"John, I think you will be just fine if you keep up that good outlook. You would be surprised how these things sometimes turn out. Just keep the faith. Now I want to go over some more details with you because a trial date will be coming soon, and we do not want any surprises from the other side when you get on the stand. Do you have any questions for me about what to expect going forward?"

"No, Jesse, I think at this point it is out of both of our hands. Not that I am giving up, even though I am a bit discouraged. It's just that I want to get this ordeal behind me as soon as possible regardless of the outcome and deal with the consequences. I have over the past couple of weeks been preparing myself for my fate and I am willing to accept it without any bitterness."

Jesse stared at him and wondered just what brought on this attitude. With the few recent inmates he had defended none seemed to accept anything except an acquittal. It was a moral and ethical dilemma for Jesse to defend people that he most certainly had doubts about their innocence. John was one that was different, and he thought a rigorous defense could all but guarantee an acquittal. Unfortunately, drugs were the one thing that most of the people in the county wanted stamped out, and the prosecutor was on a crusade to make it happen and she had the full backing of the toughest judges in the district.

"OK, John I understand what you are saying. I just want to be sure that you are not setting yourself up for disappointment. Now we are going to put our best foot forward and give you the best possible defense. I am glad that you are on board with the outcome. And you know that filing an appeal will be almost expected. I suppose this whole thing will pick up speed now and we should be in front of a judge in a matter of weeks. I want to know if the prosecutor puts anything on the table that is reasonable, regarding a plea bargain, would you consider it?"

"Yes, I think I would."

"Great I hope to see you next week and let you know if there is anything that they are offering that will get this behind you sooner and without the ugly mess of a trial. You hang in there and keep your head up. Try not to let this place get inside of you. Just know that there is an end game in sight."

John looked at him and smiled. "Oh yes there is most certainly an end game. One that we all need to be prepared for, and that includes you Jesse."

"I see." Jesse gathered his papers and quickly tucked them in his briefcase and headed to the guard that was near the door.

Chapter 19

The ceiling fan churned out a low hum as Wanda lay facing the wall. Her mind was twisting over the thoughts of how life was going to be different once the baby came. More importantly keeping her secret from John was not as appealing as Andy made it seem. Furthermore, to complicate matters she had a conscious she was going to have to suppress in order to live a lie in front of her friends and eventually John once he got released. She could not believe that this was her only option. It was getting easier to stray away from the solid path of righteousness she was so accustomed to. The deep growing fear of spiritual repercussions kept nagging at her, but she needed a way to quiet the holy spirit that was constantly sounding off. It seems that one of the good benefits of having been saturated with the word of God is that the holy spirit serves as an on-demand memory that accesses all the input of the word that had been downloaded onto the hard drive of her brain. She knew deep down that there was no way to ignore the truth of what the bible had showed her, yet she would have to be willing to ignore the inner urge to do the right thing and hope that God would have some mercy on the lie of a lifestyle. She was not all that convinced, but slowly over time she shut out the voice of the holy spirit until it was rarely heard at all.

The weeks flew by as the baby inside of her grew. She was getting more and more anxious with each visit to the doctor. Andy seemed to be monitoring her more than supporting her. During one visit he went with her to the doctor and began asking questions to the doctor about what Wanda had been doing during her pregnancy that would bring harm to the child. This did not set well with Wanda at all and she could barely contain herself in the office. She glared at him the entire visit and barely heard a word the doctor told her about the condition and progress of her pregnancy. They had barely stepped out of the lobby when Wanda began to let out her rage.

"Andy, what in the world is wrong with you and why would you think that I would do anything to hurt my child? That was humiliating to question the doctor about my pregnancy!"

She was walking as fast as she was talking and got in the car and slammed the door, started the car and sped out of the parking lot. The ride back home was very tense and very uncomfortable for Andy, as he did not know how to respond to what he did at the doctor's office.

"Wanda, I got to be honest with you, that I am getting a little concerned, because sometimes I think that you are not onboard with this."

"That is ridiculous Andy, and you know it. We went over everything according to your plan. What is it that makes me feel I am not going to go through with this? Did you think I was going to try to have miscarriage or something? How could you think like that? I think I am more invested in this than you are. Besides I have far more to lose. If I wanted to bring harm to this baby, we would not even be here right now. I could have caused a miscarriage and there is nothing you could do about it and you would have never known otherwise. I cannot believe you would think that."

"OK Wanda you have made your point. I just hope and pray you are going to follow through, because we are in way to deep and we have no way out. This baby will be here in a matter of weeks."

"That's right Andy, the baby will be here in a matter of weeks, so you better start acting like a father." She was yelling loudly and at the edge of emotional breakdown.

"And just what is that supposed to mean?" Andy blurted out.

"Are you an idiot? I need encouragement, consoling and your support. Not criticism and harsh words of indifference that I am getting from you right now."

Andy shook his head in disbelief. "OK so you are telling me that you do not think I will be a good father. Is that what I am hearing from you?"

"Don't twist my words or turn this around on me Andy. You know exactly what I mean."

"Ok, calm down, you do not have to yell and shout. I know you are under a lot of stress and I promise you we will get through this. Just hang in there and it will all be over in a matter of weeks."

"Be over! Are you kidding me? Did I hear you say be over, Andy? Tell me you are not that stupid?"

"What I meant was.."

"I do not care what you meant! I cannot believe that I actually agreed to do this with you. I am violating all of my moral principles for you Andy. And I resent the fact that you would put me in such a situation."

For Andy, those words were cold and personal. It was a shot to the heart. "I put you in that situation Wanda? Did I hear you say that? Didn't you come begging and pleading for my help when you found out John was in trouble? Didn't you reach out to me?" He hesitated briefly knowing that his next few words would be very hurtful and he contemplated not saying them, but his anger blurted out. "It's funny how your morals and principles were nowhere to be found when we were making love. You certainly seemed to enjoy it. I think you need to stop hiding behind your religion and face the fact that you are a normal human being like the rest of us. Get off of your self righteous high horse, because you got just as much mud on you as anybody else on this planet." He knew those words had stuck deep and he could not take them back.

Wanda stared straight ahead at the road barely aware of the traffic around her. Hearing from deep within the small voice that had once reassured her now came to condemn her as a horrible witness for Christ. She wondered how many other Christians were in her same shoes. And she recalled just how true it was that the Bible had stated that the devil was the accuser of the brethren. However, she never expected the accuser to come in the form of her once longtime lover and best friend. While having a stone face while she drove down the road, her eyes began to water.

Andy looked over at her to see her tears welling up. He softened his tone and placed his hand over on her leg and rubbed her gently. "I am sorry, perhaps I was a bit too . . ."

"Fuck you Andy, you bastard!" She took her right hand and slammed it into his chest with a hard thump. The car swerved slightly from the force.

It was then the tears flowed freely down her face and she cried out loud and uncontrollably. "I hate you for this and I hate John too for putting me in this position."

Andy sat there silently, not knowing what to say or do. He knew he had hurt her deeply and thought he should not have been so cruel to a woman he truly loved.

When she turned into the driveway to his apartment, she was a bit calmer but still had blood shot eyes from her tears. Andy was still unsure of her emotional stability but nevertheless he tried to console her. He opened up his door and went to the driver's door, opening it he asked her to step out. "Come on, let's go inside for a few minutes."

She made no movement and appeared to ignore him.

"Come on Wanda, please. Come inside and relax, you are way too emotional, and I was wrong to hurt you with the things I said." He reached out his hand to her and helped her out of the car. He hugged her and walked her to the front door and they both stepped inside.

Once inside he took her coat and hung it up in the small closet just behind the door. "Please sit down and I will make us both a cup of coffee if you like."

Wanda sat down on the couch and nodded yes. He rushed into the kitchen and a few minutes later emerged with two cups of coffee on a small tray and some chocolate chip cookies. He sat down beside her and held her close to him. He reached over to the tray and picked up one cookie and placed it just at the tip of her lips. "I have heard that moments like this were made for chocolate."

She gently laid her head on his shoulder and snuggled up very close to him. She looked at him and smiled and then slowly took a bite. "It's not fair that you know me so well. One of these days Andy your charm and chocolate cookies is not going to work. And lucky for you this is not that day."

"I love you Wanda, and I am sorry that I was so cruel to you earlier. I should have been more sensitive. I cannot imagine what this is like for you. I will do my best to be a bit more emotionally supportive for you. Somehow, we will get through this. Just . . .I need to know we are still on the same team because I am scared also, to be honest with you sweetheart. I am scared to death."

Wanda nodded, knowingly. "Yeah I know. I am sorry I hit you and lashed out at you the way I did. I just do not know how to process all of this. This is so new to me."

She turned his face toward his. "And yes, I love you too Andy. I really do."

She leaned in and kissed him passionately. Their passion grew while on the couch, and moments later they were entangled into each other.

For Wanda, making love to Andy again was an outlet and diversion that she desperately needed. She did not care, she wanted to feel anything to relieve the guilt and pain and shame. Even though knowing that her circumstances would not change when she left his apartment, for the next several minutes that she made love to him, it was a welcome relief to the emotional turmoil she was feeling inside.

An hour later she drove home feeling relaxed and very calm. She knew she had to gather strength for what was to come. And there was no turning back, so she wanted to concentrate her efforts on how things were going to unfold.

Chapter 20

During the next couple months Wanda increased her work load at the marketing firm. Actually, she enjoyed the fact that she was given more responsibility, as it served as a good diversion from her personal turmoil. Her relationship with Andy grew stronger and she was anxiously waiting the day that she would go into labor and have his child. Her most recent visit to see John in the jail was less stressful, although wearing oversized clothing to hide her pregnancy was getting to be a difficult task to juggle.

John seemed to be settled down into a routine that he was comfortable with, knowing his upcoming trial was only a month away. He told Wanda that if he was convicted on the charges, he would be looking at 18 to 24 months as a minimum. He indicated he was prepared to do that. She had sensed that he had resigned himself to his fate.

She was somewhat surprised to see how calm and peaceful he had been over the past several months. During her last visit she thought he was not the same husband of before who was self-centered and demanding.

"John, I have not seen you this at ease in a long time. What is going on with you in here? Don't get me wrong, I am glad that you are faring well, I was just wondering how the change happened and what is going on with that."

John was not reluctant to talk about his new spiritual birth, however knowing the gravity of his own misdeeds, he was doubtful she would believe he had a true conversion. However, for him keeping the marriage together was a top priority. And while knowing that his incarceration was a strain on the marriage and for Wanda, he felt it was his duty now that he knew the truth about God's love and forgiveness, that reconciliation could be the only course of action. He had a lot to consider regarding his legal troubles, his thoughts were always on Wanda and he wanted to prove to her that God's redeeming love could overcome even the dire circumstances they found themselves in as a family.

Though her visits to the jail were few and far between, Wanda seemed more concerned about the changes in her body. Standing in front of John while carrying another man's child proved more difficult than she realized. How much more difficult would it be once the child actually arrived?

Chapter 21

Wanda's life went uneventful in the few weeks leading up to the birth of the child. Occasionally she would have a lunch date with Angie, but for the most part she concentrated her efforts on learning what to expect with a newborn.

While at work one day she found herself daydream of singing lullabies and rocking the baby to sleep. Not knowing what sex, the child was going to be, she went to the local bookstore and got a book of names to begin the tedious task of picking both a boy and girl name. She had asked Andy a couple week earlier to come up with a male name if it was boy and she would do the same for a girl.

She was grateful that the pregnancy had gone smooth with no medical setbacks, and the baby was developing just fine. The extra weight she was carrying made her feel tired all of the time. She was amused when she looked down to see her feet swollen with the extra fluid.

The office personnel were cordial and kind to her knowing that she was going through a difficult time with John being incarcerated. At times she felt a little ashamed to be living a double life and keeping secrets from such good people who had treated her very well over the few years she had been at the marketing firm. She could only hope that they would be understanding and continue to offer goodwill if the truth unfolded.

It was a late sunny April afternoon she was sitting at her desk collecting and sorting marketing data. She was feeling lightheaded and began sweating heavily. It was a feeling she had felt before. She tried to dismiss it as just a little dizziness due to hunger as she had not eaten most of the day. She went to the bathroom and then to the employee lounge to get some snacks from the vending machine thinking that a candy bar would perhaps level out her blood sugar. Surely she would be feeling better in a matter of minutes. She came back and continued on her work, but with each passing minute she felt weaker and weaker. A co-worker noticed that she was just not herself and came close to inquire.

"Wanda are you feeling alright? You are looking a bit pale and sweating, perhaps you need to get outside and get some fresh air."

"Thanks Tammi, girl I been a bit light headed and dizzy but I think I will be ok. I have some stomach cramps also. This is what I get for not getting a good breakfast to start the day. I just went to the snack machine to get a snickers bar and hopefully that will do the trick soon."

"Well let me get you a bottle of water, you should perhaps get some air, go outside and take a few minutes."

"Thank you, that is so kind of you."

A few minutes later the coworker returned with a bottle of water in hand. "Here take this and relax. As a matter of fact, why don't you take a few minutes and go into the lounge and sit down. I will let Mrs. Parks know what is going on and I will cover for you. I will be back to check on you in a few minutes."

"Thank you, that is probably not necessary, but I will go back and be ok in a few minutes."

The brightly lit employee area gave Wanda an instant headache when she stepped into the room. She sat in one of the small metal folding chairs and put her feet way out in front of her and tried to get as comfortable as the chair would allow. Moments later she yelled out a loud cry as her stomach pains had her doubled over.

A male worker returning from the rest room, peeked through the door, after being startled by her scream. "Wanda! What going on. Hey! Talk to me!"

She was out of breath and could barely whisper. "Thank God you are here. Please . . . call an ambulance, I need to go to the hospital. I think I am having a . . . baby."

The worker was in a moment of shock and disbelief upon hear the word baby, but then pulled out his cell phone and dialed 911. He then ran up the hallway to Mrs. Parks office. Within minutes half of the office was in the break room attending to Wanda and trying to console her and began preparations to make her as comfortable as possible.

Mrs. Parks immediately took charge of the situation. She directed several employees to grab some blankets or towels of any kind they may have in their cars. After putting together a makeshift bed she had Wanda lie down on the table and put some blankets over her to keep her warm. She stood next to her and held her hand and began to softly speak.

"You are going to be OK, Wanda. They will be here in a few minutes as a matter of fact I think they are pulling into the parking lot right now. So, don't you worry about a thing. Just concentrate on breathing and managing your contractions. Are you with me?"

Wanda nodded her head.

"I am going with you to the hospital. Is there anybody you want me to call? We are all in a little bit of shock around here because nobody knew you were pregnant."

"Yes, I need you to call . . .Andy. His cell phone number is in my phone contact list."

Mrs. Parks directed another employee to get Wanda's pocket book and bring it to the break room. She got the phone and found the number and dialed Andy, then gave the phone to Wanda.

"Andy, its time sweetheart. I am on my way to the hospital. I need you to stop by the house and grab the ready bag and meet me at the hospital. The bag is in the living room closet near the front door."

"I am on my way." Andy said. "Where are you at now?"

"I am at work, and it just happened so fast. I was feeling a bit weak and nauseated and when I went to the break room suddenly the worse pain, I have ever felt hit me and I knew what it was. They called the ambulance and I will probably be there before you get there. I am sure they are going to take me to the delivery room. Mrs. Parks is going with me so I will not be alone, but please hurry."

Twenty minutes later Wanda was wheeled from the ambulance into the delivery room. The baby would not wait. Less than forty-five minutes later a six-pound five-ounce baby boy arrived into a new world.

Wanda was all smiles and tears of joy when they laid the new boy into her arms, who had been washed and covered up in a blanket. She looked up at Andy and smiled. "Do you have a name for your son yet?"

"Well I had planned on rolling the dice with Raymond. And please do not ask how I came up with Raymond. It just came to me. He looks like a Raymond to me, don't you think?"

Wanda chuckled a bit, looked down with loving eyes and amazement and said, "OK Raymond, your father has spoken. You will be forever known as Raymond Simpson."

Wanda could not help but to think that even though this baby was created through a sinful act, he was healthy and deemed innocent by most. She tried to push back the thoughts of hiding this baby from most of her friends, and husband John. But for now, she would enjoy the moment of his arrival.

Mrs. Parks and a couple of associates who went to the hospital were a bit perplexed to see Andy there as the father. No one dared to ask questions, but Wanda knew instinctively that they had doubts and reservations and endless questions about what was taking place.

She thought maybe she should address it to stop the rumors and office gossip that was sure to follow. While she could not control what people would think about her for the predicament, the truth would at least be the only thing that would be talked about.

She asked that everyone else except Andy and Mrs. Parks leave the room for a few minutes to chat in private.

After taking a deep breath, she calmly spoke. "I wanted to thank you so much for coming down here with me and how you took charge of the situation at work to make me feel comfortable. And I also want to ask for your discretion about my pregnancy." She glanced at Andy who was growing uncomfortable with what he was hearing. "This baby is the result of a growing and wonderful relationship with Andy, who is not my husband John." After a few moments of silence, Andy cut in.

"Wanda this is not the time or place to discuss any of . . .."

"Andy this needs to be said, because it is going to get out and I for one want the right story, the truth instead of office gossip. Yes, it is a bit embarrassing, but we have to deal with it. After all our lives are now changed forever as a result of our lovely son, Raymond."

Mrs. Parks could sense this was a delicate situation that needed compassion more than moral correctness. "Wanda" she began "I am no stranger to these kinds of things and trust me when I tell you that the people that work with you in that office have lived through drama and been through things in their personal lives that the best Hollywood script has not yet produced. There is no one who can judge you or Andy, and it will not change my opinion of you one bit. You are a hardworking dedicated account manager who has devoted and I am sure sacrificed a lot. We are here for you and if there is anything we can do to help you, just let us know. And if I hear something from your co-workers that is not right about this, I will be the first to professionally put proper controls in place. You have my word on that, and I am sure I speak for all the senior management as well."

The eyes of Wanda began to tear up. Andy moved closer and hugged her and Raymond. "Shsss! Baby you are going to be OK. Let's just make a new beginning for our son." He looked at Mrs. Parks. "You are a good woman, and I wanted to thank you, for helping us both."

"You guys are going to be fine and believe me when I tell you that these things have a way of working themselves out. Besides you are going to have plenty of time while on maternity leave to learn how to be great parents. I will handle all the details Wanda so don't you worry. I will call you in a couple of days so you can come by the office and sign some papers. Now I want you to take this little bundle of sweetness home and begin to raise him to be the next marketing executive at our firm."

The smile on Wanda's face was as big as the joy in her heart.

Chapter 22

When Wanda was filling out the discharge papers a day later, she was beginning to think that motherhood would be the most wonderful thing that could happen to her. She also thought it would be a great bonder of her and Andy and she sensed that he wanted that more than anything else now in his life. She was glad to see him take such a genuine interest during her whole pregnancy and wondered if John would be as caring or attentive. It had been several weeks since her last visit to see John and she wondered just how he would hold up during trial. She felt a bit comforted that he seemed to be handling things far better than she had expected. Maybe he was coming to terms with his fate and was going to turn the corner on a new life for himself. Of course, the new life as she had envisioned might not include her, as with the arrival of Raymond that was the one thing that changed everything. She did not want to entertain the thought of divorce pending the outcome of the trial. However, she also thought that divorcing John was the surest and easiest way to hide the truth about Raymond from him. For now, however she did not want the good feelings she was having to dissolve. But she also knew that the realities of this life changing event would be unfolding very quickly in the weeks and months to come. Ready or not Raymond, Andy and John were now linked for a life time, for better or worse.

The ride back to Andy's apartment was a bit awkward with Andy hesitant to bring up the subject of temporary custody of Raymond.

"So do you think this little guy is ready for life in the small place I have prepared for him?" He wanted to break the silence and gage her reaction.

Wanda looked at him and could feel the growing love for Raymond tugging at her heart and the thought of not having him with her all the time was a crushing blow and dampened the joy she felt just a few minutes earlier.

"Let's not talk about this now, OK? It can wait and we have other things to get done." Her voice sounded raspy, as she leaned over and kissed Raymond on the forehead.

"Listen sweetheart, I know this is a little bit uncomfortable of a subject, but the reason I bring it up is to make it easier on you later on. I know you want to bond with him, and you should, however your emotions will get in the way of the things that you need to do to get your life moving again and to finish what we have started here." He paused a few seconds then continued. "What I mean is . . . "

"I know what you mean Andy!" She snapped sharply then took a deep breath to speak more calmly. "I just did not think it would be this hard to have to give him up so soon. Can't I just have him stay with me for a couple of weeks until the beginning of the trial and then hand him over to you?"

"Wanda I am telling that your bond with him will be too strong and it will be twice as bad, and the pain will be even more. You will be an emotional nervous wreck and this whole thing will fall apart. Now you are going to have to trust me on this and believe that it is for the best that I start right now with custody until the window opens up for you to bring him into your home permanently. You do not want this tug of war on your heart. It will not be good for you or him."

"My heart is going to ache for him all the time he is out of my sight. How can I live like that?"

"Wanda your love for him will make you strong enough to endure what you have to endure until he is with you again. Now remember you can see him anytime you want, you know I would never deny you that."

"Just stop talking like that. Andy you don't know anything about taking care of a baby. What if there is a medical emergency, what about shots and checkups and all the other things that could go wrong? He should stay with me. Any good mother would never do this!"

"You are a good mother, and you know it. You will prove it every day for the rest of your life, and when you get the chance to have him with you again, you will know that as a good mother you did the best decision for him at the time. You have to believe that Wanda, or else you won't get through this. Now listen I need you to be strong for me and Raymond. I can be a lot more at ease and calm knowing that you are in a good place with this. Will you do that for the both of us? For all of us?"

The tears slowly welled up in her eyes, as she tried to smile. "Don't you dare put pampers on him backwards or dress him the way you used to dress!"

"I won't, I promise."

Chapter 23

The wheels of justice picked up steam over the next several weeks with a trial date set and a jury panel in place. The conversations between John and his lawyer Jesse intensified as the painstaking details were gone over. Jesse told him no good options were on the table for dismissal or reduction of charges, and that given the current mood of the district attorney, he needed to prepare for absolute hostility from the prosecution. The best chance of any leniency would have to come at sentencing time, and even that was very questionable since the district attorney wanted to make an extra effort to show the county citizens that cleaning up the recent increase of drug activity was a top priority. She did not hesitate to admit that winning a couple of substantial drug cases could convert to votes at the polls next year when she was up for reelection.

Jesse cautioned John that with a wave of no tolerance to drugs and especially distribution, a conviction was all but guaranteed and a stiff sentence was likely. However, he would most certainly put all of Johns best character and no prior offenses in front of the jury, in hopes that they would administer some goodwill toward him.

Even though John wanted his date with the jury to come quickly, he seemed more and more nervous with each passing day. It had been several weeks since Wanda last visited, and he grew even more anxious about what was going on at the home front. His last couple of letters he wrote to her went unanswered. He could only hope that she was not contemplating divorce.

There was increasing irritability as he interacted among the other inmates. On one occasion he shouted back at the food server for apparently shorting him a helping of mash potatoes. About a week later he found himself in a small altercation with a correction officer for not returning to his cell for count, after a work detail. The officer cautioned him about infractions that could be used against him at court in his trial and that additional time could be given upon conviction. That seemed to be a very effective deterrent for most of the inmates, and John was no exception. Even though he was a bit angry he managed to refrain from drawing any more unwanted attention to himself. The best he could hope for was to cope until his date with the judge. He wanted to see Wanda again at any cost, so he concentrated on what would be needed to demonstrate to her if he got the chance that he could be the husband she wanted and needed.

He still had turmoil in his mind about Cindy. He could not fully understand how she got so caught up in the drug culture, to the point that she had consistent suppliers all over the county. What nagged at him the most was why did she set him up? He had told her that anytime she wanted out of the affair he would back off and no questions asked. He was careful not to allow her to black mail him, however he was very aware of just how clever she was. One day while picking her up from the gym she opened his glove box and took out an envelope that had his address on it. She playfully waved it in front of him while noting that she was going to show up at his front door one evening in a very sexy party dress. John was furious and was the only time he had some concern about his relationship with her and wondered if she was the type who would threaten to tell his wife, if he failed to comply with her every demand. That was in fact the issue that had come up on the day he went to visit her supplier.

She told him that even though she liked him very much, there were times when he was way to smothering and seemed insecure. At every free moment he would call or text her to the point that her manager at the gym noted she was spending way too much time on the phone and not paying enough attention to her paying clients. John gave a halfhearted apology and mentioned that he had been under some stress at home and work, and that she was the only friend and outlet he had from his otherwise boring life. It was then that Cindy suggested he escape into another feeling of something good, by taking something that would make his stress and worries disappear for several hours. She also told him that she was running low on her "feel good vitamins" and wondered if he would go pick some up for the both of them. Sitting in his tiny cell looking out at the other inmates in the same type of housing, John wished he had never agreed to make that trip.

Chapter 24

On a bright sunny Wednesday morning John climbed into the prison van with two other inmates. Once seated they were shackled to the specially modified passenger compartment to ensure maximum safety and security. During the thirty-minute ride to the court house, John stared out the window contemplating if the array of houses and businesses, and the general landscape would be the last he would see for a few years. Over the next couple of hours, the future of his life would be determined by a jury of his peers. He wondered if Wanda would be there willingly for moral support or would it feel like an obligation because of her title as John's wife.

He was brought into the court room and seated at the defendants table and unshackled and the hand cuffs were removed. Grateful for this small gesture of good will, John thanked the Sheriff and then scanned the room looking for Wanda. Looking back up at the judge's bench and the large seal of Virginia in the background, he felt very helpless to alter the outcome of what lay ahead. After briefly discussing his case quietly with his defense attorney Jesse, he looked across the table to the district attorney who seemed more than eager and confidently prepared to present her case.

John felt a weakness in his stomach with every passing minute up until the court was brought to order and the judge appeared at his bench. With precise protocol the trial started, and the district attorney wasted no time citing that John had perpetuated the rampant drug problem than plagued the county and the citizens deserve to have all those who engage in such activity removed far from them, and for a very long time.

When it was time for the defense to present its case, the jury seemed so saturated with the strong words and animation of the district attorney that it was almost embarrassing for the defense to not come to the same conclusion. However, Jesse did do a halfhearted attempt to show John in a good light and that his life had momentarily spiraled out of control due to his lust and out of control infatuation with the pretty little blonde, and personal trainer. Jesse went on to say that it was not for the jury to condemn John because of his lack of moral judgement during that time of his life. And that since his pretrial confinement he had in fact transformed into a most remarkable person who had a deep spiritual awakening far beyond what anyone in the jury box could imagine. He further pleaded for the jury to let John do the most good and give back to the society he had at one time damaged by allowing him the freedom to take his message of hope and forgiveness to the other troubled souls who are searching like he was.

Several times during the trial John would look back and scan the room for Wanda, and was heart-broke when he did not see her. Surely, she would come, if she loved him at all, if there was any glimmer of hope she would come.

When the trial took a brief recess for lunch, John was escorted back to the holding cell with the other inmates who were waiting court proceedings. It was during that time that the loneliness became overwhelming, and he began to ask the guard in the hallway if there was a way to find out if Wanda had come. The guard replied that John would just have to wait until trial resumed to try to see who was in the court room.

The second half of the trial went by even faster than the morning with the prosecution and defense reiterating their positions. The jury received instructions from the judge and swiftly went out of the court room to begin deciding his fate.

After watching the last juror step out of the jury box and into the jury room, John searched again eagerly for Wanda. This time his eye caught a glimpse of her in the far back on the last bench on the left side of the room. She was wearing a light powder blue dress with white outline that he had bought her for her birthday last year. She looked tired and drained of energy. He was hoping it was due to the unforgiving metro traffic of the area, but somehow sensed otherwise.

By two o' clock in the afternoon the jury had finished deliberations and handed the bailiff a small sheet of paper to give to the judge that contained the verdict. The judge read the note and used a pen to make a small note, then handed the note back to the bailiff who gave it to the foreman of the jury.

Within seconds John and the defense and prosecution attorneys were standing waiting for the verdict to be read. The foreman's words were slow and deliberate. "On count one distribution with intent to sell a narcotic, we the jury find the defendant John Evans guilty."

The silence of the court was shattered by a piercing scream from the back-left side when Wanda cried out. "No! No! You cannot do this to him! He is a good man; he made a mistake; you don't know him like I do. He is a changed man, give him a chance! Please!"

Order returned in minutes after Wanda was swiftly escorted out of the courtroom by two officers standing near the back door.

After hearing her outburst, John wondered if that momentary loss of emotions would somehow impact his fate. His attorney told him that the judge ran a very orderly court and that he was known to gain control over anything that disrupted the proceedings.

John sat back down in the chair next to his lawyer and shook his head. He knew that the verdict would most like come as stated but still it was hard on him to be face to face with that reality. What was to come next would be even harder to accept and much more swiftly than he had imagined. By Friday he would be standing in front of the same judge for sentencing.

On the ride back to the jail, John was very quiet while contemplating what would happen on Friday. He tried not to think of the worst, but knew he needed to prepare for the possibility of a maximum sentence being handed down. It seemed that nothing could mitigate the circumstances. Certainly, the District Attorney was going to recommend the max, and the judge was well known for not deviating far from the recommendations that she presented over the last year of cases.

Back in his cell, John saw the Bible laying on his bed. Even though he knew that he was found guilty of the charge, he somehow could not bring himself to feel like a just convicted felon. He was not the same as the other hardened criminals who had been convicted multiple times on various charges from armed robbery to murder. Yet here he was, and the rest of society would not or could not make a distinction from the man who found himself caught up at the wrong place at the wrong time, from those who have decided to make a criminal career their lucrative trade of choice.

He sat down on the bunk and picked up the Bible and opened it. He began turning the pages amazed at how flimsy and thin they were, and yet this book of all books contained the very thoughts of God. Inmate Robert who encouraged him to read it, had given it to him the same week they met. John was grateful and thought it was a nice gesture but never spent any time reading the suggested parts that Robert had mentioned. At this moment however he was willing to try anything to give his mind a brief reprieve from the circumstances he now faced.

His marriage to Wanda had not found the spiritual light it needed even though Wanda was the one who maintained a Christian footing in her personal life. Now he wondered just how much of a challenge it was for her to be stronger than the current circumstances she faced.

After a few minutes of deep reflection, he sat down on the bed and began to pray, not even knowing why or what to say. "Dear God, why would you bother to take the time to even acknowledge me as a part of your creation. I have screwed my life up really bad. I thought I had everything in control, but all of my best efforts have failed and made me miserable. All the choices have brought me to this moment where my very fate is in your hands alone. I deserve the punishment that is coming my way and even though I want a way out of it, I admit I truly deserve this and perhaps more. I feel like I am in despair and searching desperately for some answers. Most importantly however dear God, I need change from the inside. I need to be the new person you describe in the bible. Please, I am begging you to show me how that change takes place. How do I become a new person with your spirit? Can you direct me to the truth of who you are and what I need to do? I have nothing to lose and I am at the point where I am willing to try anything and do anything you tell me as long as I am not the same person I am today. Amen."

While John was more rational than emotional, he could feel the heaviness of his heart at realizing the seemingly waisted potential of his life. The thought of being a failure of a husband to Wanda also brought tears to his eyes. An inmate walked by his cell and peered in when he when heard some sniffles.

"How are you holding up?"

John looked up a bit startled that anyone cared or would even ask about his feelings at this vulnerable time. "Well I would be lying if I told you I was OK. To tell the truth I have seen better days."

"It may be a while before better days come again, but I guess you already know that. It is a process before you really get to the coping mode. For me the days are as uncertain as the wind. One day I am just fine and feeling strong and then there are other times when I want to curl up in a ball and cry all day, but in here we are not allowed the luxury of not functioning. So I just put on my face and become the best damn actor I know."

"How is that working out for you?" John looked puzzled.

"Well for me my acting is going to be a very long time, and when I stop, I will be carried out in a box. You see I am waiting to get transferred to Richmond, and that will be my last stop. I am on a lifetime train ride, and it only has one destination and that is to the graveyard."

"I am not so sure I can do that." John's eyes trailed off to the bunk bed behind him.

The inmate looked at him and with a grinning smirk that took John by surprise, said "The sooner you accept the fact that you do not have a choice the better you will be." And just as quickly as he had emerged at the cell, he strode off and disappeared.

The next Thursday morning John was led into the courtroom wearing a bright orange suit that seemed way too big for him. He sat down in the defendant chair with his legal counsel. He wondered why at this stage of the court proceedings the defense council seemed to be so intense about his case. Was not this all just one big formality? Had not all the dealing and wheeling been negotiated behind closed doors? He sat there not fully listening to the lawyer explaining the upcoming proceedings. His mind drifted to Wanda and what the years would be like for her in his absence.

Less than forty-five minutes later John was led out of the court room after the two-year sentence was handed down. He should have felt comforted that the maximum sentence was not imposed, but somehow could not breathe a sigh of relief.

The next several days was a flurry of activity as the jail prepared his transfer to Richmond Virginia to the state prison. He regretted that being transferred would only make things harder on Wanda as she would have to travel about 75 miles farther to see him. The agonizing thought of his incarceration also meant that Wanda had also been sentenced to two years of loneliness and difficulty that no person, especially her should have to endure.

Recalling Wanda's antics in the courtroom John, began to think that just maybe she cared enough to stick it out for the two years he would have to serve.

On a busy Friday afternoon John was led out once again to a van with dark windows and there he took in the sights and sounds of the outside world that he would only see for about ninety minutes before being led inside the massive structure in Richmond.

Chapter 25

The loud ring on his cell phone jolted Andy from a deep sleep. Picking up the phone he noticed the time of 0305 and it was Wanda. Sitting upright in bed he cleared his throat but was barely audible.

"Hello."

"Hey, Andy its me."

"Yea, I see, what's going on? It is three in the morning. Is everything OK with you?"

"I know, I am so sorry for calling at this hour. I just cannot sleep. I think I got some anxiety and I want to see my son Raymond and you."

"Don't you mean our son?"

"Of course, Andy, it's early in the morning, give me a break please."

"Sure, I understand. Well do you really want to wake him up now? I put him to bed at about eight and he has been sleeping soundly ever since."

"No, I won't wake him up, I just want to see him and be close to him. I miss him and can't be without him long. I did not know I was going to feel this way. This is torture, not having him here with me."

Andy paused in deep thought for a few moments before speaking. He sensed something else was bothering her.

"Well come on over and we can talk about that. I will unlock the front door, just come on in. I will put some coffee on."

"No, you do not have to do that. I don't want to stay up." She hesitated. "Is it OK if I stay with you for a while, for the rest of the night? I am lonely and I need to see you."

Andy was a little nervous, but his voice never showed any concern. "Sure, you can stay. You are always welcome here." He wondered if her coming was going to grow into a regular event of perhaps her even moving in with him.

"OK, thanks sweetheart. I will see you soon. Can't wait to see that little bundle of smiles. I know you are taking real good care of him. Ok, bye."

Andy got up and went and unlocked the front door. He then went to the bedroom to find Raymond sleeping soundly. He stood for a few minutes and looked at him adoringly. Seeing how sweet and innocent he looked, he could not help but think just how hard it must be for Wanda to endure time apart. It was obvious that her motherly instincts were strong and that she wanted to be close to her child. Would he be the one person who would have to console her on a regular basis over the absence of her child?

He thought that just maybe he and Wanda should work out an agreement to balance visitation so that she could feel more connected to Raymond and keep the strong bond intact. It sounded a bit strange to think of visitation rights, when both of them equally wanted the child for all the right reasons, even if the circumstances of his existence were questionable, and most certainly deceptive.

Twenty minutes later he heard the creaking of the front door opening with Wanda calling out to him as she came into the living room.

"I'll be right out. Make yourself comfortable." Andy quickly put on a pair of shorts and tee shirt and came into the living room to find Wanda staring at a picture hanging on the wall.

"Who is this, Andy? I don't recall seeing this picture here before."

"That my dear would be my ex." He was very reluctant to talk about any of his romantic interests after his break up with her many years ago. A sudden fear came over him as he tried to quickly change the subject. "How about me and you go see our son who looks so adorable when he is sleeping?" He moved closer toward her and put his arm around her and led her down the hall and into the small room where Raymond was.

Wanda stood at the foot of the crib watching him sleep. Andy quietly embraced her from behind. She snuggled into his arms. He leaned down and kissed her left cheek.

"This is our work. Isn't he beautiful?" Andy said.

"Yes, he is. I was just admiring him myself. When I see him all I see is love, Andy. I see our love."

He squeezed her tight and kissed her again. "Yes, so true, I was thinking the same thing. What a remarkable thing that our love created him."

She turned to him smiling and whispered. "I need to talk to you about something. Let's go to the bedroom. I don't want to wake him up."

Andy looked a bit startled at the tone of her voice and the serious look on her face. "Honey he is sleep, and I am sure whatever it is you are going to say, he would not know what you are talking about anyway. You can talk to me right here . . ."

She cut him off abruptly. "I want weekend arrangements. I want to have him on the weekends."

He looked at her for a moment motionless, pondering why she would ask that. "Did I hear you right? You want to keep Raymond on the weekends?"

"Yes, I cannot bear to be without him. Look, it won't be a problem. I work Monday through Friday and I am off on the weekends. I can pick him up right after work, take him home and bring him back late Sunday night or early Monday morning on my way to work. It will be fine, just trust me."

Andy grabbed her hand and slowly led her back to the bedroom. They both sat down on the bed. He put his arm around her and gently leaned in. "Wanda, you got to believe me when I tell you that I want you to be with him as much as possible. But we simply cannot take a chance on you getting found out or having all of this blow up in our face. What if you have company come over, or a co-worker or one of your friends and they start asking questions about this baby?"

"I am not ashamed of my baby and I am not going to hide him from anyone. Besides half of the office already knows I have a baby. Remember I went into labor pains at work, even though most people didn't know I was pregnant." She was getting annoyed at the thought of Andy suggesting that Raymond be a personal secret.

"Wanda I am not telling you to be ashamed of your baby or to hide him from anyone. But this whole thing will unravel if we don't do it as we laid it out. Remember you agreed to this, and said it was the best course of action. And don't forget that this child does not exist in theory until John gets out of prison. And if one of your friends or anyone who knows you sees this child, the word is going to get out, questions are going to be raised. We need to make sure not to bring any attention or suspicion to ourselves about Raymond. Listen the only way I would even consider letting you have him on the weekend, is if you were leaving town."

She sat listening but seemed uninterested. Slowly she spoke. "Why don't we just try it ok? And see how it turns out. Let me have him next weekend and if all goes well and feels comfortable, we can continue. I just cannot stand to be away from him. Besides I need the time to bond."

"Sweetheart I know how hard this must be for you. But please understand that for you to even have a remote chance of raising him long term you are going to have to endure this short separation. And remember I will make every opportunity available for you to see him. If you want, you can come over during the weekdays after you get off of work for a while. Would that be ok?"

She reluctantly gave into his point of view. "This just sucks! I cannot stand this. This is the one thing we did not count on, Andy. Now we are way past the point of no return. I am surprised that you can be so cold and calculating about your own son not spending time with me."

"Did you hear what I said?" Andy blurted out.

"Yes, I heard you, but that still does not make me feel any better, and neither should you. But of course, you do not care as much as I do."

Andy shook his head in disbelief. "You are not being reasonable. You are acting from a selfish emotional point of view."

"Well somebody has to." She stared at him.

"That is not fair, and you are fighting me on this for all the wrong reasons. Can we please just change the subject?"

"Yes, that is very convenient for you because you don't want to deal with it."

Wanda did not want to fight with him, after all they were going to have to share a special bond and the responsibility of raising Raymond for the next two years, and possibly more. Even though she did not want to admit it, deep inside she knew he was right in that, if word got out about Raymond, it would wreak havoc on their plans.

"I am sorry Andy, you are right. I apologize, I should not lash out at you. I'm just a little nervous about all of this. Especially now that the baby is here. I just don't know what to do, how to feel, or how to act. I do not like this whole deception thing. But still I feel drawn to you and having feelings I should not have. I am married and my husband is in prison and I don't know if I can go on pretending to be in love with him, when I am starting to feel something totally different."

"So, what are you feeling that is so different?" He was tense with anticipation.

"Well I don't know what the future will be like when this ordeal is over. Actually, I don't see it being over. I cannot pretend that things will be the same. The lies, the deception, all of it. And yes I know I am just as guilty, but I do not need to hear that from you or anybody else right now."

Andy brushed the hair back from her face. "Listen I cannot tell you that I have all the answers, but I am here for you. I know things may get a bit rocky going forward, but I will still be here. I promise I am not going to let you ride out this storm alone. We will get through this, Wanda. I need you to believe in me. Believe in us."

She looked at him and could see the tenderness in his face that had not been there earlier. She needed that side of him to reassure her. "OK, I will try. Just be patient with me."

He pulled her closer to him and softly kissed her. "Done. Come on let me get you tucked into bed. You need a good night sleep."

She grasped his head and pulled him down on top of her. "I don't need sleep, Andy. What I need is a good night of love making."

Seconds later the two bodies that had once been dressed now lay naked and bare and panting from the rising tide of passion that swept over them.

Chapter 26

The house was very quiet as Wanda busied herself cleaning, and vacuuming. She enjoyed the free time she had available on Saturdays to get all of her chores done, and even take time to pamper herself. She had scheduled a manicure and pedicure with a cut and style for her hair later in the afternoon. She seemed to enjoy this free time even more now, because while John was in the home, he discouraged her from taking the time to do something special just for herself. He would sleep in on Saturday mornings until about eleven, and that just drove her crazy, because by the time he had showered and gotten dressed, half of the day was over. He was less than helpful when it came to the many things that needed to be done or fixed around the house. More than once she became infuriated with his lack of urgency for her needs wants and desires.

John also seemed unmotivated and unwilling to initiate any family activity. To her he seemed way too self-absorbed with his computer, and video games or reading. Now that he was gone, she could finally explore the desires that had been denied and stifled.

She found herself spending a lot more time at the gym and actually enjoying not only the intense work outs but the additional attention of guys who seemed to have transformed their bodies from 'junk to hunk' in a matter of weeks.

The sound of a ringing doorbell pierced the silence of the house. She went to the door and glanced at the clock and wondered who would be visiting at nine in the morning. She found Angie smiling at her, dressed in jeans and a pink blouse. And even though she would never admit it, secretly she envied her near perfect body.

"Well hello, come on in, this is a pleasant surprise. What brings you out so early on a Saturday morning? Are you out doing errands again?"

"No, girl running errands makes me tired. I was just thinking about you and had not seen you in a while and decided to come over here and check in on you. You know just spend some time with you and get caught up on your life and give you some moral support."

"Well that is so nice of you. I am hanging in there one day at a time. That is about all the strength I have for these days."

Angie was slow to speak after sitting down on the living room couch. "Hey Wanda, I hope this is not too intrusive, but I was wondering, if umm, I could go with you the next time you go see John for visitation. How is he holding up by the way?"

"He seemed to be doing pretty good the last time I spoke with him. I have not seen him in several weeks because they transferred him to a different prison in Petersburg or Richmond, I think. Between the cost of gas and the long drive down there and back, it is hard for me to see him as often as I would like. But yeah, sure you are welcome to come with me. I don't know when I will see him for sure, but it could be as early as next week. And I will let you know."

Wanda did not want to make a full commitment to Angie regarding seeing John, however she did not want her to think she had totally abandoned John. "I cannot promise you for next week, but I will be sure to let you know the next time I set up a visit."

"Ok Wanda that is just great. I hope you know we are all praying for you. We have banded together to keep your family before God. We pray for God to give you the strength you need to endure."

The guilt that Wanda had suppressed for so long came flooding back in an instant.

Chapter 27

The routine of prison life did not come quickly or easy to John. The days dragged on a lot slower than he had ever imagined. The sheer size of the institution overwhelmed him, and the deafening noise caused him to miss the quiet solitude he valued so much before his incarceration.

As he took in all the new sights and sounds, quiet whispers from some other inmates who were making a return stay spoke of the reputation of the warden, Bill Hayden. Bill had gained a reputation of being a father figure, often stopping at the cells and spending a few minutes talking to the prisoners about their dealings with life. He seemed to really care about how they were handling the stress of prison life. He would give encouragement, and wisdom to anyone willing to listen. He often joked that he wished all of the prisoners would put him out of a job.

He especially gave attention to those who were nearing the end of their sentence, as he did not want to see them come back through those gates again on his watch. Every prisoner had a one on one with the Warden as a part of the in-processing routine. And as if life were a full circle, every inmate that was due to be discharged also met with the warden for words of wisdom to keep them on the straight and narrow path. He also spoke to every inmate that was headed to the execution chamber.

John wondered what words the warden would have for someone who is going to their death, and in that instance, he was very glad that he would not have to find out personally.

The twelve by seven cell that would now be his new home was surprisingly more spacious than the cell he had in Prince William County, with one notable difference; no windows. Even though the prison was old, it had been remodeled over the recent years to handle the ever-growing population and to meet the stringent codes to be called a maximum-security facility.

Life inside was hard, and the prison was running with a cold efficiency by design to ensure safety, and to get the message across that unlike the movies, there was no fun or glory of being a prisoner of the State of Virginia. As John looked around, he could see the stress on some inmates and wondered for a moment what changes he would go through as the next two years unfolded. He had all but forgotten to expect regular visits from Wanda, knowing that she would not be able to afford the added expense of driving to Richmond, with the rising gas prices. The two times he called her was an emotional outlet that he did not want to relive over and over again, because of the guilt he still felt. He told her that he was making his peace with God and that he had faith that God had forgiven him, but he had difficulty erasing the memories of his life of deception that had caused her so much pain and suffering.

Chapter 28

Wanda sat at her desk, staring at her computer screen unable to concentrate on the work at hand. Her mind was consumed with thoughts of Andy and Raymond. It had been several weeks since she had visited John in Richmond. It tugged at her heart and made her feel a bit awkward for spending time that could have been devoted to seeing John, with Andy.

On Friday afternoons her heart was filled with joy at the thought of seeing Raymond and having him for the weekend. Over the past few weeks, Andy seemed a bit more relaxed and was getting more comfortable with the visitation arrangements.

On a particular Friday she had worked only a half day and was going to pick up Raymond very early and she had also planned a surprise outing with Andy as it was his birthday.

She wore a beautiful red dress with a very low-cut V-neck that revealed way too much cleavage. As she stood in the mirror sideways looking at how the dress made her curves stand out, she smiled at the thought of Andy not being able to resist her when she wore anything that showed off her great features that had gotten better over the years. And she was even more surprised that her post baby weight had fallen off.

Andy had jokingly teased her about the baby fat, saying he wanted to hold onto it for as long as possible. To which she replied, 'You had better take a good hard look and take a picture, because this is going to be off of me in six months.' "How can you be so sure?" he asked.

"Well I know a personal trainer at my gym who had two kids, and her body looks like she did in high school. And I told her, whatever you do, make sure my body looks like that after I have Raymond. So, she said she will personally work with me until I am satisfied."

In route to Andy's house she stopped by CVS and picked up a birthday card. After filling out the card she reached in her purse and pulled out two tickets and dropped them in the card and sealed up the envelope. She had arranged for a babysitter so that they could go out for the evening and celebrate. This weekend she had planned on staying over at Andy's place. She was beaming with joy and excitement when she rang his doorbell.

"Wow! You look stunning! My God just how did you get that dress to paint on you so well?"

"It's called years of practice, hun!" She gave him a lingering hug and a kiss. "I have missed you a lot this week and our son. Happy birthday baby!" She pulled the card out of her purse and handed it to him. "Let me see our custom creation. Has he been sleeping well?"

"He is fine and yes I can tell that he longs for you. Sometimes he wakes up in the middle of the night and I have a hard time getting him back to sleep even after a bottle. Nothing works except soothing music and gently rocking."

"That is because that is how I put him to sleep when I have him, and I spoil him probably a bit too much, but he is so worth it, and I cannot help myself."

She strode down the hall and into Raymond's room to find him playing in the crib. She reached out her hand to pick him up. "Mommy's here, mommy's here! How is my little munchkin? Just look at that smile, are you happy to see me? Aww that is so sweet, I am happy to see you to. Yes I am." She gave him some kisses on the cheek and bounced him up and down a few times until he laughed out loud. Minutes later she put him back in the crib and carefully wrapped him up in a blanket.

Andy appeared in the doorway with an astonished look on his face.

"What's the matter sweetheart? You look like you just seen a ghost or something. Are you alright?"

"Wanda, Oh my God! How did you find concert tickets to Jason Aldean! I am the happiest man alive! I can't believe you did this! What a total surprise. Come here." He pulled her close to him and hugged her and gave her a long passionate kiss. "This is the best birthday ever!"

She winked at him. "Oh, you just wait and see baby, I promise you it is going to get a whole lot better before the night is over. I promise you a night you won't forget!"

"Oh, I like the sound of that! And I am so glad today is my birthday and the chance to celebrate with the woman I have fallen in love with all over again. But how are we going to go to the concert together? We cannot take Raymond into. . ."

"Shhh I have already taken care of that my dear. I have arranged for a babysitter to watch him while you and I go out this evening. She will be here at six, and that gives us enough time to still make the concert and get to our seats by seven."

The doorbell rang and when the door was opened a young twenty something girl with long blonde hair and big blue eyes greeted Andy. She came in and was directed to the baby's room where Wanda had a list of instructions to go over with her. Wanda found it difficult to trust Raymond with anyone other than Andy, however on the recommendation of a co-worker who had used this babysitter before, she decided to be a bit more accommodating.

Standing in line waiting for security check at the concert venue, Andy held her hand and they both laughed and joked at the different sights and sounds that they encountered with people who were decidedly country. Wanda was not as immersed in country music as Andy was, but did like hearing the way he could relate every song heard on the radio to a part of his life. He often told her that the key to understanding his heart and his view of the world was through country music. And because of that she took a keen interest to what he was listening too. All too often she heard songs about past loves and wondered if he were thinking of them more often than her. He assured her that he was not, and that there was nothing wrong with reliving the good memories that brought joy and happiness to him. She wanted to make even better memories with him.

After the show the two went to a local Friendly's restaurant for ice cream. It was nice to feel free even for a few hours to feel like carefree lovers again. Andy did not want the night to end, and actually dreaded having to go back home. "I wish we could run away together just the two of us for a few days." He listened for her reply.

"That would be nice, but you know I cannot do that. I cannot take off any more days from work and I need to be with Raymond as much as possible."

While slowly eating his mint chocolate chip ice cream, Andy's mind seemed to wander and drift. He had a blank stare that Wanda found to be uneasy.

"What's on your mind and why the sad face?" she said slowly. She held his hand across the table.

"What are we going to do about each other when John gets out?" His eyes searched hers for the answer.

"To be honest, I have not thought about any of that yet. I just can't think much past where we are right now. Why do you ask?"

"You know how I feel about you, and I am not sure if I can be comfortable with you having a life apart from me with him, knowing that we have a child together. Bottom line is I was thinking you would want to start a new life with me. Tell me am I reading too much into this, with you and I?"

"Oh, Andy please do we really have to talk about all of this now? It is just a bit overwhelming to think about right now. Why don't we see how things unfold after he gets out? I do not want to make any promises and I do not want any pressure about it. I am sorry if I cannot tell you what you want to hear."

"Well, Wanda the truth from your heart and not your head is the only thing I want to hear."

"Well I hate to say this sweetheart, but it is becoming more and more difficult for me to even know what the truth is when it comes to my heart. I want to have life the way it was, meaning a happy marriage and a bright future to look forward to. His incarceration has changed everything except a small glimmer of hope. And there are days when that is doubtful."

"I can't believe you still want a life with him, after all he has put you through. How are you going to pretend everything is ok after you get back together with him? Now I know it seems selfish of me to ask you to divorce him, but that is exactly the way I feel. We have a child together Wanda. Doesn't that mean something for the both of us?"

"Of course, it means something Andy. But what am I supposed to do, just walk away from all of this without a second thought? It is just not that easy or simple. Have you tried to put yourself in my shoes? Could you just leave it all behind so easy?"

"Yes, I could if I was in love with someone else. But maybe your love for me is not strong enough to make you leave him. And if that is the case, Wanda I need for you to tell me so that I will not set myself up for a major heartache, or keep hoping for a future with you and Raymond that will never happen."

She looked at him and tears began to flow. "I love you; I really do. I wish I was not in this position and I hate that my circumstances have put you in this awful position. I need some time to figure this all out and get the peace I need for my decisions about the future. Do you understand that?"

"I understand that we both are going to be in a lot of pain until you do. And that was why I was wanting for us to get away just the two of us, and maybe we can work through that together. But at this moment I do not want to influence your decisions in any way, so it is best that you figure out what you want to do, because it is your future happiness that is at stake."

"I know and believe me if there was an easy way to know what I really wanted; I would have figured it out by now. The truth is I haven't. But don't worry I do believe the answers will come, and we both have to be willing to accept what those answers are. Are you OK with that?"

He looked at her closely and squeezed her hand gently. "Yes, I suppose I can be." They drove home with more silence between them than normal.

Chapter 29

The rigid routine of prison life seemed to be the thing that John needed the most to make the time pass quickly. The weeks turned to months and then a year, and then a year and eleven months. With only a month to go before his release, he was getting a bit uneasy about transitioning back into society. He had learned a few trade skills, while working in the metal shop stamping out license plates. He did not really want to get back to work so quickly after release, and the transitional unit that he was transferred to was more lectures about socialization than work skills. He sat in classes very attentive even though he wondered how some of the long-term inmates would adjust to a world that was so different. His two-year term meant that not much had changed other than science and technology, and a new president and the downward spiral of morals that plagued the country even before he was locked up.

With his newfound life as a baby born again Christian, he found it rather fascinating and sad that the world was truly blind to the knowledge of the saving gospel of Jesus Christ. He also had a deep fear that once he got back on the outside that the pressures of the world would drown out his newfound convictions. That fear drove him to read the bible even more and pray to get close to God and hope that God would not let him slip back into his old thought patterns and habits that derailed his life, not long ago.

He was keenly aware that his thoughts would eventually lead to his destiny. He kept saying over and over as a mantra, 'Thoughts produce feelings, feelings produce action, action shapes your destiny.' It was the most reliable and accurate measure of what a person would become and where they would end up. The thousands of other inmates in prison with him served as a stark reminder daily of that undeniable fact.

The visits from Wanda were getting more emotional for him as he still did not know how to make up the time lost and most certainly did not know if Wanda would still accept or respect him as a husband. Even though he wanted her to believe that he was changing from the inside out, he also knew that the damage that he caused would not be forgotten and that Wanda was going to be on edge for a long time to come. He gently shared with her the things he was learning in the bible and the revelations that had come to him. However, the nagging thoughts that he was a hypocrite seemed to neutralize his best efforts. He talked with the chaplain and some other believer about this matter. The best advice they gave him was to let his life be the proof and not his words.

It was hard to think of the future at times because he did not have a solid plan. Wanda asked him on several visits what he intended to do when he got out. On one such occasion he tested the water to see how she would react to his level of faith.

"I know this is not the answer you want to hear, but I am going to allow God to give me some direction so that I am sure of what I want to do. I realize that he put me here for a specific purpose and that I will not have a very fulfilled life until I am functioning in his purpose and plan. I read in the Old Testament that God's love toward the people of Israel was so great, even after they had messed up really bad and their sins led to them being in captivity. He still says about them, that, the thoughts he has for them is for good and not evil, to give them hope and a future. I claim that verse as God speaking to me in the same manner, because I know he loves me and even though I have been through this bad period in my life, I am convinced that he can make it for his purpose and good can come out of it."

"Well, I hope so for your sake, John. Forgive me if I do not feel so optimistic. You will find me to be a very different person when you get out. But I guess you already know that by now."

The truth is he did not know just how far different she had become. And the unveiling would still be a couple months away.

Chapter 30

Wanda grew jittery as the date approached of John's release. She was scared and did not know what to expect or just how she was going to hold up, knowing she had a child with another man. The days seemed to grow longer than the summer days of prolonged sunlight and warm humid temperatures of July. She had worked out arrangements with Andy to continue visits as often as possible. She told him that as soon as possible she would gesture the idea of having another child with John and hope that he did not flat out reject the idea. She was thinking that John would want to please her in any way possible to reconcile their marriage. As a matter of fact, she had every intention of getting any and every request she could possible think of while it would be fresh in his mind upon his returning to home. Andy cautioned her not to push him too far too fast, because he was going to need some time to adjust to life back in the mainstream. And even though the thought of John laying in the arms of Wanda drove him crazy, he knew that he had to keep his cool until the whole story unfolded as planned.

With only two weeks until he got out, Wanda spent as much time as possible with Andy and Raymond, even taking off more time from work than she had on the vacation books. This got the attention of the senior marketing executive, and on one Wednesday afternoon he called her to his office. Mark Vandenberg was a rising star at the firm, and he ran a tight ship and demanded a lot of his subordinates. It was Mark who saw the talent and potential that Wanda had, and he was the one who lobbied hard to the president and CEO to bring her on board and to trust her with some of the most lucrative accounts. He wanted a driven woman who had the talent to close the hard deals that no one else wanted to touch for fear of not delivering as promised.

She stepped into his spacious office and admired the beautiful furnishings, and the wonderful view of the large window that overlooked the garden courtyard. She knew that upon her next promotion, she would have an office of similar size and beauty. She had always kept the next rung on the ladder in mind with all of her business dealings along her career. She was good at what she did and the company always recognized her accomplishments.

Mark looked up from behind his desk. "Come in Wanda, and please have a seat." His tone was pleasant but businesslike and firm. "How have you been?"

"I'm ok, just taking life one day at a time." She was reluctant to reveal too much about her personal life. She always felt that career decisions could be hampered by what the company knew about one's personal life. She had seen that play out time and time again, as soon as a woman announced a pregnancy, her accounts were shifted to someone else, and somehow they never got back to her again.

Mark smiled at her. "One day at a time, I suppose that is all any of us can manage. Speaking of which, I see you are on the Rosenthal account, and I must say you are doing a great job so far, however they were expecting you to meet last Friday with their VP of operations. Russel and I get a call that said you never showed up. I was wondering if you could explain why?" He sat back in the chair and looked at her, with the stern look of a future executive to the most sought-after marketing and advertising agency in the area.

Wanda hesitated for a moment while squirming in her chair. "Oh, my goodness, oh my goodness, I am so sorry. I forgot all about that meeting with Russell, and I scheduled a doctor's appointment on Friday afternoon instead. I will send him an email and give them a call to reschedule."

"A doctor's appointment? Are you OK? Have you been sick or something? Because I see here where you have been taking a lot of time off that is not accounted for and that Friday afternoons you have been leaving very early and on one occasion Mrs. Parks did not know where you were for our own quarterly accounts meeting. Is there some explanation for this? What is going on with you?"

She sat back in her chair feeling like she just got kicked in the stomach. If she were to reveal all the things that are taking place in her life, the firm would lose confidence that she would be able to make good decisions and function well with all the stress. Yet she needed the job the most at this time in her life because it was to be her only escape from the chaos that was to come in less than two weeks with John coming back home. Furthermore, she was going to be the sole bread winner, and had no faith that anyone would give a drug felon a chance for employment.

"Mark, I got to be honest with you, I am very reluctant to say this. First, I am sorry that I have not been a hundred percent lately. I do a pretty good job of holding my own, but the last two years have been extremely tough for me. I have had a crisis in my life pretty much the entire time. I had assumed with all the office chatter that everybody knew by now, but perhaps not. My husband . . . John, did something and has been incarcerated for the past two years and is expected to get out next month. But this has taken a toll on me personally and emotionally. I just did not want it to get to the point where it affected my job, as I know how much faith and trust you have in me."

Mark, listened for more and then asked, "OK, what is going on with you missing so much work and especially on Friday afternoons?"

"He is locked up in Richmond and knowing how the traffic is here on Friday's I have been leaving early so that I can go visit him during the selected hours available, because it is over two and half hours driving even when traffic is moving."

"Ok, I am trying to be very understanding and accommodating here. Of course, you got to realize that you have been placed on some very high and valuable accounts, and we need your best effort on this. We need your attention and focus. Now tell me should I consider someone else for this account while you take the time to sort out your personal life? And how are you going to handle the transition when he gets out and comes back home?"

Wanda seemed to be daydreaming for a brief moment. "To be honest, I do not know."

"Your accounts are in good order and you have made a lot of progress and we all are very proud of what you have done so far. I would hate to have to pull you off of this, however with all that you are dealing with, I think it is best that you take some time, get things sorted out in your personal life, so that when you get back you will be fresh, alert, an able to function at the level that is needed. So, I am going to authorize up to another month of LOA. How does that sound, and will that help free up some time you need to get back on track?"

A leave of absence was not what she wanted or needed now. She wanted every minute away from the house especially if John was going to be coming home in a chaotic and confused state of mind. And she needed the money.

"Mark I am deeply thankful that you would do that for me, however I think it is in my best interest to stay on and work, and it will be very therapeutic during this time of transition. I hope you understand. I think if I pour myself into work, it will be the best thing for me to get my mind off of all this."

"Wanda, I know you are a go getter and I love that quality about you. But there are times when you need to step back and slow down and allow a reset. And I think this is one of those times. You won't be much good if you are dragging in here with a head full of emotional garbage from your personal life nagging at you while you are trying to land the biggest client we have had in a while. I really would rather you take the time off, keep me posted and come back when your plate is clear. Wanda, I know you can be stubborn and very hard on yourself. You are just like me in so many ways, and that is why this is not for negotiation. I want you to get with Mrs. Parks and get the paperwork filled out. I will sign off on it this evening before I leave. Is there anything else I can help you with?"

"No sir, thank you very much."

He looked at her knowing that she was still thinking about ways to tie up loose ends with the client. "Listen do not worry about Russell I will have someone follow up with him and reschedule another meeting. We may have to sweeten the deal a bit more, but he will come around. You have already done the leg work and the hard part. Let us handle it from here and don't worry. OK?"

She smiled and said, "I promise I will not call the office except to gossip!"

"Great, I am glad to hear that."

She stepped out of his office feeling even worse than when she entered. Now, like it or not she would have to confront everything that was coming in the next few weeks. She did not have the job to rely on as a crutch and would have to figure out another way to handle it.

Chapter 31

John could hear the heavy footsteps of the guards coming down the tier. It was the best sound he had heard in two long years. Because it would be the last time the guards would open the cell door of 347 and escort him out. Shackled and cuffed he was escorted to the warden's office for the famous out bound processing talk. It was rather brief with the warden doing the procedural review of the last two years of conduct within the facility. Knowing that John was regarded by all the correction officers as a model prisoner, he had full confidence that he would adjust well on the outside. Processing was still a long tedious process and John felt the same anxiety he had two years prior.

It was a very clear day with sunlit skies when he stepped through the tall gates and waited for the electronic wall to come down behind him. Looking up he saw the cameras still watching his every move. He smiled, and gave a courtesy nod, knowing that the guards watching on the other end would find it amusing, and that another bet would be placed on his return to prison as was the case of so many others who stepped through the gate on parole.

He took a deep breath and turned his face toward the sun, glad that this was just the beginning of many brighter days ahead. Wanda was running a few minutes late and he was glad to have some alone time to take in his new freedom. He prayed silently and was thankful to God that he had survived and asked for wisdom for the road ahead. He felt an unusual sense of calm and peace come over him. He recalled reading a scripture about having 'peace that surpasses all understanding.' This was one of those moments.

Wanda arrived with her own set of anxieties as she turned into the parking lot and was cleared pass security to go meet John. She was thankful for the long drive to Richmond, as it gave her time to collect her thoughts. When they met and embraced, he was overjoyed with excitement. He hugged her tightly and picked her up and twirled her around, followed by a long passionate kiss.

"You are the best thing I have seen in two years, and . . ." He could not speak as his emotions overcame him. He began to sob.

"It's ok, sweetheart, I understand. It's all getting better from this moment on. Remember you are leaving this all behind." She hugged him tight and smiled. "Come on let's get you away from here before they put you back in. I am taking custody of you now."

The drive back home was a bit awkward with John, staring out the window taking in all the sights and sounds. He seemed to not hear all of Wanda's rambling about the last two years without him. She looked over at him and could tell he needed to adjust to life and freedom on his own terms and at his own pace.

Stepping into the house John was glad to experience the gentleness of the door closing quietly behind him. He stood in the middle of the living room for a few seconds to bask in the serenity of his new environment. Wanda looked at him not understanding what he was feeling at the moment. "Are you OK?" she asked.

"Yes, I just needed a moment to experience the peace of here. I take nothing for granted anymore and life has a way of taking on a whole new meaning when you have been deprived of the very basics. Freedom has a sweet taste that you may not understand unless you have been where I have been."

"It's alright, John. I know this is going to take some getting used to. Take your time to adjust. You will get back to normal again in no time, I promise you. Soon you will be fully engaged in life . . . your new life." She could only hope that her life would unfold over the next several weeks with the same excitement hopes and dreams that John was longing for.

They spent the rest of the day home, with Wanda cooking his favorite meal, spaghetti.

She had a bottle of wine that was left over from her last encounter with Andy and thought this would be the perfect time to share it.

John was very impressed at how she had managed to not only run the house but decorate it and make some improvements that he had procrastinated on for months before his incarceration. "Are you still the queen of HGTV? This place looks like you have spent a lot of time at Home Depot."

"I am and yes I have. I am glad you like it. It was a lot of work, and it was also the reason why I could not visit you on the weekends as often as I would have liked." She needed to drown out the guilt she was beginning to feel.

Sitting on the couch she laid her head on his shoulder and took his hand. "Look I cannot imagine what you went through in there, and I will not pretend that I know how to help you get back to normal. All I know is that you will, and that I am here for you. We got a long road back to where we were, but I guess it begins with one step. And I have been thinking that it also begins with the one thing that has kept me from healing . . . forgiveness."

He looked at her, hanging onto every word. "One thing I know Wanda is that forgiveness does not come easy and it is often the hardest thing you will have to do when it is under these circumstances. If you are not at the point of forgiveness, it is OK, because to be honest with you forgiveness is really not in your power to do. I have come to know that it is the power of God to forgive. After all that is what he did for us all. A good example is that it has been hard for me to forgive myself for what I did, and yet he has forgiven me. I just have to get to the point of realizing that his forgiveness of me is good enough for my forgiveness of me. I hope that makes sense."

She gently squeezed his hand. "Yes, it does." Her mind drifted to Andy and wondered if John could be able to forgive both of them for the deeds of the past two years. She took a big gulp of wine hoping that it would soon kick in and begin to drown out the thoughts of her mind. She put her arm around him and squeezed him tight. "You know what I heard is the best cure of two years of incarceration?"

"No, I have no idea." He looked at her perplexed. "What?"

"All night love making in our bed, starting right now." She quickly grabbed his arm, yanked him up and pulled him toward the bedroom. He was smiling as she began to undress him, knowing that what was going to happen next was just what he had longed for every time he closed his eyes in the small cell in Richmond.

Chapter 32

Passion consumed them both and the hours passed quickly. The faint light of day began to fill the room as the two lay naked under the covers. A small moan from Wanda awakened John.

He turned toward her and slowly stroked her face. "Hey, you look like you just had an all night session with a guy who has not had sex in over two years."

"Yeah, I was thinking the same thing. We both have a lot of catching up to do. It has been way too long."

Wanda finally swung her feet over the side of the bed and put on a red bath robe. She quickly stepped into the kitchen to begin making morning breakfast. John soon appeared in the kitchen wearing just his boxer briefs. He stood by the entrance way just watching her and smiling. He admired how effortlessly she moved about the kitchen. He had always been impressed by her efficiency and on more than one occasion she reminded him to have a seat and let her master her domain. She did not like anyone moving about in the kitchen with her or distracting her or talking while she was concentrating on preparing a meal. She had a routine that made sense to her, even if it seemed like organized chaos to everyone else.

John was taking in her beauty and anxious to ask many questions. Minutes later, they both were eating breakfast very quietly. No sounds could be heard, accept the occasional fork tinkering against the plate.

The ringing of her cell phone pierced the silence between them. Believing it to be Andy, Wanda let it ring.

"Aren't you going to get that?" John asked.

"Oh, it's just marketing calls. I get them every morning about this time." It was a lie she had to tell instantly, because she instinctively knew it was Andy as he always called in the morning to check on her and update her on Raymond.

"Listen, why don't we both go back to bed and lay around for a few more hours. I am not in a rush to get the day started so quickly, and I want to spend as much quality time with you as possible to get reacquainted. I thought having breakfast would be nice because we both worked up an appetite. And who knows we just may again, and that could take us to lunch." She smiled at him and slowly walked by him toward the bedroom.

They both laid in bed over the next couple of hours talking and laughing about some of the funny things that John had seen while locked up. Wanda did not think much of it was funny on the surface, but the way John told the stories made her laugh. John always had a very weird sense of humor, and he often was sarcastic with most of the things he said that would bring him attention.

Even though the time spent that morning was wonderful, Wanda still could not feel totally at ease with John, knowing that she was living a double life of massive deception. But she felt she was way in over her head and had to play the act all the way through. She had lost John for the last two years and feared that if she confessed her awful secret to him now, he would leave and she would lose him forever. She looked into his eyes and could see that he was a man filled with much hope for the future. She wanted so badly for his dreams of the future to come true, and she reasoned within herself, that if her deception could bring that about, then so be it. She knew there would be consequences, no doubt, but for the moment she wanted to share the best moments she could with him. Regardless of what John had done, he paid the price and he deserved the best she could offer him. She still had a role to play as the good wife, and the one who would build the bridge back into their relationship. That would have to be her focus for now. It was her job to complete the mission.

She was grateful that her Leave of Absence was brief. The firm was strained with rumors of a merger with a competing marketing agency that had gained far more market share than any other company in the region. She breathed a sigh of relief when they asked if she was come back to the office and resume her duties as soon as possible. She agreed to come in the next day.

The following morning she was very tired as she picked up her car keys and pocketbook and headed out the door for work. Knowing that she was still the only bread winner in the household still made her feel a bit angry, but she knew that John needed some time to beat the odds and get a job. The hiring rate for felons was declining with each passing day, and she knew that John was going to need a miracle to land a job anywhere. She thought that perhaps she could network with some people at work who might be willing to give John a break and hire him to do anything. And then there was Andy who most certainly knew people that might give John a chance. She decided she would see Andy after work to check on Raymond and talk about getting John some work.

The office was busy with activity when she arrived. A visit from the CEO of the competing advertising agency had stirred things up. There were whispers about a merger and some major personnel changes. She needed to focus on her work at hand and not get caught up in the office drama of the hour.

The day dragged on agonizingly slow. The sheer exhaustion she felt from being up all night was taking it's toll. She went to the bathroom and took a longer than usual break. She texted Andy and told him she was coming by after work but would not be able to stay long because she was very tired and needed to get home and rest. Minutes later she was back at her desk and putting the final touches on a marketing proposal.

Her mind wandered back and forth from thoughts of Raymond, to Andy and John. It was sheer torture to juggle so many things at once. She clearly was not doing her best work and had to force herself to stay focused. When she clocked out at the end of the day, she was grateful that a bright sunny afternoon greeted her as she walked to her car.

The text reply from Andy, asked if she was OK, and why she was so tired. Of course, he did not want the truth, but asked out of habit. "I'm on my way, will talk when I see u." she replied.

She felt uneasy when she rang Andy's doorbell. The thought of asking him to try to find a job for John felt like betrayal, knowing that if the truth be told he did not want John in her life. On more than one occasion Andy said that John did not deserve to have her back after the hell he put her through. He thought it extremely selfish to hurt her the way he did. Wanda could not disagree but being married to him raised the stakes very high, and even though he caused her great pain, in her mind him, and for the sake of her marriage was worth at least an attempt at reconciliation. It would not be easy, but she would have deeply regretted not even trying.

Andy opened the door slowly, and motioned for her to come in. "Hey, I'm glad you could stop by. Our little Raymond has been missing you. I just finished changing him and put him down for a nap."

"Oh, I see. Are you getting better at this daddy thing?" She strode past Andy to Raymond's room and stood next to the crib. "I want to pick him up and hold him but he might not get back to sleep, and I know he needs his rest."

"Well I don't know if I am getting better but am getting more efficient."

"Efficient? You act like he is a machine you have to operate."

"Wanda, will you please give me a break, I am doing the best I can here."

"Ok, OK, I am sorry. That was not fair or a nice thing for me to say. I know you are trying and I must say you are doing a very good job. I guess being a mother who is absent from her child makes me critical. I should not take it out on you. Can we go in the living room to talk?"

"Yeah. sure. Can I get you anything to drink or eat? I was just about to fix a sandwich."

"No thanks, I am fine."

Andy looked at her, and slowly shook his head from side to side. "No Wanda that does not look like fine. I can read your face plain as day. What's wrong? Is it John?"

She sat down on the couch and leaned back and closed her eyes for a few seconds. "Yes, it is John, but not what you may be thinking. He just got out of prison and trying to start life over is not easy. It is especially hard when you do not have a job and the chances of getting one are next to none because you are a recent ex con and felon. I told him I would do the best I can to put him in touch with people who could be of help." She looked at Andy hoping he would not be too critical at this moment.

"And somehow you think I can be of help? You actually believe I want to help?"

"Stop it Andy! I got enough crap at home to deal with. I do not need any crap from you! I know what you think of John, and maybe you have some valid points, but I can only deal with the here and now. And right now he needs a job of any kind. I came here hoping that you would find it in your heart to help him, and in doing so you would be helping me. Can you for once stop being selfish and think of someone other than yourself?" She was at the verge of tears.

"Listen Wanda, I know you are trying to be the dutiful wife and be supportive of him as any good wife would. But I got to tell you that he does not deserve your support after what he has done. You are calling me selfish. What about him? Was he thinking of you when he decided to mess with drugs? Remember Wanda, he stole over two years of your life and made it a living hell. How can you be so eager to take him back, and think that all is going to be fine the way it was?"

Tears were streaming down her face. "Shut up! Don't you think I know that? You selfish bastard! All you care about is getting back together with me, especially now that we have a baby together. That is not an option and it is not going to happen Andy. Yes, I do know you have been there for me during this whole time and I am grateful. But now I wonder what your true motives were. I did not think we would have to have this conversation. I thought you knew that when he got out of prison that me and him were going to try to reconcile. Remember that baby in there is a big part of it, or have you forgotten the plan that you insist that I stick to?"

"I cannot help if I feel what I feel. But for your sake, not his, I will see what I can do and call a couple people and try to get him hired on somewhere. It might be something off the books under the table until he can find something more legit. I am not making any promises, but I will try."

"Thank you. And even though you don't want to hear it. He thanks you also." She stood up. "I wish I could stay longer, but I have to get back home. He does not know I am here."

Wanda could sense the pain that Andy felt in that moment. "I am sorry, I just got to get in a routine that won't cause him to ask too many questions. Please understand, Andy."

He hugged her goodbye. "I will call you or text if something comes available."

Chapter 33

She found John sitting on the couch reading his bible when she returned. "Has that become your favorite book?" she asked.

"Yes, as a matter of fact it is. How was your day? You look very tired." He stood up walked over and hugged her. She melted into his arms and had longed for his embrace that reminded her of the first years of their marriage. "Listen sweetheart I know things have been tough for you the last couple of years and you are a very strong woman. But you are not super woman and you will not have to do it all alone. As soon as I can find some work, I will be sharing more of the load."

"I know sweetheart. It's ok, things are going to work out for you I just know it. I can handle this for now." She looked up at him smiling and kissed him. So, what did you do all day?"

"Well to tell you the truth not much of anything. I just took in the serenity and basked in my freedom to enjoy all the little simple things that I had taken for granted for so long. It is amazing how little things that people on the outside get to enjoy every day is a long sought-after luxury to inmates. Things like hot water, a window, sunlight, a television, carpet and most of all the freedom to move about when and where you want to without chains, and shackles. You know it really is a whole lot worse than what you may have seen on television and in the movies. Trust me when I tell you that the outside world does not know any of the horrors that can go on inside of a place like that."

"I know it must have been awful, baby. But I am so glad you survived, and you are here with me now."

"I feel lost, Wanda. I do not know where to begin, making my way back to be the husband you need me to be."

"It's ok. We will figure it out, together." She smiled and slid from his embrace. "Listen I am going to take a shower and change and then I am taking you out to dinner. How does that sound?"

"Great, you know me, I am not a very hard man to please."

"Yes, I like that about you."

She strode off to the bedroom and shut the door. After getting undressed down to her undies, she sat down on the side of the bed and began rummaging through her pocketbook for birth control pills. She had been taking them regularly but forgot to ask the doctor for a new prescription with her last checkup. She found the bottle and counted two little pink and white tablets.

She picked up her phone and called the doctor's office. The receptionist told her the doctor was out on vacation and would not be available for about two weeks. "Does he have someone covering for him and taking care of his patients in his absence? I need my birth control refilled now. I am down to two pills." Her voice was near panic as she explained that she forgot to ask for a refill with her last visit.

"Mrs. Evans can I schedule you for an appointment next week on Thursday?"

"Next week! Do you have anything sooner? Listen I don't you think you understand. My husband just got home from a very long . . .deployment and we have not had sex in over two years, and I am not ready to conceive a child this week. Do you understand my situation here? It is rather urgent!"

"I deeply apologize Mrs. Evans but that is the only time slot we have available unless someone calls and cancels."

Wanda slumped back onto the bed with the resignation in her voice of despair. "Oh, no this is not good at all. Please call me if something changes, please."

"I most certainly will, Wanda. You have a pleasant day."

Hanging up the phone she sat back up on the bed, wondering how she would explain to John that they would have to put sex on hold for a week. She knew he did not like to wear condoms, and that was made clear while they were dating. But perhaps with his strong needs that should be met, he would have a change of heart.

An hour later the two were sitting across from each other at a small booth at Applebee's, enjoying a couple of drinks and food. Even though Wanda was smiling, she was feeling nervous and tense on the inside, because of the things she wanted to discuss with John. John seemed not to notice her, as he looked around the room and took in all the various sights.

"So, how does it feel to be in a place like this after two years of dining with people who all have the same uniform?" Wanda asked.

"Well, I can tell you that it is nice to be able to sit down without having hundreds of other guys around you, with all the noise and wondering if you will get through your meal without a fight breaking out, because somebody from a rival gang wants what you have."

She looked at him and frowned at the thought of having to fight over food. "I would imagine it is nice to know that you can eat a meal in comfort without worrying about your safety."

Her nervousness became apparent to John, when she picked up the teaspoon and began twirling it in between her fingers. It was the exact thing she did on their very first date, when she told him that when she gets nervous or uneasy it is a calming method to channel her energy.

"Is everything OK? You seem a bit anxious."

She took a deep breath. "I'm sorry to be honest, I need to talk to you about something that has been on my mind for the last several months. I do not know why I feel so nervous talking to you about this now, we have not had any real bad communications problems in the past, in spite of all that has happened."

A growing fear inside of John caused him to think that perhaps this was the moment she was going to tell him that she wanted a divorce. "Wow, I would be lying if I told you that I am not a little scared at this moment. Why do I get the feeling you are getting ready to tell me about a life changing event . . . like divorce?"

In that moment Wanda contemplated for a few seconds how easy it would be to confirm Johns notions. After all it had crossed her mind several times during the past two years, and Andy all but insisted on it. Even if divorce was inevitable, this was not the time to inflict such distress to a man who was taking his first steps to normalize his life. She smiled back at him, cherishing the fact that she had a secret he desperately wanted to know. Just as quickly she thought of the secrets, he had been keeping from her which led to his incarceration.

"No, I was not thinking that at all John. I am surprised that you would say that, unless of course it is something that has crossed your mind. However, what I am thinking is a life changing event that will benefit us both. As a matter of fact, I think it could very well be the thing that will bring our marriage back together."

John's interest was now peaked and he gave her his undivided attention. "Oh, this ought to be good. It sounds interesting. I am all ears."

"I think we should have a baby." There she had said it. She put it out there. She sat back and waited for a response, hoping she did not give him a heart attack.

"Did I hear you say, you think we should have a baby? . . .OK"

The only other time he had heard Wanda mention a baby was six months after they got married. They both had decided that it was not a good time, because John needed to focus on his career, and Wanda had just started the job with the marketing firm. Wanda had never mentioned it again over the course of their marriage, and John was hoping that she would simply forget the idea. He was a little surprised that she would bring it up now.

"Well you were absolutely right when you said a life changing event. May I ask, how long you have had this on your mind?"

"It's not on my mind John. It's in my heart. Am I to assume that you are not too thrilled with the idea?"

"No, Wanda. That's not it at all. I was just a little taken by surprised, because we have not discussed this in so many years. I mean the last time the thought of us having a child came up, we had just gotten married and starting our careers. We agreed that the timing was not right. To be honest, I never brought it up, because I was thinking that you became so absorbed in your job that perhaps motherhood was not on your radar at all, especially since the lost of Jasmine."

"I know, you are right. I had put it out of my mind for all these years. However, I have been thinking about this for a while. I think it is something we should seriously think about or at least consider. I am getting older and my biological clock is ticking. In fact, there is no doubt in my mind that being a father would be very good for you. It would give you something to focus on. Regardless of what has happened between us you are starting over, and what better way to celebrate a new beginning than with a new life. What do you think?"

"Well, I am not totally opposed to the idea. However, my situation right now is vastly different from when we first got married. I just got out of prison and need to focus on rebuilding my life, our lives. That means a job or career. A baby at this time would most certainly hinder that. I am open to the idea; I just think the timing is very bad."

She reached out and held his hand. "Listen I know your having to deal with a lot, and this may be way too much for you to even contemplate right now. Think about this; I am still working full time; I can make ends meet. If we have a child regardless if you only have a part time job, it would be the perfect scenario, because you could stay home and be Mr. Mom. I think you would be a great stay at home dad."

He beckoned her to lean across the table closer to him. He stared into her eyes and smiled. "Who are you and what have you done with my wife Wanda?"

She gently stroked his cheeks and pulled his head even closer and kissed him. Looking into his eyes she said, "I am the woman who wants to give you a child, so that we can begin our lives again. What do you say to that?"

"That is a very big decision and step to take in our lives. I think it requires some serious thought and wisdom from God. So even though I do not want to spoil this moment for you. I will delay giving you an answer until I have prayed about this. Is that all right? Don't you think that is a good idea?"

She wanted to scream at him for being so dismissive but realized that he was not the same man who agreed to just about everything she said, several years ago.

"OK, but do not wait too long. My clock is ticking, and I cannot be an old mother. It is just not cool or fair to the kid."

"I hear you. I promise you I will get back to you on this. For now, though let's have a desert." He looked at the dessert menu with childlike anticipation. "Oh, yeah! Mint chocolate chip will do it for me. My God I have not tasted that in so long. I can't wait."

On the drive back home Wanda's thoughts drifted to Raymond. She still wanted to spend more time with him but knew that John's suspicions would be raised if she acted on her impulses. Over the next three weeks of job searching for John, she made a point to see Andy and Raymond on a more consistent basis after work. She often would call John just before leaving work and tell him that she was going to be following up with some contacts about hiring him. She would be out till evening leaving John with the responsibility of both cleaning the house and preparing a meal. While John was very grateful, he also wanted to see more of her, and focus on building their marriage again. He was getting increasingly frustrated as the days passed by.

On an early Wednesday morning John strode into the local unemployment office in search of some advice about how to best go about disclosing and talking about his criminal record, as undoubtedly it would come up in a job interview. The recruiting administrator looked up from her desk and smiled at him.

"Good morning, how can I help you?"

"Hello, my name is John Evans and I need some help and advice for filling in details about a two-year absence from working. Could I speak to someone in private about that, as it is a sensitive and personal matter?"

"Sure, I can help you with that. Do you have a resume that I could review for you?"

John leaned in a bit closer to her and lowered his voice to a near whisper. "No, I do not. You see to be honest I was just released from prison about a month ago and I am trying desperately to get back to work. For now, anything will do. It is a little embarrassing to talk about as you can imagine, but I am willing to confront my past, because I have faith in my future."

The recruiting administrator was reassuring and put him at ease. "Don't worry John, we have seen your situation before and I can tell you that with some effort and persistence, you will be working again. The best thing you can do is to be totally honest with any employer you are applying to and explain the details in the interview. You would be surprised at how many employers are open to giving second chances to folks in your circumstances. What you want to do on your resume or application is highlight your skills and accomplishments up to the point of incarceration and if you have taken any training or schooling in prison, you want to show that also."

About 30 minutes later John walked out of the office with a stack of information on how to best reenter the job market, and how to best present himself both on paper and in an interview.

Having to walk virtually everywhere, John thought it would be a good idea to get a bike so that he could be on time for appointments and cover a lot of ground for interviews if he ever got any.

Later that evening when Wanda got home, he told her about his plans to get working again and that he was confident that he would be helping out financially at the house.

"Sounds like you have made a lot of progress in a short amount of time. I have been talking to a lot of my contacts and telling them about your situation. I am sure someone is going to give you a chance John." Wanda was glad that he had taken the time to get out and explore. She did not want him to feel trapped at home while she was at work.

"I need a bike so that I can get around town and make my job interviews when they come up. I was thinking about looking in the papers for one or maybe the bike shop has a few used ones for sale. Is that something you could help me with?"

Wanda hesitated for a moment, a bit stunned at his desire to pay any price to get back to work, but very glad that he was going to be occupied while she was away. She had forgotten that his license was expired. "Wow, it sounds like you really got a plan to make things happen. A bike would be good for a while, but what you really need is your license, that way you could use the car while I am at work. I think the DMV has extended evening hours on Friday, maybe we can get by there when I get off work this Friday."

"That would be great. Listen I wanted to say thank you for your support, it really means a lot to me. We are going to make it work Wanda."

"Of course, we are. I can see you making a comeback better than ever."

"Well, it is not all that I am doing, as much as what Christ is doing. His word has promises that I believe in and I totally trust what he says. He has been very faithful to me over the past two years, Wanda. I could not have survived without putting my trust in him to take care of me under those conditions."

"I know sweetheart and I am very glad that you have found new faith to help you." If only she could say the same for herself.

Friday after work she went home and picked up John and drove to the DMV office. The long line was expected but surprisingly it moved faster than usual. After the documents were processed and a photo taken, John was holding in his hand a license.

"This represents a major milestone, because while it may be mundane to most, it is something that I will never again take for granted. You know I learned a lot while locked away. One of the things that has stayed with me is realizing just how fast and how drastic your life can change. It can all be over in a heartbeat." John was smiling as he put it in his wallet.

Chapter 34

The next several weeks passed by mostly uneventful, but for the occasional complaint from Wanda about her not getting pregnant as she had hoped. She had been taking the pill regularly and having sex almost daily. John was trying to be as sensitive as one can in his position.

One morning he asked her to go to the doctor and get a checkup. "It is better safe than sorry Wanda. Maybe there is a reason you have not gotten pregnant and you need to find out what it is. It is not for a lack of trying." A big grin came to his face.

"OK, but what if there is something wrong and I can't get pregnant. Then what? I do not want to disappoint you."

"Hey! Stop talking like that. I just want you to get a professional opinion and maybe there is something that you or we can do to increase the odds of you getting pregnant. I just want you to be proactive. That's all I am trying to say. OK? And besides you know me, I am fine either way."

"Yeah! Well I'm not and I am going to have a baby!" She stormed out of the room and picked up her purse and keys and started heading for the front door.

"Hold up! Where are you going?" John was startled at her sudden change of mood.

"I am going to the doctor, alone. I will see you when I get back." She then walked out the door and seconds later was heading out of the driveway with much fury.

John was at a loss for words to understand how she could be so calm and then in less than a minute be angry and agitated. He accepted it as something he would not easily understand, because through the years he had heard about the emotional ups and downs of women during pregnancy. That's when it hit him that perhaps just maybe she *was* pregnant.

The doorbell rang and Andy opened it to find Wanda standing there looking very nervous and tense.

"Come in, what a surprise to see you at this time of day." He hesitated. "Ok, I have seen that look before on you. What's wrong?"

"I am at the doctor's office right now trying to find out why I can't get pregnant, and John is waiting at home expecting some answers when I get back!" She pushed past him and sat down on the couch.

"Excuse me?"

"Look I know you don't want to hear this, but John and I have been having sex, while I am on the pill, and now he is starting to worry about me not getting pregnant. So, he suggested that I go to a doctor and find out why. So here I am."

"In case you hadn't noticed Wanda I am not a doctor. You are absolutely right; I don't want to hear about you and him having sex. So, when and how are you going to break the news to him that you cannot get pregnant?"

"I am not sure. I was hoping you could help me figure that out." She sat up eager to hear his brilliant mind.

"Look Wanda, I do not like the guy, and you know that, but he is no fool and I think he is going to see right through whatever excuse you give him. I am not sure if I can help you with that, because if this thing comes unraveled you are going to have to live with that. It's not that I do not want to help, but the stakes are very high here and we both have equal amount of loss if something goes wrong."

"Loss! Andy don't tell me about loss. That baby of ours, Raymond is not going to be part of any loss!" She stood up and began backing Andy up toward the bedroom, with her voice rising to the point that Andy put his finger to his lips to calm her down.

"Calm down please, I just put him down for a nap. Do not wake him up."

"OK, Andy, I am sorry, but I am scared because we are at the point of no return when I tell him that I cannot get pregnant and still insist on taking in a child from foster care. He may not be open to the idea of that. He told me he is fine either way, whether I am pregnant or not. However, if I insist that I have to have a foster child, it may not sit well with him, and I just cannot take not having Raymond with me. He is going to want to know why I am pressing the issue. What do I do then?" She was almost in a panic state, when Andy put his arms around her.

"Well, to be honest, I do not know how he will react. However, this is one time I am going to ask you to trust him. I cannot believe I am saying this. After all you have made it clear to him that you think a child will make for a good start to help rebuild your marriage as well as his life. So, if that is important to him, I think he will come around. Just emphasize that to him again and again until he has no choice but to make your desires of happiness his desires also."

She pulled him closer and looked up and smiled. "I knew you were the genius I thought you were."

"If I truly were a genius this situation would be me and you planning our wedding instead of this charade we are trying to master now." He thought at just how he could be a husband to her knowing that she was determined to go to all lengths to be with John. How was she still willing to take him back in spite of all the suffering she endured over the past two years. Was it love or something else that had made her so irrational?

"I have to ask," he inquired; "why are you doing this? Why are you so hell bent on having a relationship with him, knowing what he has done? I know you must have thought at least one time or another that he might do it again. How can you live like that? Is he really worth all of this? And no, this is not my jealousy talking so don't hand me that crap!"

"Yes, you are jealous, and you just don't have the balls to admit it! I don't know! OK? I really don't. All I know is that I have to try and that he is not the same man who went into prison. He is much different now and yes it scares me, but what choice do I have? I thought that marriage vows meant that you have to show up for the good and bad, and that is exactly what I am doing even if I hate it and don't feel like doing it. Do you think this is easy for me? Every ounce of me wants to pack my stuff and run as far from him as possible. But then what? You have never been in this position Andy, so you don't have a clue how I feel."

Andy could barely keep himself under control. How dare her to think that John's prison conversion was something more than a ploy for her to take him back.

"You know, I find it very interesting that while he was in prison, he had this sudden awakening to how bad he has been treating you and then decides to do something about it. It seems convenient that knowing he was getting out and that you would forgive him if he told you what you wanted to hear and take him back. Jail house conversions usually don't last Wanda, and I do not want to see you get hurt again. But if you insist then I guess there is nothing I can do."

"Andy I am sick and tired of your jealous bullshit! Just stop it, OK?"

"Well what the hell am I supposed to think or feel, Wanda? That child in that crib is a creation of our love. Am I supposed to stand by and feel great that you are going to take a symbol of our love and be with another man?"

"He is my husband, Andy. Regardless if we like it or not, that is the way things are." She wanted to say, "at least for the moment", but that would give Andy false hope, and she wanted to spare him that. Yes, she did love Andy and it was difficult to have to protect the heart of two men. She just wanted this whole thing to go away, even if for a little while. "I cannot take this pressure from you Andy. I got enough to deal with, so please be the friend that I desperately need right now. Can you do that for me?"

He smiled at her. "You know maybe it is me who needs a shrink, for thinking that this is going to work out to be ok to everybody. Yes, I will stand by you best I can, but please know that I am a bit sensitive in this area about us. I guess if I did not love you or care at all about you it would be much easier to take. But real emotions like this surface because my heart cannot hide what I feel. This is tough on me, but I know it is even harder for you. So let's get back on track and see this thing through."

She stared at him wondering all the time what the next several months would mean for the both of them when Raymond would be in her care and custody.

"OK, just how do we get at the heart of our adoption plan? I mean. ."

"I know what you mean. I just do not know about all of that right now. This stuff is not easy to draw out, because there are things involved beyond our control. All we can do right now is do our best to make sure he does not find out that you have had this kid with me. That is where we focus our attention for now. Give me some time and I will work out the details of the rest."

"Alright, I just need to be up to speed with what you have in mind and what you think is best, so that I can slowly move John toward this idea without causing alarm or suspicion."

"OK, fair enough. Just do your part and let me know how he takes the news of your infertility. All I know is that this whole process as it unfolds is going to be interesting."

He gave her a big hug and walked her to the door.

On the drive back home, Wanda began daydreaming of the day she would look in the rear-view mirror and see a car seat with little Raymond sleeping quietly as she ran about her errands. She thought of the nighttime bed stories and the endless hugs and kisses they would share before tucking him in alongside a soft and plush teddy bear.

Arriving back home she found John finishing up breakfast of oatmeal and toast when she stepped into the kitchen. He looked at her but was a little hesitant to speak because of the attitude she had when she left. He wanted her to be the first to reveal what the doctor had told her and decided to wait and gage her mood.

"I was about to clean up here, but would you like anything?"

"A cup of coffee would be great."

"Sure, coming right up. I think you like that with three sugars and some cream. Correct?"

"Wow! I am impressed, you actually listen when I am describing the things I like. I think I am going to like this new John." She smiled at him, still nervous about proceeding with the conversation.

"Well I have been making an extra effort to listen to people and actually understand them. I just wish I had done that with you a whole lot sooner and then I could have perhaps avoided the last several years."

"I also think if you had talked a bit more, no a whole lot more about what you were feeling, then we could have worked on some issues before they got out of control. But let's not drag up the past. We are on a new path now with new beginnings."

John was more than curious now as to why she had not mentioned anything about the doctor's visit. Perhaps this was a good time to test the waters.

"I hope your doctor's visit went well and you got the answers you were looking for." He paused and stared at her quietly.

"I did get answers, but not necessarily what I was hoping for. There appears to be a blockage in my fellopian tubes preventing me from getting pregnant."

"Ok, that sound pretty serious. Is there anything that can be done about it?" John was a bit relieved to know that it was not a lack of sexual performance on his part, but still the thought of her not getting pregnant for medical reasons was disturbing.

"The doctor said it is extremely rare and because there is no substantial testing and research into it, there is no known cure at the moment. Canada is doing some medical trials and trying to develop a drug, but it is at least five years from approval, and there are not enough case studies to know the effectiveness of it."

"Do you think your case should be considered for research?"

"I do not want to be a guinea pig for any doctor, especially something as serious as a pregnancy. So, the answer is no."

"Wow, I am so sorry to hear that you cannot get pregnant. I know how much that meant to you to have a child, to have our child."

"It's ok, John. These things happen and besides there are other paths to having a child." She looked at him, knowing that this is the moment that would start the process of having Raymond, be with her permanently.

"So, where do you go from here? What do you have in mind?" John for a brief moment hoped that she would put the idea of having a child on hold for a while, at least until he was stable enough and felt comfortable enough to fully function back in society with a job.

"I want to adopt. I want to adopt a child who desperately needs a home and a loving family. Just the other day I saw an ad and a public service announcement about children who need to be placed in a home, and I am going to start looking into adopting. It will be great for us John."

She knew that getting John's full support of adopting a child would be an uphill battle, but because he did not fully reject the idea, she thought in time he would warm up to it. Besides once he took a look at Raymond and saw how cute and adorable, he was, surely, he would want to keep him as his own.

"Do you know what all is involved in adopting, Wanda?"

"Yes I do, and we can handle that. It just takes a will to not quit and jump through any hurdle thrown at us. I mean look already at what we have overcome. Don't you think we are getting stronger by the day as a couple?"

"Yes, and we have a long way to go, and that is the reason I would suggest going slowly and not taking on too much at one time, because as I have told you before I am not too stable yet, and I still have to check in with my parole officer, and he is wanting to see real job progress."

"What a good statement it would be to see that you are a family man and handling all the responsibilities that come with it?" She looked at him and grinned.

"You are impossible sometimes Wanda, and I can tell there is no stopping you so go do what you got to do, and I will support you with the adoption. But give me some time to adjust to a new baby in the house, OK?"

She smiled and hugged him tight. "Thank you, sweetheart. It is going to be OK; you just wait and see."

Two weeks later and much to the surprise of John, Wanda announced that her new baby boy would be coming home the following week, to stay. John was taken back not understanding how a process such as an adoption could take place so fast. Furthermore, he had not been contacted, interviewed or screened regarding this child.

"How is it that you have not consulted me about this Wanda. I mean yes you told me you were going to adopt but I have not heard anything and today you announce the child will be here next week. Don't I have a say in this? Has the agency stopped interviewing the adoptive parents?"

Wanda grew tense with nerves as she was beginning to think that it would be more difficult to pass her child off as a legitimate adoption.

John continued sounding a bit agitated. "How is it that this adoption goes through in just two weeks, and I have not had one phone call from anyone, or any questions. I have not had the chance to go see the child. What's going on here?"

"This was an emergency placement John, and an emergency placement fast tracks the adoption process. And to be honest it is a whole lot easier than the conventional way. A lot of the red tape and formalities are forgone."

"Well I find that rather interesting. How is it that the adoption agency or the birth parents know what kind of home their child is going into?"

Amused that she could come up with a lie so quickly and on command, Wanda smiled.

"I am glad that you mentioned that, because I have decided to invite the father over for dinner when he brings the child next week."

"I have not seen you making any preparations for his room, and two weeks is very short notice don't you think?" John was sounding very frustrated that this child was going to be forced upon him regardless of his reluctance.

"John, listen everything is going to be ok, I got everything under control. Don't you worry. Our little bundle of joy will be here shortly, and you will see that it was the right thing to do. He is so cute."

"I see, so what is his name and what does he look like? Do you have a picture of him?"

"Raymond Mahoney. I do not have a picture of him yet, but I will certainly get one the next time I go to the agency or the temporary home he is now in."

She did not panic at the thought of Andy coming over to bring Raymond or about the possibility of John recognizing him, as her long ago ex-lover. However, she needed to think of a clever way to disguise Andy so that he would not be easily recognized.

Later that afternoon Andy's phone ranged with Wanda on the other end.

"Hey Andy, how are you and my little bundle of joy?"

"Well I am just fine. And don't you mean our bundle of joy?"

"Yes, yes, Andy; our bundle of joy. That is exactly why I am calling you."

"Oh! What's up?"

"Listen I know it has been a very long time since you and John have seen each other, way back in the day when we were dating. But I cannot take a chance on him recognizing you, when you bring Raymond over to the house. So, I am asking you to do something you may not be thrilled about, but please understand it is the best thing to keep drama away from John."

There was a long silence on the other end of the phone. Wanda had never gone this far with deception and she questioned how she could even remotely call herself a Christian. But at the moment none of that mattered. All that mattered was getting Raymond home to be with her.

"What exactly are you up to Wanda?" Andy's interest was now piqued.

"Oh my God, I cannot believe I am asking you to do this, Andy, but I need you to disguise yourself. I mean a total transformation, like shave your head, grow a beard and put on glasses. And from this moment forward you need to think of yourself as Larry Mahoney, that is your new name."

"Ok let me get this straight, Wanda. This Larry Mahoney that you have in mind has a bald head, glasses and a beard. Does he have an accent? I don't do accents."

No Andy, I am not asking you to have an accent, wait correction; no Larry I am not asking you to have an accent. Just be yourself but look totally different. That is all I'm asking."

"OK fair enough. Now listen I can shave my head in a matter of minutes but the beard, that is going to take a lot longer to grow, at least three or four weeks. How does that fit into your timetable of getting Raymond?"

"Well if you have to, go to a costume shop and buy a fake beard."

"Wanda, you are getting way to good at this. Did you dream up all of this by yourself? Or did you have help?"

When Wanda heard those words, she froze in silence. She was faced with the realization that her lying had gotten out of hand and in the back of her mind the biblical assertions and warnings that come with lying surfaced to the front. Clearly, she had read God's thoughts on what he intends to do with all liars. Was not the book of Revelation specific on saying that "all liars shall have their part in the lake which burns with fire and brimstone"? Had not the fall of mankind began with a lie from the devil, and did not Jesus Christ refer to the devil as the father of lies? She did not want to think that she was truly associated with someone so capable of great deception, yet this current plot seemed to play out way too easy.

"I have learned from the best. Now get back with me as soon as your disguise is in place. Now remember I am going to be inviting you over for dinner and that means you may be showing up at the house several times to check on Raymond, so you will have to keep this up for a while until all is clear, over the next few weeks."

"Wanda my dear, usually situations like this the people placing the child in a permanent home do not have much or any contact with the child after giving them up. So you had better tread carefully about that."

"OK, I will. Thanks, talk to you soon."

Chapter 35

John had a growing frustration and even anger, because of the stubborn way Wanda went about the adoption. With only a few days before the child was to arrive there was a million things to do in preparation for the new arrival. He tried to make out a list on the obvious things that would need to be done right away. The list mostly consisted of items to buy on the income of only one person. He wanted to be supportive, but it was becoming obvious that something was very wrong because the tension between Wanda and him caused more than a few arguments the last few days. Because he did not like confrontation, he mostly sulked with his emotions, and would speak little to encourage her at all regarding the adoption. He knew the more he argued against it, the more of a crisis it would become. That week he found himself very withdrawn and distant from her, saying very little during the day and virtually no communication or physical contact at night.

He began to think that she was being very selfish to push this onto him at a time when he needed her more than anything else. Was this child going to be a distraction from him, and the whole event that took place over the past several years? Was she going to throw all of her time and energy into raising a child so that she had the perfect excuse not to engage with the difficult challenge of repairing a broken marriage? And where did he fit into all of this? He was still tethered to the corrections system and had to make check ins with his Parole Officer. One was scheduled in a couple of days, and he did not know whether or not to tell him about the new addition that was coming.

The lingering thought of honesty was tugging away at him two days later as the doorbell rang. On the other side was Officer Warren Keller, a face he was going to see on regular intervals over the next couple of years.

"Come on in Mr. Keller I have been expecting you. It is nice to see you." Well maybe not.

"Hello John"

"Did you have any trouble finding this place tucked into this sprawling community?" John was trying to not sound nervous.

"Well to tell you the truth John I would be totally lost without the greatest invention since the map, that we call GPS." He smiled and sat his briefcase down on the floor.

"Come on in here to the dining room table where you got more room, sir." John led him to the small kitchen and pulled out a couple of chairs. "Can I get you anything to drink? I got sodas and water."

"No thanks, John. I just finished a cup of Dunkin Donuts coffee on the way here."

A few seconds later he pulled out some forms and a small tape recorder. "John, I use a tape recorder as a way of keeping notes because I have to file so many detailed reports of my visits with different people, I have found this to be the best way to keep organized. Are you OK with that?"

"Yes, sir do what you got to do. I have nothing to hide, at all." John said.

"OK great. I just want to start off by getting a little info on how you are adjusting to life since you have been released. Tell me what you have been feeling and what has the adjustment period been like for you."

"First of all, Officer Keller I . . ."

"Warren, you can call me Warren." As an official of the state it was his job to not only conduct follow up visits, but also to actively guide new parolees into integrating into society. Recent training emphasized the need to have a more warm and courteous conversational tone with any parolee and that meant taking down the invisible barrier between the state and the subject.

"OK, Warren I wanted to say that I am extremely grateful to have my freedom and I will take full advantage of getting my life back on track. I know it won't be easy, but I can say that I am making some progress."

"I am so glad to hear that. Tell me what has the adjustment been like for you?" Warren asked.

"Pretty good. My wife Wanda has been a big help. She has been more than understanding and is getting me through some of my doubts. She has did a lot of networking with family and friends to get the word out that I am in need of a job, and I am proud to say that I have been on three interviews and I think I may have landed a position with an auto body and detailing shop. I hope to hear some good news later this week." He did not want to mention his growing frustration with the upcoming adoption and thought it best to keep the first visit positive and upbeat.

"Well that is great John. Let me know how you make out. Is there anything I can do to help?"

"No, you have more than helped enough by giving me the chance to prove myself again."

"John, I have been in this business over 20 years and you are most certainly one of the most deserving that I have come across in recent years. I think with the help and support of your wife, that you will do just fine. Please let me know if there is anything I can do to help and be sure to make your call ins on time."

Within minutes John said goodbye to Warren and sat back down on the couch. He was thinking of all the changes a new baby would bring to his personal life. It was apparent that Wanda was on a fast track pace for the adoption and no amount of reasoning would stop her. He closed his eyes and began to pray silently.

He heard off in the distance the faint sound of his cell phone ringing. He quickly dashed into the bedroom and pick up his phone off of the nightstand. Looking down at a number he did not recognized, he slowly picked up the phone and began to speak.

"Hello, this is John." A few seconds of silence brought a sense of nervousness to him.

"You sound well John; it has been a bit. How are you doing my friend?"

That faintly familiar voice John was listening too, became all too clear by the end of the sentence.

"If this is who I think it is, you have some nerve to call me and dare to call me your friend." The steam of emotions was beginning to stir up deep inside of him. "Do you know what my life has been like, because of you Cindy? How could you do that to me? What did I do to deserve that?"

"John, listen I know you are upset, but believe me that is why I am calling, to begin to build a bridge of healing between us and to ask for forgiveness." Her voice trailed off faintly as she thought of the betrayal many years ago.

"Cindy, look I do not need any trouble from you. I just went through hell and barely came out alive and in my right mind. I put Wanda through hell and I still don't think she is ever going to forgive me. She is a good wife and did not deserve that."

"John, there is no doubt that what I have done is awful." Cindy said. "And we have not had the opportunity to talk about this or do any reconciliation, and that was one of the reasons for my call. I feel responsible for being the person who destroyed your life. I want to make a good faith attempt to help you put the pieces back together. And I am begging you to give me that chance. I know it will never change the things that I have done to you, but it is important that you know how sorry I am and that I have deep regret for what I have done to you."

"I think it is way too late for that Cindy, way too late. There is nothing you can do now. I have already had my life wrecked. What more can you do?" John had a growing frustration that she would think that his life could be back to normal with a halfhearted phone call.

"I'm very sorry John, and I know that is the truth, and believe me when I tell you that I feel powerless and helpless to make you feel any better. But let me help you to put some of the pieces back together. I am in a position now where I can help you instead of hurting you.

"And what exactly Cindy is it that you think you can do for me? There is nothing that you can do for me but leave me the hell alone!"

"John, please wait. Just hear me out. I know you are going to need a job. I have connections. I am working at a temp agency in Alexandria, and I have connections to a lot of people who would be willing to give you a chance at employment. Look, I know you may not be willing to do that for me but think about it for your wife and do it for yourself, to at least give yourself a chance to put your life back together."

"Cindy, I do not like the sound of this at all. You were the devil that destroyed my life, and now you want to be the angel to save it?"

"John, I know this does not sound good, but I am begging you to stop being so stubborn and let me help you. I am in a position to help you, now please put down your pride and look at the bigger picture. It is my only way of trying to undo the damage that I have done. Please let me help you. Help me to help you. I am not doing this for selfish motives John. God knows I am not."

As John listened, he thought of his probation requirements and how he wanted to be able to report to his parole officer again that he had found a job. And it was even harder to have to allow Cindy an inch back into his life, even if she did have noble intentions. But he had to admit that he needed all the help he could get, and if that meant putting his pride aside and allowing her to help him get a job from a guaranteed source that would hire a felon, then so be it. He would reluctantly consider it.

"I am not at all cool with this. But because I seem to be over a barrel, I am going to take your help. But you better not screw with me." He reemphasized again. "You had better not screw me up again. If you were to ever set me up again, I just might sacrifice it all and beat you to no end. Do you hear me? Do you clearly hear me."

"John I hear you, and I would not dare to hurt you again. Now listen, we need to meet somewhere, like my office so that I can give you some contacts. And I might be able to bring in one or two people who owe me some favors and will sit down and do an interview with you at my office. How does that sound John?"

"It sounds like I am talking to the same manipulative, conniving woman who got me in prison years ago. The one who only wanted me to go pick up a package."

Cindy realized that John was not going to make it easy for her at all. After all she had violated his trust and caused a lifetime of hurt and pain. She surmised that this was the price she would have to pay to make things right again with him.

"You are right John, I know it sounds like the manipulative person that you mentioned. I do not know how to tell you or rather show you that I am a changed woman other than you trusting me enough for you to come see for yourself, that I have your best interest at heart. I care about you John, and I know I do not have the right to say this, but it is coming from a place of love for you."

"Don't talk to me about love, Cindy. You don't know nothing about love. As a matter of fact, while I was locked up, I had the opportunity to find out what real love is about. Something that you will never know anything about. And unless God changes your heart, you will never be capable of loving anyone else."

"You are right John, so very right. Believe me the whole time that you have been gone I have thought of how to ask for your forgiveness. I have even asked that my own life and heart could be changed to do better and become a better person and find a way to reach out and help people more. So, this temp agency position allows me to help people in a real way, and you were on my mind to help in this way."

"OK, so what do you need me to do?" John was still very frustrated.

"How about you come meet me at my office this Wednesday at noon, and I can show you what jobs are available, and have you meet a few people."

"Alright, text me the address and phone number and the name of the agency."

"Sure, it is called Work Right Agency in Old Town Alexandria. And John you can put your mind at ease, because the people I want you to meet already know your situation and they will not judge you about your past. They won't hold it against you because of a setback."

John was furious. "A setback! Is that what you call this? You don't have any idea what I have been through and still will be going through for some time to come, thanks to you."

"Alright, sorry. That was a bad choice of words. I hope you know what I mean."

"Yes, I think I know what you mean. I will see you Wednesday at noon."

"It was so nice to talk to you after such a long time. I hope this will not be our last talk. I will be in touch to see how things are going with you after you land a position. Besides I want to know about how you were able to get your life back on track while you were inside. I have to confess that I have been keeping tabs on you the whole time you were gone because I care about you. A friend of mine, Suzanne, I think you may know her. She used to date one of the corrections officers who was at your place in Richmond, and she told me that he said you were a model prisoner and that you found religion and that it made a world of difference for you and other inmates.

I was so glad to hear that, and I was hoping that you could share some of that experience with me sometime. I would like to get the same results."

John chuckled at the word results. "Results! This is not about results, Cindy. It is about a personal relationship with Jesus Christ and having him transform your life. But you might not know anything about that." He wanted to recall his last few words, but it was too late. He knew that hearing her stirred his anger and that it was opening up old wounds and the hurt was spilling out."

"Maybe not, but you could teach me and show me how, John. Maybe we can get together sometime to discuss that. Listen I have a meeting I have to attend shortly, but it was nice talking to you and I look forward to seeing you Wednesday. You will not regret this John."

"Well, that remains to be seen. Goodbye." He hung up with his head spinning in disbelief that he spent time talking to the one person who threw his life into so much chaos a few short years ago.

He tossed the phone onto the bed and turned around slowly to see Wanda standing in the doorway to the bedroom.

Chapter 36

If looks could kill, Wanda would have been facing murder charges for the deep penetrating stare she gave John.

"Tell me, I did not hear you talking to that bitch that ruined your life and our marriage! I know I must be dreaming. Surely the man standing in front of me was not talking to his slut whore and planning on seeing her again. That is not what I heard. Because I thought that man was trying to do everything in his power to keep this marriage together and start a new life. So please enlighten me on what I just heard, John."

John began to shake his head slowly and let out a sigh. "I should have known this was going to be a test today from the enemy when that phone rang, and she was on the other end. Yes, Wanda you heard me talking with Cindy. And before you go off the deep end without all the facts, let me tell you that I was not as comfortable talking with her as you would imagine. I was reluctant to talk to her and believe me when I tell you that I was very distant and cold to her after all she has put me through."

"Believe you!" "Ha Ha" Wanda began to laugh sarcastically. Yeah, of course I am to believe you. After all you have only lied to me about her for several years while you were sleeping with her and buying dope from her!"

"Stop it Wanda! Shut up! I don't need this crap from you right now, and I was not sleeping with her."

"Fuck you! John, I don't give a damn what you think right now. Just as I am trying to come to grips with all that has gone down and all the hurt and anger that I set aside so that I could have a chance at forgiving you and this is what you do to me behind my back! You and your whore can kiss my ass. And you can get the fuck out and go live with her, and let her help get your life back, because I am done."

The tears were instant, and she began shaking uncontrollably. John moved quickly toward her to put his arm around her. The fury was relentless as Wanda let loose a barrage of hits and slaps, kicks and punches that escalated into an all-out fight, with plenty of bruises and samples of John's blood.

When the fight was over with Wanda wailing on the bed, John looked at her in shock and disbelief. "Wanda, we cannot do this to ourselves. We cannot have police in here to deal with this, and any violence is a violation of my probation. Now I need you to think about this and calm down."

As she started to wipe the tears from her eyes, she looked at him and in a whispered voice said, "You know John, I think I have thought about this, and I just do not see any way forward for you and me. I think we are going to have to come to grips with the fact that our marriage is over. I don't have any answers, and I do not have any solutions. I am emotionally spent, and I do not have anything else to give. We cannot help each other under these conditions, and I need to figure out a way to save myself."

John looked at her and was slow to speak. "We are so close Wanda, and if we give up now, then the past several years of my incarceration is in vain. We have never had to be this strong before, and this test has so far showed us that we individually have strength we did not know we had. Just imagine what we are together, if you will only join forces with me and not abandon me now. As for me I still do not claim any strength on my own, but to be honest it was God. And what I am asking you is to let him channel his strength toward you. Are you open to that?"

Wanda put her hands up. "Stop just stop with all of that God stuff, because I do not see it working for us, not in this situation." She was reflecting back on the deception that she was in the middle of and pondered why she would even bother consulting God anymore about anything. She had used her free will to push aside any conscious that would have restrained her from the adultery and the cover up she was now in the middle of, with no way out. "God has not been very strong in my life since you left John. All I know is that my life has been in turmoil and I had to do what I had to do to survive."

"I know, sweetheart and you have done a great job. After all we are still standing, even if for the moment. We need to think of a way forward. I know we can do it; we can do it together. Our lives will be so much better for it when we rise from the ashes again. We just have to find a way to keep putting one foot in front of the other. I will do all that I can to show you that I am worthy of your trust again and will do everything I can to earn it."

Trust. That was the one word she did not want to hear, especially since she had betrayed him in such a personal way. Could trust ever come back into their relationship?

Chapter 37

The next morning, after John left for another day of job hunting and filling out endless applications, Wanda dialed the familiar number of her baby's daddy. After a few rings, "Good morning Larry, how are you this morning and how is my Raymond?"

After a brief pause, the sound of throat clearing was heard on the other end. "Larry? Who is Larry? More importantly why are you calling me Larry? Raymond is fine."

"You would make a terrible actor, Andy. You have to get into your character and actually become someone else. Can you do a better job of being Larry? You will be coming over for dinner tonight Larry and I do not want to see any trace of Andy. Can you handle that?"

"I think you are enjoying this too much Wanda, but yes for you, Larry will be the only person you will experience until this whole thing is done. What time shall I bring Raymond to meet his new parents?"

"Seven, and we will keep it short, the shorter the better. Most likely the next time you see me after tonight you will hand off Raymond."

"Is there a story line that is needed in case John starts asking a lot of questions." He was concerned that something might trigger John's memory of long ago.

"Well, I think it is best that we keep a very simple narrative of how we met and what the circumstances are about Raymond. Something along the lines of you became a temporary foster parents for kids who could not be placed otherwise, on a short-term basis of three months or less. You will be deploying overseas soon and will not be able to continue to keep Raymond and wanted to make sure he got placed in a home as soon as possible. The agency agreed to expedite the process and decided under the unusual circumstances to cut through the red tape of the placement and screening procedures."

"My God, Wanda I thought you said a simple narrative. How am I supposed to remember all of that?"

"You have until seven to work on it, and I suggest you get started right now. I expect Larry and Raymond to be on time. See you both then. Goodbye"

After hanging up the phone, she breathed a sigh of relief that John was going to be gone most of the day job hunting. This gave her the opportunity to make sure everything was in place for the night to come. She went to the local grocery store and picked up a few items, and then headed to the gym for a one hour work out to work out the jitters and nerves that had been nagging at her since last night.

She needed this to go perfect as it was the single most important piece to the life she wanted to have with John since his release from prison. The thoughts of the incredible deception and lying still plagued her, but she kept telling herself that it was for the greater good of saving her marriage and helping John make a full comeback.

About six o clock that evening John came home and stepped inside to find a nicely decorated dining table and the smell of fresh baked biscuits.

"Wow, you are really doing it up big for this." John knew it was important to her and he wanted to be as supportive as possible even if it was a bit overwhelming and way faster than he would have liked. It was far too late now, and he could only hope that he could adjust quickly to the family that was to grow by one in less than a week.

"Well, since I do not get the chance to have a formal baby shower and all the things that normally go with having a baby, this is the best I could do." She was smiling and bouncing with joy.

"I am glad that this baby will bring you so much joy." John said.

"Bring us joy, John." She looked at him sternly.

"Yes, of course sweetheart, he will bring us both a lot of joy and laughs. I think it will be good to have a future high school athlete that steals the show on and off the field." John was trying his best to get his mind to think more positively about the new family addition.

Wanda smiled at him. "I just hope you can throw a ball and keep up with him. It requires a lot of energy you know!"

"What! Girl what are you saying? I have energy. I am not over the hill, just so you know."

"And you have never had to keep up with a growing boy for 18 years either. We will see how much energy you have, when Raymond wakes you up at 0200 in the morning needing a diaper change. Yeah! I think you will have a different opinion about your energy after a year or so of that! Now I need you to hurry along and get cleaned up, they are supposed to be here at seven. Go!"

He shook his head and smiled at her before turning into the bedroom.

As she was making last minute preparations to dinner, her phone beeped that was laying on the counter. Looking down at it was a text message that simple read, "Larry and Raymond are on our way, be there in 15 minutes." Her reply was a simple "OK".

The meeting went better than expected and Wanda realized that the knots she had in her stomach was undue anxiety. John was warm and accepting to the little baby boy that was cradled by Larry. Larry came into the house and began to introduce himself and the child with a big smile that was heartwarming.

As a bit of caution, Wanda interjected and tried to control most of the conversations and questions to make sure that the rehearsed script Larry had worked on was the only one to be told.

She needed to make sure dinner went off without a hitch and that Larry and Raymond were back out the door within the hour.

"Well I sure hope that you are hungry, because I have dinner that is going to get cold if we don't get to eating it real soon." She motioned them all to the dining room.

John quickly pulled chairs back and began to bring in the food from the kitchen.

"Wanda fixed some really nice biscuits, Larry, and she is not the kind who likes to see them hanging around after dinner, so please eat what you like. And tell me does Raymond have a big appetite or not?"

"He looks like he is not going to have any trouble eating us out of house and home." Wanda interjected quickly.

Larry looked at Wanda a bit startled by her response but continued to speak. "The past few days he seems to be eating a bit more. I can tell that he is growing very fast and has gained about 7 pounds since his last check up."

"Well that is very good as we most certainly want a healthy boy. He is very energetic. Does he sleep well at night, and how many times will he be waking us up?"

Larry shot a glance over to Wanda and slowly smiled. "Well for the first few weeks, I did not get much sleep but after we got on a schedule and settled in a bit, he seems to go to sleep right away and mostly sleeping right through the night. I don't think you will have much problem with that."

"Don't worry Larry, I can assure you he won't be the one with blood shot eyes from waking up. Besides I have been waiting for this moment for a long time and it will be some of the most loving memories that I can make with him. We will be just fine." Wanda seemed to want to end this visit, before the conversation went in a direction she could not control.

"Hey, listen we can all get caught up on the details of little Raymond next week when he comes to stay, but for now I need you all to eat up. Your food is getting cold. And I am sure Larry you are wanting to get Raymond back home and into bed soon." She looked at him with a sterner look. He easily got the message.

"Yes, I do need to be getting the little fellow tucked in. I am going to hate giving him up, as we have gotten so close to each other. But I am very glad that he is going to a great loving family that will take care of him and raise him right."

The rest of the dinner was a bit awkward in that there was deafening silence as they all ate the rest of the dinner. After dinner was over, Wanda quickly began to put dishes in the dishwasher. Larry got up and went to the small bedroom where Raymond was laying in the cradle. Moments later he reappeared holding Raymond who was smiling and playing with a small plastic toy.

"Do you want to say something to your new mommy and daddy? They are going to love you and take care of you beginning next week. I am going to hate to hand you over, but I will visit you often." Larry knew he needed to be leaving while this was still playing out as planned.

"We are so glad to meet our little Raymond, and thanks for bringing him by. I cannot wait to have him next week. I will be in touch with you later this week to get some of his things from your place and sign all the documents."

John offered an open invitation for Larry to visit often. "You are welcome here anytime and I think you should come by and check in and interact with him as much as possible while he adjusts to his new home."

"Yes, I would like that." Larry said.

Wanda could barely contain herself in that moment. "Oh, that is so kind of you honey to welcome Larry back like that." For her it was a mixed bag of emotions. She was glad to have the opportunity to see Larry more even if it was in a very controlled setting, and on the other hand she would be concerned about the growing relationship between John and Larry and if any conversations between those two would expose the cracks of deception that was playing out right in front of him. "Yes, Larry please come back often to make sure Raymond is adjusting well."

A few minutes later the door closed, and Larry and Raymond were gone.

Chapter 38

The following morning Wanda woke up with a since of peace and calm she had not felt in a few days, knowing that the dinner last night had went off very well, with the introduction of Larry to John. All she had to do now was concentrate on getting through the week and on Saturday morning Raymond would be in his permanent home. She kept very busy at work and also at the gym working out as a way to calm her anxiety and nerves. By Thursday she had completed the final touches in Raymond's room.

She had Friday off and thought it would be a good time to spend with Andy since she would have limited time to see him after the arrival of Raymond.

After making breakfast for Raymond, Andy could hear the faint ringing of his cell phone in the other bedroom. He looked down while picking it up to see the smiling face of Wanda.

"Hello."

"Hi, Andy, or should I call you Larry still?"

"Well only you have the answer to that Wanda."

"Yeah, I know. Listen the reason I called, I wanted to tell you that I was so glad that things went well the other night when you were over and I know you were not very comfortable with doing that, but thanks a million for your discretion. I can't wait for you and Raymond to come tomorrow.

I need to know if you have the papers available for me to sign, and they have to look authentic."

Yes, as a matter of fact I do have them. I have a friend of mine who works as a social worker and has connections with the foster care intake department at Family Services. She owed me a favor and was willing to get the papers produced as needed. One little thing however is that they do not have a raised seal stamp from the public notary. Let's just hope that these papers do not come under close scrutiny, if you know what I mean."

"OK I think I can live with that as long as everything else looks authentic."

"Don't worry, I got the actual template for the adoption papers that the department uses, and all you have to do is sign at the highlighted tabbed locations."

"That is great. I am off today, and I was thinking about coming over there and spend some time with you and Raymond. You know this will be the last time you and I will get to spend any time or even see each other for a while because of our new arrangements."

There was a long silence on the other end. "OK I see, and yeah I guess you are right since you put it that way. What time would you like to come over?"

"I should be there about noon. We can go out for lunch all three of us, and then spend the rest of the day and part of the evening back at your place."

"Aren't you concerned about perhaps being seen by some of your friends and word getting back to John?" Andy was puzzled and curious of her boldness.

"Listen Andy or Larry, I am only thinking of you right now and today. Is that understood?"

"OK, enough said. I will see you at noon. How does the 99 Restaurant sound?"

"That is just fine. See you soon. Thank you, for being there for me during all of this. I want to show you just how much it means to me and how much you personally mean to me."

"Well Wanda we have a unique history, and I think regardless of what happens in our lives we will always be there for each other. I just know that you are doing all of this from a good heart, even if I do not fully agree or understand why you would go to this extent to make a life with a guy who put your life through hell. But enough of that, just come and we will make the most of the day."

"Great that is just what I wanted to hear. Bye."

The rest of the day went better than they both could have imagined. The three of them went to the mall and did mostly window shopping with Wanda occasionally putting on a fancy hat and doing her best impression of a famous movie actress. Little Raymond was all smiles as Wanda pushed him around from store to store. More than once a smiling stranger would stop and shower Raymond with praise and giggling laughter, while the doting mother would beam with delight.

Wanda was fully enjoying the possibilities that motherhood could offer. She could only hope that her husband John would be as supportive as Andy. She tried to think positive and know that tomorrow would be the start of a new life and hopefully a new marriage. Yes, indeed life was going to be good.

After lunch, they drove to a nearby lake and slowly walked along the bike path that winded along a scenic garden. Pushing the stroller and walking arm in arm, they took a few selfies and talked about what life would have been like if they both could make a life together with Raymond. Andy wanted to be sure that things were going to be ok with her and John.

"I know that there is nothing I can do to change your mind about all of this. But please do not be blinded by your personal ambition to the point that you do not react to yet more emotional abuse from John. I know how strong you are, but taking on abuse is not strength, it is fear. Good, bad or ugly I am here for you if you need me. And I got to tell you it will not be easy coming over to visit you with the new life you are making for yourself, but because I love you, I am not going to show my selfish side, and will try not to act on my jealous side."

His eyes trailed off into the distance. Wanda could see the pain in his eyes but knew that there was nothing she could do to alleviate it.

"I understand how you feel, and I feel bad that this puts you in a difficult situation, regarding your feelings for me. I will be just fine, and I promise if I really need you, I will reach out to you. I have to make this work for so many reasons. For me and John, failure is not an option, because this is our last chance to save this marriage. I have wanted to walk from the moment I found out about his drug problem and cheating on me. At one time I thought that I owe it to him to do this for us, but that is not the reason I am doing this. I just need to know that after tomorrow you are going to be alright."

Andy smiled at her. "I will be ok. Things will be a bit different and maybe even a little lonely without my little man to see every night."

"You know you can see him any time that you want and as much as you like. As a matter of fact, I expect to see 'Larry' at least weekly." She pulled his arm and placed it around her waist and turned toward him. He leaned in and kissed her until the deep well of passion began to spring up. "Come on let's get him back home and put him to sleep."

Chapter 39

The early morning rays of sunlight bathed the queen-sized bed, as John and Wanda lay entangled on the soft cotton sheets. A slight moan from Wanda was just enough for John to acknowledge that she was not only awake but would most certainly be anxious for the arrival of Raymond.

"I love that look on you in the morning." He said.

"What look are you talking about?" She never thought of him as overly romantic, so this was a bit surprising.

"The look that says your heart is pounding in your chest because today you get the one thing that you have wanted for a very long time. For you today is Christmas."

Wanda looked at him and smiled with the thought of Raymond coming to her in in about an hour. "Yes, you are right. This is the day I have longed for. And you know what? It is also the day of our new beginning. So yes, I am more than glad. I am very happy for both of us. So, what are you thinking about today? And please nothing negative!"

He smiled and turned toward her while putting his hand on her cheek and brushing it slowly. "You know I been doing a lot of thinking. And just as God gives me a second chance every day, I am glad to know that we have been given a second chance to put our relationship back on track. I am here for you and Raymond and committed to raising him as our own. The challenge of raising a child can only make the both of us stronger. It will force us to solve our differences and make the needed changes to go forward. That is what I need right now to feel like I am contributing to society."

"So good to hear that from you, sweetheart. How is the job search going? Did Cindy keep her word and help you the way she said she could? I notice you did not tell me how your meeting with her went. I did not want to press the issue but was hoping that you would talk to me. No, I am not all that happy that you have reconnected to her, but if she can help you get a job then I am ok with that. But you got to put yourself in my shoes and think about how that would make you feel if the situation was reversed."

"Yes, I do understand, and yes she is working very hard on my behalf to get me placed by a temp agency. It may not be permanent, but it is at least a start. And right now, I need a place to start. They had me take a skills assessment test and they will submit it to various employers to make a match. We will see what happens from there."

"Ok, if there is something, I can do to support you, let me know. And John I am glad to see that you are taking steps forward, that puts you miles ahead of other people who have been in your situation. I know I have not told you this, but I am very proud of you, because I know it is not easy to have the burden of a conviction and make a comeback in life. I know you have only experienced the angry wife over the past several months, but I think it's time to put her in the past and move forward. I will make the effort and knowing that you are making an effort is what gives me courage to make the changes in my own life. In a strange way you are an inspiration."

He looked at her, leaned in and kissed her on the cheek. "OK, thanks. Now let's get out of this bed, because Raymond will be here shortly."

The doorbell rang at 0815 and a big grin consumed Wanda's face, as she opened the door.

"Oh my God! There he is. My little Raymond has come to stay." She was elated beyond words. "How are you Larry, please come in. Did you bring all of his stuff?"

Andy smiled and looked at her momentarily amazed that in an instant he was once again thrust into the acting role of Larry. It almost caught him off guard. "Oh yeah! Umm I got all of his things and the paperwork to go over."

John surfaced at the front door and helped with the boxes of toys and baby essentials for his new adopted son. He did not know if he would be comfortable with fatherhood, but knew it was a challenge that would make him grow more as a person. Prison had taught him a bit deal of patience and he regarded parenting a child in much the same way. When he saw how happy Wanda was now that Raymond was finally home, he just knew that it was the right thing for their family.

The next half hour the house was buzzing with activity as little Raymond began adjusting to his new home. Larry and Wanda completed the papers that would need to be filed in the public domain. Larry assured her that all the follow-up vaccinations were completed. The visit was short, but Larry told them he would be back just about every week. He left thinking that the fate of Raymond was out of his hands. While he did want to see Raymond, mostly it was because he wanted to have the inside scoop and see first-hand just how Wanda and John were moving forward. It was horrible and very selfish of him to want their marriage to fail, but in truth that is exactly what he desired.

The days and weeks seemed to fly by as John, Wanda and Raymond began to make a life together. The days were also hectic as Wanda continued her full-time job and John occasionally went out on sporadic work assignments from the temp agency. Finances were a little strained as Wanda was for the most part the sole bread winner. With the addition of Raymond came more food, tons of diapers and the much needed childcare for the days that John could not be available.

They tried to keep as much routine as possible, with family dinner a priority to vent out the stress of the day and plan for tomorrow. Wanda seemed to like the new arrangements and the mothering instincts grew with each passing week. John also began to shine as a father. As a matter of fact, it was hard for Wanda to believe that John who did not seem to be very mature or responsible a few years ago, was now taking on his new role as well as any seasoned veteran. This new John she seemed to like very much and made her even more comfortable with her decision to rebuild the marriage and most of all the decision to bring Raymond into their world.

Larry was showing up on Sunday afternoons to play with Raymond and of course to keep his unique connection to Wanda. When at their house he was careful to act out his crafted role like an award-winning actor. He would however ask a lot of questions that involved Wanda and John's relationship. He played the role of counselor and communication expert, which is something in truth he was very good at. He perceived that things were going very well between to the two of them, and was a little heart broken. But he had been in this role before over the years many times and knew that with enough time a crack just may appear and that an unmanaged crack in a relationship was subject to mounting pressure. He knew it was selfish, but he wanted to be there when it failed for the only purpose of swooping in to rescue Wanda and reclaim Raymond. He was willing to wait on the sidelines.

Finally, after showing up on countless temp agency jobs, John landed a full-time position as a van delivery driver for a printing office. It had full time benefits and decent pay so that he could relieve Wanda of some of the financial burden. He was very grateful that someone was willing to give him a second chance. He knew that it was no small thing for a company, any company to put an ex con and convicted felon on their payroll. He had a lot of people to thank, beginning with God, but also the one person who he knew pushed hard for him when nobody else would, Cindy.

The week before getting the job offer, he got a call from Cindy who told him that he would be doing three days of temp work for them, and that they were actively looking to hire two drivers. "John you are building a good work record and that goes a long way with people these days. I see you have been on several different types of jobs and all of the employers have good things to say about you. As a matter of fact, United Van Lines would love to have you as a full time CDL driver, but their hiring policy prevents them from taking you on due to DOT regulations. They mostly get their loading help from the day labor pool in the local area they are servicing, which is why we were able to connect you to them last week."

"Cindy thank you so much for working on my behalf, I know it is not easy to place a guy who gets released from prison."

"Hey! What did I tell you? I owe you this and so much more for destroying your life for several years. Anyway, listen I have some even better news. There is this print and design company in Northern Virginia called Corporate Graphics/Ikon, they are wanting to hire two drivers and they told us to send them our best candidates for three days next week and if they like what they see they will hire them. I gave them full disclosure about you along with your desire to turn your life around and your proven track record of good work ethics. They said they like the comeback kid attitude and would be open to taking a look at you. Isn't that great?"

"That is the best news I have heard probably since the day of my release. I can't wait to share the news with Wanda and get started."

Cindy could hear the joy in his voice and she smiled on the other end of the phone. "Well you most certainly deserve it. And listen promise me if you land this job as a full-time gig that we get together and go out and celebrate. Alright?" She was beaming as though she reeled in a big fish.

A long pause of silence as John was contemplating if it would be wise to spend any time with Cindy and shatter the fragile but growing relationship he was building with Wanda. "Well, now Cindy I am not sure if that is a good idea, and I know you have good intentions, but Wanda may not be that understanding. You know she was very reluctant to allow me any communication with you at all. And the only reason she did is because she believed that you were going to try to help me get a job. I do thank you, but I just don't think I should. Can you understand why?"

"Well invite her, she can come along. And did I hear you say that you have a new addition to your family, a boy named Raymond? I would love to see him also."

"Listen this is not a good idea at this time. But I tell you what, let me think about it and maybe at some other time when things are settled down a bit more, we can get together for lunch. She is not the kind of person to warm up to you Cindy, she still harbors some bad feelings toward you, and I do not want to stir up any distrust in her about me and you. Don't push so fast."

Her disappointment was obvious, but she understood. "Ok, I guess, but promise me that after you get this job that you won't forget about me and be a stranger. You can call me and let me know how you are doing. I will always be interested in your progress. I will make sure you have the address, phone number and the dispatch manager name to report to next week. I am so happy for you and glad that you are getting your life back on track. Hope to hear from you soon. Goodbye."

The next two years were virtually uneventful with Wanda, John and Raymond bonding as a family. John had gotten several raises on the job and was one of the most admired drivers for the company. He had earned unsolicited customer appreciation awards for outstanding service and on time performance.

Wanda was crafty at living a balanced life of work and being a full-time mom to Raymond. One of the highlights of her week often centered around the Sunday afternoon walks with Raymond and John after church at the local public athletic field. There they would talk and dream of the life they wanted to build for Raymond and themselves. Of course, Wanda also loved the fact that Larry was a regular at the house just about every week, even if for only a few minutes. They managed to play their respective roles quite well, with Larry pushing the envelope on occasions just to be reprimanded in private by her. Larry and John slowly began to treat each other as mutual friends and enjoyed the playfulness of competition with impromptu sports trivia that Larry would spring on John while holding his smartphone at the ready to confirm the answers given. Yes, things were well, and this is the exact life Wanda had imagined that was possible. Raymond was going to be three soon, and Wanda wanted to throw a big birthday party and expand their circle of influence to include local neighbors, some of John's work associates and of course Larry.

She asked John to invite as many of his work associates as possible. He told her that even though he was well liked on the job by all, he had only managed to establish a close friendship with one, an older gentleman named Tyrone. Tyrone and he bonded very easily mostly because while no one else at the company could understand the unique challenges of rebuilding a life after incarceration, Tyrone in fact had. He had done five years for being a look out for a bundled armed robbery about seven years earlier. Tyrone was the best possible person for John to bond with and look up to as a social mentor. It was during the many shared lunch breaks together that Tyrone and John discussed the challenges of reintegrating back into society. Tyrone shared with John the struggles of acceptance from his once close family and the loss of a long list of friends.

John confided in him the uncertainty he felt about his marriage to Wanda and his ability to raise a child.

"OK, but don't be surprised if nobody shows up. Maybe Tyrone will."

"From what you have told me about him, I think he will. I will be stopping by the store to make sure I have everything I need for the party. Do you need or want anything?" She was very thoughtful of him.

"No, I think I have everything I need."

She looked at him from across the room and smiled. "I am so proud of what we have accomplished since you been out. Who knew that in such a short time you would be working full time at a decent paying job or that we would be raising little Raymond, and that we would be putting all of this mess behind us?"

"Yes, it is quite remarkable. And all the credit goes to God for putting all the pieces together and creating the right circumstances. I really want to thank you for sticking by me through all of this. It means a lot to me."

"I know it does." She winked and smiled at him and headed out the door.

Chapter 40

The day arrived with Raymond bouncing up and down in his crib. He had a restless night which prompted several visits to his room from Wanda. As a very energetic child it was not unusual for him to be up at two in the morning, playing or laughing out loud and giggling.

Wanda appeared into his room to greet him with a hug and a kiss like always. After a diaper change, bath and breakfast, she sat Raymond down on the couch beside her and played with him for a while. "My little man is growing and becoming quite the stud, aren't you? Look at you with your little cute self."

By two o'clock that afternoon the house was fully decorated with the table set and party balloons filled. A Happy Birthday Raymond banner hung from the dining room ceiling. Wanda was thrilled to see invited guest starting to arrive at three o'clock. Regarding entertainment and parties, Wanda was a perfectionist, so seating assignments was a natural thing for her to plan and demand of some of her guests. She had placed Larry and Raymond side by side with her and John on the other side, with all the other guests surrounding them. When Larry showed up, she quickly escorted him to his designated seat. One of the last arriving guests was Tyrone who sat directly across from the birthday party.

Wanda thanked the guests for showing up and John voiced his appreciation also.

"Wow! I really do not know what to say! I am kind of speechless, which is rare for me. But anyway, I thank you all for coming. This is really special. And while I expected all of you to come, what I did not expect was for all of you to bring gifts." He pointed over to the gift pile next to Larry. "Don't be shy, we have plenty of food, cake and ice cream. Please eat and enjoy and I guess we had better get this party started, by singing happy birthday to a little boy who came into my life three years ago when I was going through some difficult times. God blessed me, rather us with him and he has made me learn new skills ever since. So here we go, Happy Birthday to you. Happy Birthday to . . ."

Raymond, not knowing why the three yellow candles were in front of him on the birthday cake, clapped his hands and giggled even more, with Larry mocking his every gesture. Larry and Wanda both assisted Raymond in blowing out the candles.

John asked Larry to begin to pass the presents one by one to Raymond and help open them and teach Raymond the same.

It was very amusing to watch the interaction between Larry and Raymond as they both opened presents using the same gestures and facial expressions.

Immediately afterwards, Wanda stood up. "Oh, my goodness! How rude of me. Does everybody know each other in here? I should have introduced everybody when you arrived. I am so sorry. If you would, just go around the table and introduce yourself and we will go from there. I apologize."

Tyrone was the last person to introduce himself, and in his usual comic way made a few jokes that had everyone laughing. His last remarks however were not as humorous to the birthday host and hostess and especially Larry. Tyrone motioned to Larry, "I'm sorry I am not sure if I got your name, did you say it is Larry?"

"Yes, I'm Larry."

"Ok, because I have been looking at you trying to picture you from somewhere. You look familiar and I just cannot put my finger on where I have seen you before. The guy I am thinking of and had in mind, I am not sure if his name was Larry or what. I thought his name began with an A or something. I just can't recall his name. It could be Aaron, Andrew, Albert. Not sure. But you know they say we all have a twin somewhere. I sure wish my twin would pay all of my bills on time." Laughter broke out at the table as Tyrone continued to eye Larry. "Oh by the way Larry you did a great job of teaching Raymond how to open the presents. I mean he even started copying your every move. As a matter of fact, the more I look at you too the more you look alike."

He laughed it off with a smile, but it did not go unnoticed by Wanda, or John.

An awkward silence fell over the room as people reflected on the insinuations of Tyrone regarding Larry and Raymond. But after a few forced smiles the conversations resumed. It was more than obvious that Wanda was not at all pleased with Tyrone's comments. She stared at him with a sheer look of disgust on her face. John also seemed a bit puzzled but realized that Tyrone was known for blunt direct speech.

As the guests left, John and Wanda thanked them all for coming, and making Raymond's birthday party very special. After the cleanup and dishes put away, John broke the silence between them, as Wanda put Raymond down for a nap.

"Sweetheart, that was a total success. You did a great job, and Raymond was all smiles and giggles the entire time."

Wanda was contemplating whether or not to mention the remarks of Tyrone but decided it would not be best at this moment. Maybe she should speak to Larry instead. "Oh yes he was overjoyed, and I am so glad the guest showed up. We will have to do something even more special in the years to come."

John pulled her close to him and put his arms around her. "You know when I first got released from prison, I had a real hard time thinking that my life would ever get to the point it is right now. I mean who would have ever thought that a convicted felon could get out, get a job, get his lovely wife back, start a family and make progress. It is though I picked up right where life would have been if I had never gotten locked up."

She looked at him and smiled, hoping that indeed she had pulled off the impossible. "And yes, I think we should focus on keeping it that way." She leaned in and kissed him with just enough passion to make him walk her to the bedroom while they both made a decent effort at getting undress while bumping into the hallway wall.

Chapter 41

The next day allowed for Wanda to see Andy before going into work at ten. She did a short work out at Planet Fitness and drove over to his house hoping she could catch him before he left.

Pulling up into the driveway she breathed a sigh of relief to see his car. Moments later the door opened, and Andy was smiling from ear to ear.

"Come on in, I was hoping you would come see me. I must admit that we put on the best performance ever, last night." He was beaming with pride until Wanda abruptly cut in.

"How long have you known Tyrone, and don't you think he recognized you last night? Jesus Christ, Andy, John is getting a bit suspicious and even though he did not say anything, I can tell from his manners that something is stirring in the back of his mind about Tyrone questioning who you are or if he has seen you before. This is not good Andy. How do we fix this?"

"Slow down! There may not be anything to fix, if we do not put it in focus and act normal around John."

"John works with him daily and I bet they talk about everything because Tyrone was locked up before too, and he is like a mentor right now to John. If he keeps planting the seeds of doubt in Johns head, it is just a matter of time before they grow and then this whole thing falls apart."

"Well let's just take it one day at a time and do not pull on the strings to unravel anything, that is the best I can offer."

She looked at him and smiled. "You did put on a great show, Larry. I think that you missed your calling as an actor! Last night's performance was Oscar worthy."

Andy smiled and politely bowed. "Thank you and forgive me as I did not have an acceptance speech prepared."

Wanda turned for the door, "Well I think you should work on that." Moments later she sped down the road to work.

Lunch time was not exactly granted even though it was a legal requirement at Corporate Graphics. John did not seem to mind grabbing a bite to eat at any fast food restaurant and he had perfected eating quickly, mostly while at a delivery stop. A crackling of the two-way radio interrupted his lunch on a Wednesday afternoon when his dispatcher needed him to come back to the office to assist another driver with the delivery of a huge book order for a government office in Washington DC. Upon arriving back at the job, he found Tyrone loading up his van with a mountain of books. The dispatcher called him in the office and told him that he would be riding into Washington with Tyrone for this delivery.

After about 30 minutes of stacking the van from floor to ceiling with boxes of books, the two were heading north to Washington, with Tyrone behind the wheel.

John was very observant anytime he was with another driver to pick up pointers on how he could be a bit more efficient at the job. Tyrone was one of the top drivers and John found that to be impressive and was eager to learn from him.

"Do you often get big jobs like this?" John asked.

"Every few months the Pentagon prints up new publications or new release updates to all of their training manuals and we get the contract. So, since I have already have security clearance for the Pentagon I usually get the run. It's pretty good and pays well, although I must tell you that we will be there a while, because we have to go to different places on all five floors. They have cargo elevators, so your back will thank you."

"I see, well that is good to know." John was reluctant to approach the subject of the birthday party but thought he would have to break the ice. "Listen I wanted to thank you for coming to Raymond's birthday party, he is becoming quite the little man."

"Oh, yes my pleasure, and it is good to see you getting back on your feet. If there is anything I can do to help you let me know. But I have to admit that I know nothing about raising a child, so you might be on your own there."

"Well I am learning as I go, besides if there was a book to tell me how to raise him, I would not read it anyway. I am just glad we were able to finally adopt him."

Tyrone glanced at him. "Tell me what you know about his real parents and why was he in foster care?"

"Well I cannot tell you too much other than Larry has had him for about two years or so."

"Do you know anything about Larry? The reason I asked is because for some reason I think I may have seen him before, but I am not sure where."

"The only details I know is what Wanda has told me. She is the one who has put together all the adoption details and made all of this happen. I think she did a good job and it went very smoothly and quickly."

Tyrone was silent for a few minutes as they navigated the congestion on I-95. "You know I am glad you were able to adopt but didn't you want to have your own child? Was there a reason you had to adopt?"

"Well we tried but for some reason she could not get pregnant, and she wanted a child so bad as a way to help start our lives over, so adoption seemed like the best alternative."

"Your parole officer must have been very busy submitting reports and doing intensive house visits. You are very fortunate as it is rare that they will place a child into a home that was subject of drug charges. Sometimes I think they go too far. I recall they denied this guy who was in jail for about 30 days for having part of a joint in his pocket when he was arrested on a shoplifting charge. And because of that he was denied the ability to adopt. There is like a permanent punishment that goes with it. Almost like sex offenders have to register for life and can never be around children again, the system seems to be applying that logic to all drug offenses."

"Well my parole officer did not seem to have much input at all about that. All of our visits were routine. He was mostly concerned about me checking in like I should and wanted to make sure that I was actively looking for work. After I told him I found a job, he was fine."

"Did he know you were adopting? Because he would have to disclose to the adoption agency your circumstances and history as required by law."

"To be honest Tyrone I do not know all the details that go into it, like I said before Wanda took care of all that and set everything up."

Tyrone seemed puzzled with each answer he got from John.

"You know I don't know how to say this but, something that struck me as rather odd at the birthday party is, I observed the nuances between Larry and Raymond, and it seems to me that they might have more in common."

John seemed taken back. "What exactly do you mean by that?"

"Well I can't be sure, and I am not saying that they look alike, but I noticed some of the same gestures the two shared, and even a slight resemblance. For some reason I am thinking that I have seen that guy somewhere before but can't put my finger on it. But anyway, I guess it does not matter. As long as you and Wanda are happy, that is all that matters."

"You know what you are saying is not comfortable to hear." John stared out the window as his mind began to wonder about the things Tyrone was saying.

"Listen don't let it upset you, I was just making a little small talk. Let's get these books delivered and hopefully get back to the office before the evening rush gets really nasty."

Later that evening John walked into the house to find Wanda sitting on the couch in the living room bouncing Raymond on her lap.

"Hello, my handsome husband, how was your day?" Wanda was all smiles as she looked up at John.

"All is well. Had a huge delivery at the Pentagon that took longer than expected which put us in the evening rush hour, but other than that a good day. And how is our baby boy Raymond?" He bent down to kiss her and then picked up Raymond and held him high in the air. Laughter and drool came from him.

"I had a feeling you were running late, and I saved you some dinner. It is in the microwave. It is chicken and rice. I will go and warm it up for you." Wanda sprang up and within minutes prepared the plate for John. "You can put him back into his play pen to nap while you eat."

"OK, I will be there in a minute." John put Raymond back in his pen the whole time wondering how or if he should confront Wanda about the doubts Tyrone had about Larry and Raymond. He did not want to think that something wrong or sinister could be playing out in front of him. After all Wanda chose to endure his incarceration, and she wanted a child to help bring their marriage back on track. No, he would give her the benefit of the doubt, because right now all was going well and most people under his circumstances do not get a second chance to bounce back at life or a strained marriage. He wanted to concentrate on building their future together as a family, and being the husband and spiritual leader as he had learned from the many hours, he had spent studying the Bible.

They exchanged hugs in the kitchen and then sat down to eat. John took her by the hand and looked her in the eyes. "Hey, I wanted to tell you how much I love you and that I am very grateful and thankful for all that we have been through and all that we have become. We owe it all to God and we need to show our gratitude by the life we live. Part of my responsibility as your husband is to be the spiritual guide and leader in the home. I am learning more and more each day how to do that, and I would hope that is something you want."

Wanda looked at him with mixed feelings. Where was this coming from? How come he was not this leader many years ago when he strayed? Yes, this is what she wanted and needed, but his actions had caused her to deviate from the loyal, faithful wife she once was. She was conflicted, because her spiritual life had suffered and spiraled out of control to the point that she was living a lie and immersed herself in sin. At this time, she almost resented anyone or anything that reminded her of the devoted spiritual wife she once was. She had stopped going to church, and no longer hung out with her girlfriends who had been trying to support her so much while John was away.

Moments like this, and hearing John talk like this made her feel so awful. The guilt came rushing back and was raw just like the first moment after she and Andy made love, while John was in prison.

"Well, it cannot be a bad thing, and yes, it is something that we need."

Chapter 42

Her routine of going to the gym for a hard workout, and then the commute to the office was a warm welcome and something she looked forward to. She was given the responsibility of landing a new client for the firm that would add to the bottom line and most certainly guarantee her a promotion. She felt good knowing that stability was coming back into her life that had disappeared for so long. She was glad to know that John was taking a more active role in helping to raise Raymond and felt good that they were bonding with each other as a father and son should. It was a role she had never seen him in and had to admit that he was far better at it than she thought he would be.

Her workload at the office was increasing now that new clients were turning to the firm due to the merger and her expertise in marketing their products. As a result, her hours were getting longer, which at any other time she would not have minded a bit, however as a mom she found her heart longing to be at home with Raymond.

She sat quietly at her desk reflecting on the future ahead as a woman juggling multiple roles as a wife, mom and career professional. She was jolted from her daydream state with the ping of a reminder on her cell phone. She picked up the phone from her desk to see the notification of a doctor's appointment for Raymond at 3:00pm. She had forgotten all about the appointment and had scheduled it for today in the hopes that she would still be out on personal time. She could feel a near panic well up inside of her, knowing that Raymond could not miss this appointment. He was to start preschool in the fall, and it was mandatory that proof of a current physical and up to date shot and vaccination record accompany every child attending classes. She wanted to take him herself, however, knew it would be impossible to leave the office in the middle of such increased and valued business. She would have to let John take the lead. John was home because had earned a paid day off as a reward for safe driving for the past quarter. So, he was available to save the day.

She dialed home and John picked up on the second ring. "Hi, I'm so sorry to have to spring this on you, but I need you to take Raymond to Dr. Fielding for his physical and vaccination update. I had scheduled it for today thinking I would be off, but I just cannot get away from the office. He will not be able to get enrolled in school in the fall without it. Could you please get him there at 3:00?"

John smiled listening to his wife who seemingly never got frazzled about anything and who was meticulous in running the household affairs, sound semi shocked. "Don't you worry sweetheart; I will be glad to take him. He is sleeping now but I will get him up soon for lunch and then we will be on our way."

Wanda felt so relieved. "Oh, thank you so much. You don't know how much this means to me. I'm normally on top of these things, but we have been so busy here at the office that it just slipped by me. Thank goodness I set a reminder on my phone when I made the appointment. Can you believe our little man will be going to school in September?"

"Imagine the day when we are seeing him walk across a high school stage for graduation in about twelve years from now." John was smiling as he thought of how proud he would be to cheer and applaud his son as he strode across a stage with diploma in hand.

"No, John now you just stop that. I don't want to lose sight of him as the sweet baby boy he is right now. Listen I can't talk much because I am at work, but all of his records are in the security safe in the closet. I will most likely be home a bit later than usual tonight because I have to get caught up with some things that piled up on me. But text me when you finish at the doctors to let me know how things went, and I will see you when I get home. Call me if you need anything."

"We will be just fine, and I will text you. I will keep a plate for you in the microwave. Goodbye."

Wanda tried to regain concentration of the work at hand, but her mind flooded with thoughts of Andy. Somewhere deep in her heart she still had a longing for him even though she knew it was taboo and very wrong of her to entertain the thought of them being together. However, she could not easily shake the memories of the wild and passionate love making that had produced Raymond.

She still marveled at how she could think of Andy and still know that she had a legal obligation to John. She felt as though she most certainly had to put in the effort with John for the sake of their marriage and the new start she wanted with their family. Even though the betrayal and pain of the hurtful things that John had done to put her life in turmoil several years ago was enough to consider a divorce, she thought that she owed him at least a good effort of commitment.

In hind sight she realized that she was no longer the same woman she had been before he was incarcerated, either. It had been over two years since she last went to church, and she had all but abandoned her girlfriends who were steadfast with their emotional support and encouraging her through the most difficult time of her life. She felt guilty for alienating them and not attending the various church functions and social gatherings that they consistently invited her to. The guilt kept piling up every Sunday when she would wake up and find herself driving by the church on her way to Planet Fitness. The guilt was even worse when she drove by it on the way to Andy's house for yet another sin laden session of forbidden love. Her Sunday's also served as an alibi to see Andy. John was blinded to her routine of the Sunday morning ritual that supposedly led to the church door, when it actuality it led to Andy's bedroom.

Later that afternoon John opened the bedroom door to see Raymond sound asleep. He looked peaceful and seemed to be smiling. He hated to wake him up during a much-needed nap, but he did not want to explain to Wanda why he missed a vital appointment. He decided he would let him sleep just a couple minutes longer while he searched the safe for his records. He went back to his bedroom and opened the closet door and pulled out the white security case that still had the key inserted. Upon opening it he found a dark brown binder laying neatly on top of the other hanging files, with the word Raymond on it.

He quickly opened it up and began thumbing through the papers and documents one by one, scanning the title as he thumbed along. He stopped abruptly when one document had a gold seal from the State of Maryland caught his eye. He pulled the document closer to the light to see an authentic birth certificate for Raymond Andy Evans. Wait, surely, he did not read that correctly. Raymond Andy Evans. He stared at the name on the birth certificate while recalling the child in the next room as Raymond Simpson. The birth father line was typed as unknown, the mother however he was all too familiar with. It was none other than Wanda Evans. He looked in disbelief at the name, and then the thoughts came rushing in of the conversation he had with Tyrone. The shock began to creep onto him. He felt his breathing increase and the unease of emotions that were beginning to crash onto him.

He sat down on the floor in utter disbelief of what was just revealed to him. Maybe there is something wrong, perhaps a mistake. But quickly his mind snapped back to the reality of the authentic birth certificate, realizing that a government document with a state seal, was indeed the real deal. Regardless of how he wanted to displace the truth of the finding, the reality was that Raymond Simpson or Raymond Andy Evans was in fact a love child of his wife Wanda who had been conceived by another man.

He continued to move through the folder looking at different notes written by the adoption agency. Toward the back of the folder he saw another separate vanilla folder with the name Raymond Simpson written in bold red letters. He opened it and pulled out several pages of documents from the Barker Adoption Foundation located in Bethesda, Maryland.

Quickly scanning the pages, he looked to see who had signed the various pages authorizing the adoption. He only found two names with various signatures from each. Wanda Evans and Andy Simpson. John's mind began to whirl with curiosity about the Barker Adoption Foundation and wanted to run to the computer and look it up. All of a sudden Andy Simpson was the most person of interest to John. However, glancing at the clock on the wall he knew he had to get Raymond up and going to the doctor, because after all the traffic at that time of afternoon was unforgiving and unpredictable. He put all the paperwork back into the folder and brought the entire file with him to the dining room table. He quickly got Raymond up and dressed and within a few minutes he was pulling out of the driveway to the local doctor, with the file laying on the front seat.

During the short drive, John occasionally glanced at Raymond in the back who was slumped down in the car seat with his head leaning to one side. It was clear he was about to doze off yet again. John's thoughts began to plague him about the birth certificate and the obvious knowledge of Wanda's infidelity. How could she? Was this the price he had to pay for his incarceration? Had his absence put so much of a strain on her that she felt the need to. .no, he just could not get himself to agree to it. There was no acceptable excuse or reason, he would not allow himself to even condone it for a moment. He just had to function and get through the rest of the day. However, the undeniable event of confronting her about this would change their lives going forward. All of his Christian knowledge and spiritual growth seemed useless and powerless for the test of life that was just hours away.

The appointment went very smoothly and in less than one hour the doctor had signed off on papers verifying that Raymond was up to date on all of the required vaccinations and that he was a very healthy boy.

John thanked the doctor and then headed for home with Raymond yet again nodding out during the ride. It was an agonizing ride for John going back home. On more than one occasion he had thought about calling Wanda and exploding his growing anger onto her. Of course, the rational side of him knew that it would be useless and what he needed more than anything else was answers. He needed answers from her and from God about why this was happening in his life. The questions began to flood his mind. Why did he not pick up on it? Had the suspicions that Tyrone had about Larry been right all along?

With each mile his heart grew heavier. The thought of having to confront Wanda and face the truth of her infidelity was more than he could bare. Even though his heart was breaking, he did not have the luxury of letting his emotions consume him. It would still be a few more hours before Wanda was to come home.

Pulling into the driveway he found Raymond still sleeping soundly. He looked at him for a few seconds and wondered how many children came into the world under unusual circumstances. He thought of his own birth and how to this very day there were a lot of unanswered questions of why he had never seen his birth parents. His name he wore as a badge of honor to the parents who conceived him out of wedlock. While he hated the fact that he had been abandoned at birth, he at least could give them moral credit for not having chosen abortion as the solution to their problem.

Minutes later after feeding and changing Raymond, John gently placed him back in his bed hoping he would be sleeping when Wanda came home.

Still emotionally exhausted, he went to the living room and sat on the couch and turned on the television. The same old negative news story of the day was playing out on NBC. He changed channels but nothing could hold his attention or take his mind off of the consuming thoughts of his recent discovery. He turned it off, took a deep breath, picked up his cell phone and sent a text to Wanda informing her that the doctor visit was complete, and that Raymond had been medically cleared for school registration. He was grateful for the quick but simple response of "thank you." He needed some time to think about how to confront her and what strategy to employ to get her to reveal the truth that he already knew.

A deep sense of regret came over him as he thought and reflected back on the times he had treaded outside of the bounds of marriage. It had always been the emotional closeness that he had with various women that filled his need of engagement and contentment. Sure, there were very attractive women physically, but John savored the pillow talk and three-hour conversations with women who wanted to be listened to and vice versa, far more than the few minutes of sexual bliss. In truth he doubted his sexual performance with the younger women and did not want to risk the worst kind of rejection that would surely shatter his ego. He was well along in his midlife and did not know that the deep sense of adventure and unbridled and forbidden passion was slowly coming to the forefront of his thought life before he was incarcerated.

Even though that life seemed to be a million miles away, he was still fearful that under the right circumstances he would revert to his old ways and start down a path that he would not easily get off of. He had read in the Bible to be cautious of putting oneself in situations where temptation would overtake him. He tried to rationalize how unfair this was. Didn't he get a new start with God, and made a determination to go in a new direction?

His mind began to wander about how to cope with a most certain confrontation with Wanda. The nagging thought of living with a cheating wife and the possibility of it continuing was now the thing he had heard from dozens of women he had talked to over the years. Had she given herself over to the hunt, the thrill, the enticement and forbidden fruit? Had she gotten comfortable in her ability to live two lives? Was this now her vitality for living and would it become her need? Or was it validation that he could not please her?

A familiar fear gripped him again as it had on the day of his arrest. He rehearsed in his mind the conversations with her about her inability to get pregnant. And just who was this Larry that Tyrone had so many suspicions about? Was what he was facing an act of karma or some other spiritual test that he needed to be victorious over. Perhaps this was the time to reach out for help, which meant he would have to be humble at a time when he felt like projecting anything but. He wanted to get some advice from the only person who perhaps would be sympathetic to his situation and also give some sound wisdom, before his confrontation with Wanda. That person would be Tyrone.

The phone jolted him from the nap he was taking in a rest area on I-95 north, just south of Baltimore, Maryland. For a moment Tyrone thought of ignoring it, but since his break was ending soon anyway, he decided to take the call.

"John, are you lost again? Is that why you are calling me on my break and much needed nap?"

"How ironic that you would say that. The truth is I am lost. Lost for words and I do need directions. But it has nothing to do with driving."

Tyrone was intrigued with that remark. "Oh, so tell me what's going on."

John could barely get the words out as his breathing increased. "Wanda has cheated on me, and Raymond is her child."

"Whoa! Now wait a minute. That is some heavy stuff you are saying. What do you mean exactly?"

"I saw the birth certificate. It is Wanda's baby!"

"Oh, my. Have you talked to her?"

"I haven't confronted her yet. I don't know what to do or what to say to her. I am afraid of the confrontation and that is why I am calling you to get some advice."

"Does she suspect that you know? What led to you finding out?" Tyrone felt a bit nervous that his friend had discovered such shocking news and wondered how he would handle it.

"No, she is still at work. Raymond had a doctor's appointment today that she had forgotten about. She called me from work after getting the reminder on her phone and asked if I could take him. She told me where his records were in the house. So, as I was getting him ready to go, I pulled out the files and stumbled across the birth certificate. Anyway, she is going to be coming home in about an hour or so and I don't know how this is going to go down."

Tyrone felt a little uneasy in being the point man for giving anyone advise, and especially on matters of this magnitude. "Umm. I just am at a lost like you are John. You know how much respect I have for Wanda, considering all that she has been through over the past several years."

"I know and believe me I am not wanting to believe any of this, but I know what I saw on the birth certificate."

"So who do you think the father is?"

John was reflecting back over the birthday party for Raymond and the uneasiness that Tyrone had about Larry. "Well, remember how you had some reservations about Larry? I suspect digging into who he is and his history might reveal some answers."

"OK, and what are you going to do? Remember that whatever you do you cannot violate your probation and you don't want your emotions to get the best of you when you talk to Wanda."

"Well I am actually hoping that she will come clean with everything when she realizes that I know the truth." Truth. John almost laughed out loud at the thought of any truth that had been told over the past few years. How could he be so blind?

"John, this is way bigger than you and certainly far more than you can handle. You are going to need some guidance and wisdom. I suggest you pray about this before you do anything. As a matter of fact I am willing to pray with you right now over the phone, so that the Holy Spirit will give you guidance and peace as this situation unfolds. Are you OK, with that?"

In that moment, John realized that it was possible that even he, had a false sense of security when it came to his faith. Yes, he became born again in prison, and had grown a lot in knowledge of the Bible, but what he was now facing would put his faith to the test in a way that he was not sure of. He remembered the familiar mantra of the prison chaplain, 'We walk by faith and not by sight.' How appropriate he thought, since he truly did not see any of this coming.

After a few minutes of praying with Tyrone, John hung up the phone and sat back on the couch. About forty-five minutes later, he heard the key turning in the door and Wanda appeared.

Chapter 43

The pounding in John's chest only increased with each passing moment as Wanda greeted him with a hug and a kiss. John could not help but think of the same gesture that had been used over 2000 years ago when Judas betrayed Jesus to his captors, with a hug and a kiss.

"So how was your day honey? Thank you so much for taking Raymond to the physical for me. I don't know how it slipped by me."

The knots and butterflies in his stomach he hoped was not visible to the outside. John spoke slowly and softly. "My day was rather revealing. Quite an eye opener."

The contortion and frown that took over the smile on Wanda's face was the biggest indicator that something big was in the air. "OK. What is that supposed to mean?" She looked perplexed.

"It means that you and I have to have a discussion about Raymond."

"What are you talking about? Wait a minute. Let me go check on him and I will be right back."

In a flash she disappeared to the back bedroom to check on Raymond who was still sleeping soundly. She quickly pulled off her work clothes and dawned sweatpants and a pink pullover t-shirt. Her pace quickened down the hall to the living room where she saw John staring at the floor looking dejected.

The tone of his voice began to drudge up her worse fears regarding the health of Raymond. Had the doctor discovered something devastating?

"So, what's going on with Raymond? I thought you told me the checkup was fine."

"The checkup is fine. Raymond is fine. I just want to know whose child he is, Wanda." He looked at her eyes with a stare of desperation, hoping that it had been a big misunderstanding and that the woman in front of him would have an explanation that would give him a sigh of relief from his suspicions.

Wanda began to feel weak and lightheaded with instant nausea increasing upon her. She had the same feelings just prior to passing out in the police station a few years earlier. In the moments that passed before she opened her mouth to speak, her mind replayed all those nights with Andy and the precise planning that had gone into bringing Raymond into their lives. If only Andy were here now to give her instant calm and guidance on this unraveling of the truth.

She slowly approached the couch and motioned for him to come sit beside her, with her arms folded and slowly began to rock back and forth. She tilted her head back and closed her eyes tightly as if trying to contain the pain. "Oh John. I have something to tell you and you are not going to like this. Raymond is my child. I am his birth mother. I'm sorry, but you are not the father." She wanted to quickly blurt out who the father was, but emotions overcame her and a long pause set in.

John was processing what she said when he pressed for more. "Is there anything or anyone you want to add to that?" He was calculating and deliberate with his wording.

The gut-wrenching emotions hit her again. "The father is my ex, Andy Johnson."

"Andy Johnson. Do I know him, or have we met?"

"Yes, you do know him, and you met him at the birthday party. Larry and Andy are one in the same." She dropped her head in utter shame and buried her face into her hands.

John pulled her hands away from her face and looked into her eyes searching for the lost soul that was once there. "I don't know what to say. I'm numb, just numb from hearing this from you. Maybe there is something wrong with me for wanting to know all the gory details, but

I do. How and why may not do anything for our future, but I think you owe me that much."

It felt horrible saying that she owed him anything considering what he had put her through over the past few years due to his incarceration and infidelity. However, his statement did not go unnoticed by Wanda.

"Owe you! Yeah, I owe you! I slept with another man because of you John! Because you left me, and I felt abandoned and vulnerable. So yes, I turned to the only person I had. How dare you to pull your 'holy than thou' shit on me. How do you like it John? We are both mirror images of each other!"

"Wanda, a minute ago you were ready to spill your guts about what you had done. But what you are saying now does not sound like a confession but rather an excuse to justify your deeds. My wrongs, don't exonerate you."

"Whatever!"

The next few minutes of intense arguing left them both mentally and emotionally drained. They hurled insults and harsh words that cut deep. Neither seemed to be mindful of Raymond who was crying in the other room.

The reality of the worse scenario of his marriage falling apart weighed heavily on John. He knew that from this moment on he would have to come to terms with him being half of the trouble and blame for its demise, but he needed to test the waters to see where her heart was at in this moment of marital crisis. "So, where do we go from here?"

She looked at him with the tears freely streaming down her face. "There's no where we can go. Even if Andy and I had not reconnected, this marriage was long ago vacated by the both of us." She began to sob loudly. "We have to see it for what it is. Our unhappiness didn't start recently. I have felt alone in this marriage for many years. There wasn't much difference between the loneliness I felt when you were locked up and the way I felt when you were here. The fact that you felt the need to cheat on me tells me that I am not enough for you. So, there is someone out there who is, and I want to give you the freedom to go find her."

He could barely swallow the lump in his throat as the words hit like a sledgehammer to his chest. The pain crippled his thoughts from being vocal. He could only ache. The passing but fleeting thought of divorce had crossed his mind from time to time, but after hearing it from her as an only option, he became scared. He did not want to admit just how vulnerable he was in that moment, and yet if he let the stinging words of divorce reverberate it would most likely be the dominating theme of any and all future conversations between them. He struggled to speak.

"Umm. . . I know you have valid concerns and I know that I have contributed a lot of things that have gotten us to this moment. But for me, there is a moment after. There is a tomorrow. A tomorrow that I want you to be a part of."

She butted in, "Tomorrow! There is no tomorrow between us John! Nothing will ever be the same between us."

He looked at her and could see a woman who had a lost soul and he saw a woman who wanted to know what would happen next. "We are not in a good place right now. I think we both can see that. And you are right, that nothing will be the same between us. Nor should it. It needs to be better. We are at rock bottom here, so the only direction left is up." He paused while assessing to see if there was a glimmer of hope in his words. He wanted to see the fighter she had been in years passed. A part of him said that to see if he could muster a comeback after taking her down to the depths of despair. He envisioned two drowning people in the ocean struggling to save each other, all the while needing to preserve their individual lives at any cost.

It was in that moment that a verse came to the forefront of his mind, like a lightning bolt that crackles the atmosphere. 'But when he saw the wind, he was afraid and, beginning to sink, cried out, "Lord, save me!' "You know we are not in a position to save ourselves here. Listen, I know you don't want to hear this, and to be honest I don't want to say it, but we are going to have to feel what we feel for now and then get help getting back on track both as individuals and as a couple. We are both lost right now, Wanda."

"You are lost? I thought you were the man who Christ found and all that Christian bullshit you have been telling me the last couple of years." She regretted the words the moment they parted her lips. She spoke in anger, disgust and remorse about her own departure from the Christian faith. Maybe he was right in that she was lost and needed to find her way back as a person before they could possible hope to repair the marriage as a couple.

"Well to be honest, that is the one if not the only thing we have in our favor. I know that we both at one point in our lives have been called and set apart for the discipleship walk with Jesus Christ, with the end goal of transforming our lives into his likeness. I have no doubt in my mind about that. Do you remember the story of Peter who saw Jesus walking across the lake and he was in the boat? How he mustered the faith to get out of the boat and literally walked on water toward Jesus? As you recall he took his eyes off of Jesus and looked at the huge waves and heard the storm that frightened him so much that he lost hope and faith in that moment and began to sink thinking that he would drown. He cried out the only words he could get out in his moment of crisis. He did not have time for a prayer meeting or to deliberate how he was going to keep from drowning. He yelled out at the only person capable of saving him. He did not sugar coat it or make it sound reverent. He cried out what we or anyone in trouble and drowning like we are should say, 'Lord save me!'"

She looked at him while wondering if he was just repeating something that was programed into him from the many bible sessions he attended while in prison. Although she wanted to easily dismiss what he said, somewhere deep inside she knew that for the moment what he told her was what she needed to hear even if it was something that she was not ready to fully accept. It would be something to consider at another time, because in the back ground she could hear the faint cry of Raymond.

"Saving, yes that is something we all need from time to time I suppose. And right now, I need to go save Raymond." She got up and quickly walked to Raymond's room, where upon entry it was abundantly clear that a diaper change was in order.

Chapter 44

That evening was exceedingly uncomfortable for the both of them. The long stretches of silence between them only magnified the trouble their marriage was in. John was in the living room where he escaped into the online realm with his computer, fascinated by the new technological advances that he had missed out on while incarcerated.

Wanda was in the bedroom trying to stay engrossed with a marketing book and taking notes on ways to close on some of her biggest clients, while the tv played with low sound in the background. Her attention and focus however wandered every couple minutes to the marriage crisis that loomed large in her mind. After a couple of attempts to read and comprehend the tedious tasks of the marketing book, she put it down on the nightstand next to the bed. Her thoughts turned to Andy.

She knew that sooner or later she would have to tell him about the discovery John had made and that new boundaries would have to be set. Even though her secret had been discovered and it was devastating to her personally, it also in a strange way was very liberating. She needed to talk to Andy not knowing what to expect after revealing that the affair had been exposed. Certainly it was not realistic to hope that reconciliation could take place between him and John. But nonetheless she had to confront him about everything that had taken place, and even though she did not know what the future held for her marriage, she did not want to mislead

Andy or give him false hope that they would be together. If there ever was a time to do the right thing, perhaps now was it.

She picked up the phone and called his number.

"Hello." Andy's voice sounded relaxed.

"Hi! I hope I did not catch you at a bad time."

"No, not at all. I'm just chilling. What are you up to? And how is Raymond?"

"Oh nothing much. Raymond is fine, we all are fine. Are you going to be home about nine tomorrow morning? I want to stop by for a few minutes before work."

"Yes, I will be here. Come on by. Will you be wearing your yoga pants that make you look so sexy and hot when you finish the gym?"

"Andy, I don't go to work in yoga pants, so no I won't be wearing them. Listen I have to go for now, but I will see you in the morning. Bye."

Andy was a little taken back by the briefness of the phone call. He thought that perhaps John was monitoring her every word. It had been several weeks since he heard from her, so he was anxious to connect with her again. He needed to know if the charade was still holding up as they had planned. For him, however he had other ambitions of trying to swing Wanda's love from John to him. He knew it was a long shot, but perhaps time was on his side.

The next morning John woke up early and turned to over to see Wanda sleeping soundly. His heart ached at the thought of losing her and Raymond because of his sins of the past that started them both down the road to infidelity. In reality he knew Jesus would forgive, but that did not mean that consequences would be avoided. As he looked at her, he wondered how close to God she was or had all the family turmoil made her bitter to anything spiritual related. The thought made him remorseful and realized that even though Wanda was responsible for her part of the marriage demise, he too had become a stumbling block to her. Now he just wanted to be a supporter and help her grow and gently entice her to come back to God's grace. Regaining her trust and respect would be extremely difficult. He did not have a clue of what to do or where to start, and in that moment a familiar verse came to mind. 'Lean not to your own understanding, but in all of your ways acknowledge him, and he shall direct your paths.' With those words ringing in his head, he got up and began his day, while meditating and praying that God would indeed direct him.

Her nervousness grew stronger with each passing mile as she made the short drive to Andy's house. She did not have a clever plan other than to tell him the truth and hope that she was not to emotional. She did not want a confrontation but just to establish the boundaries that needed to be in place between her and Andy.

Andy opened the door and greeted her with the boyish grin that often made her heart melt in years past. In that moment she knew she needed to be strong but could not deny the overwhelming desire to make love to him and in a fraction of a moment a thought came to her to even justify doing so. After all wasn't she contemplating the end of her marriage to John? The affair was out in the open so what further harm could another love making session do?

"Hi, come on in, I have been longing to give you a hug since our brief talk last night." He pulled her close to him for a long embrace, while slowly moving his arms in a long slow circular motion over her back and dipping his fingers with a gently caress of the small indentation along her spinal cord. He heard her softly moan, and then she pulled away with definitive force.

"Please, stop! I'm not going to be able to stay long and I am not here for that."

"Well, then, what are you here for?" Andy asked.

She felt an uneasiness with the way he said it. A fast and direct blurt should be blunt enough to get the butterflies to subside. "John knows about us and Raymond."

She searched his face to see if it would betray his thoughts. Only a blink of his eyes registered that perhaps he even heard her. Nothing in his facial expressions indicated that he just heard some shocking news about the massive long term charade being exposed. For a brief second it made her feel uncomfortable to know that perhaps the man standing in front of her had become way too good at living the lie. With each passing second of silence growing between them, her mind was becoming inundated with scripture on the subject of lying, liars and the end consequences thereof. The one that spoke the loudest with the most impact was, "All liars shall have their part in the lake of fire."

"Did you hear what I just said? He knows all about us and our scheme regarding Raymond. I reluctantly told him everything. I had no choice because of his digging around like a detective and a small mistake on my part."

"Why are you telling me this?"

She could not believe he was so emotionally removed from this conversation. Had he prepared himself for this moment and was this a way to soothe his guilty conscious?

"Are you even listening to me Andy?"

"If I was not listening I would not have asked you a question." He blurted loudly. "So the game is over, we deal with it and move on!"

She was furious. "We deal with it and move on? What the hell is wrong with you? There is no easy closure like that. This changes everything, between you, John and I."

"Ok so what do you want me to do and where do we go from here? I mean weren't you the one who said that having a baby with him would put you two back together? So it sounds like to me that you got what you wanted, and it's time to put your life together again with him. I have played my part and have nothing else to add. I will eventually deal with my feelings, and I think that it is time for you to deal with yours!"

"Listen I never wanted any of us to get hurt by this, and I know exactly how you feel. But we have to have some boundaries to make any of this work. So can we agree to that and still be friends?" Her softening tone of voice seemed to suggest a sadness that she was not prepared for.

He looked at her with that longing desire still begging her touch, and her kiss. "I suppose we don't have much of a choice, now that you have sealed your fate and mine."

"Please Andy, just stop. Don't do this to me. Do you know how hard it was for me to tell him the truth? Do you really think I could have gone on forever with this lie? I'm sorry, but even though you have seen me in my time of weakness, my spirit is a bit stronger and I have to believe that somewhere in me is a woman that wants to do the right thing. I have to get back to being the wife and now mother, that I was meant to be."

"You know a part of me says that I played the fool and that this is the price I have to pay, thinking that you would want to be in my life as more than a summertime fling."

"Summertime fling! Is that what you think this was? You still don't get it do you? She stared at him wondering what happened to the guy she had admired so much.

"Oh I get it alright. And that is the problem that I *actually* do get it. You know I have a heart with feelings too you know. Damn it! How could I put myself through this crap again?"

"You did it for love Andy, and that is not a bad reason, regardless of how it unfolds now."

He hated the softness in her voice because it told him that she had already resigned to her new life with John and just wanted to soften the blow for him, and her. He wondered if it was working.

"So, are you and him at peace with all of this?" Andy searched her face for any sign of doubt or regret, knowing that he would again come rushing in to rescue her, even if it was against his better judgement.

"You know, it's a bit surprising, but yeah, I think we are going to be OK. We put it all out there on the table and since we both have did each other wrong and cheated, it was like a breath of fresh air to let it all go and forgive and get a new slate. I'm not saying it's easy, and yes it will take some time, but we are going to let God do the heavy lifting when it comes to putting our marriage back together. We believe he can do it."

"Well good, I hope that works out for you?" He knew the moment he said it in a condescending manner she would easily pick up on it.

She shook her head. "Andy listen you don't have to pretend that everything is alright. I know this hurts even though I didn't want it to. I know it's not what you want to hear right now, but the truth is that you are going to heal and all of us are going to be alright. Just give it some time. In the meantime we probably should figure out our visitation arrangements for Raymond. Are you open to that?"

Andy wasn't sure what hurt the most, the fact that she was going to make a life with John or that she was so calculating in her method of dissolving the relationship she had with him. "It seems like you got it all figured out, and you seem ok with the way this is going down."

"Andy, please give me a break and cut me some slack. This is not easy for me, knowing how good you have been to me over the years and you have been there for me when I needed you most. We were both wrong to do this, and you know that."

"Don't you dare lecture me about right and wrong!" She flinched as he shouted.

"Ok, I'm sorry. I don't know what else to say."

A few minutes later she was driving off to the office, grateful that she had a job that would be a welcome distraction to all the emotional events in her life.

Chapter 45

Over the next six months the ebb and flow of very intense emotions surrounded John and Wanda. The fresh sting of betrayal opened up a deep wound inside John that he found to be increasingly harder and harder to ignore. The lingering guilt of his own infidelity burst to the forefront of the reasons why he thought Wanda did the same in kind. He had always known her to be a loyal and faithful partner and never once did he question her devotion to him. Now after coming face to face with his new reality, he questioned was it unreasonable to expect such devotion from anyone who was a member of the flawed human race. He was not naive, and he knew that having the title Christian did not exempt one from the common sins of mankind. His mind drifted to several verses to hear that "nothing is new under the sun." In a strange sort of way he found it comforting to know that what he and Wanda were dealing with and their exact experience had been duplicated over and over since the creation of Adam and Eve. Truly they were standing in the middle of a long line of sinners. Of course, equal to any of their sins he knew was the grace and mercy of a loving God. But could he bestow the grace God had given him to Wanda?

He struggled with forgiveness for his own sins and now he had to bestow to her what he could barely claim for himself. To him this whole situation was even uglier with the thought of having to raise a son that was not his. He knew he could not look at Raymond with hate or disgust and yet that is exactly what he felt when he did any meaningful interaction with him. More than once the thought of divorce entered his mind and he began to more readily justify the outcome of going through such an ordeal. Restarting life all over again as a single man seemed to be more appealing with each passing day. Yet he equally felt guilt even from the notion of divorcing her, because of how she endured his time of incarceration. Yes, she fell into adultery, but she still stuck by him in an unexplainable sort of way. Didn't he owe her something for that? His mind was torn with the thoughts of divorcing or the painful struggle to regain the shattered trust between the two of them.

The intimacy between the two of them had all but vanished. The phone calls when they were apart were short and brief and the silence spoke volumes. They were cordial to each other and did not try to engage in hostilities toward each other, but it was obvious that with just the right stimulant, the flames of anger would flare up. John seemed to be losing control a little bit at a time. How could a man who had been born again, now not have a clue how to navigate this turmoil in his life? He needed help and advice and more importantly he needed someone to vent his frustration to. He wondered what the impact of Tyrone's incarceration was like to his family or significant other. He would know better than anyone what it was like to try to pick up the shattered pieces of a home life and put it back together.

The next day at work, John texted Tyrone asking him to give him a call at his convenience.

Wanda, had managed to land another large account for the marketing firm and the company made sure that she was the one to give her full attention to keeping the new client happy and satisfied with their services. She welcomed the challenge and the added responsibility and felt that for the first time in a long time, she was actually needed and wanted. She just wished it had been equally so at home.

The strain of raising Raymond was ever present in her mind, as she juggled the duties of being a full-time mom and a woman who was setting her sights on ambitious career goals. John was doing his part, but because of the tear in their relationship all of his efforts seemed to be only out of obligation and maybe guilt driven. She wondered when they would have a heart to heart talk about their future, if there was a future for them. It was clear that some resolution had to be made because while they both were dealing with their demons privately, they could not keep up the outside appearances to the world, and especially to those who wanted to help get them back on track spiritually.

More than once Wanda hung up on some of her girlfriends who wanted to get together for a Sunday afternoon lunch gathering. While they were understanding to a point, it caused them to organize an intervention of sorts. Wanda had been sporadically attending church, and every time she walked through the front door she was overcome with the guilt and shame of her previous secret life. The road to redemption she knew had started with her full confession to John, but it did not ease the turmoil she felt inside. She had only asked for forgiveness as a obligatory thing to do, knowing that Christ had paid such a heavy price for her sin to be forgiven. Most of her life while she was at one time was very close to God, she never quite felt the freedom from sin that other Christians had seemed to experience on an ongoing basis. How come she could not get her heart to feel broken and contrite over what she had done?

The impact of her deception had other consequences that she could not easily ignore. She missed the once closeness she had with the church family. She missed the outings and crazy times and endless laughter that her fellow church members seemed to enjoy. She felt like she belonged and could count on these people for a lifetime of support. Now she felt alienated and distant and way to ashamed to tell anyone what was really going on. Of course, her distance was not lost on any of the other members, because in many prayer sessions her name came up with pleas to God to nurture and bring the sister back into the fold.

The pastor had made a couple phone calls to Wanda as a courtesy wellness check over the last three years and offered to come by and talk to both her and John after he was released from prison. She thanked him for the offer and thought it would be needed once John was a free man.

Now she was beginning to wonder if perhaps she should have called on him a lot sooner. With some determination to give her marriage the fighting chance it deserved she thought that maybe her and John should put together a real strategy for the hard work that needed to be done between them. For her it was an all or nothing gamble, because she could not keep living a lie of fake happiness just because John was no longer in prison. All the anguish she had endured while he was in was still fresh and it gave way to resentment and some bad arguments between them over the past several weeks. Something had to be done, or else it would all be in vain.

The cell phone ringing jolted John from his mid afternoon nap while on his lunch break. He often would sleep in the van at a secluded area in the large industrial complex just behind his office building.

"Hey Tyrone, I am glad you called. Are you on break yet?"

"Rolling to Burger King as we speak. What's up?"

"Well to be honest I am having a hard time adjusting to my new reality about Wanda, and Raymond. I don't like the feelings or the thoughts I am having about it."

"I have not been in your exact shoes regarding adultery or deceit that happened to you, but I do know that it's normal to feel whatever you are feeling. And I also know that God knows exactly what you are going through and his grace is more than enough to get you past this."

"I am lacking in love and forgiveness for her Tyrone, and she knows it and I am sure she can feel it."

"Of course she can, and you know what? She can feel love that you have for her just as easily if you let it be the dominating thing in your heart. But that will not happen until you surrender your emotions to God and let him do the healing in you. You cannot love her with your own heart still hurting. What I am saying is that you will need to love her and see her though the eyes of love and compassion that is greater than you. And as a result you will grow like never before."

Johns listened to him intently. "Ok and how do get to that point?"

"Prayer and surrender. Pray until your heart is surrendered, because it is at that point that God's love takes over to love her. In other words, he will be loving her back to himself through you. You will have to let yourself go and remove yourself and your ego to let it happen. Will it be easy? No, not at all. It is a process, a growing process for sure. But in the end you will be amazed at how transformed your life will be when you allow God to love her instead of you. Yes, you are the conduit, but it is his love that gets the job done."

"I know you are right. I did not know I would be in this situation where my faith would be challenged and put to the test this way. I wonder if I am up for it."

Tyrone was smiling on the other end of the phone. "Up for it? Tell me one thing that God cannot do?" A long pause of silence came between them. "I mean if you can actually think of something, you would be the first."

"I think I see your point." John said.

"No, I want you to see HIS point. It's the only point that matters."

"Yes, you are right. Well thanks for the chat I got to get going again. I might see you back in the office. Take care." John hung up and silently prayed for God to soften his heart and allow forgiveness and love to flow through him to Wanda.

Chapter 46

The next several weeks seemed to go unchanged, however every morning John quietly lay in bed as he was coming out of sleep and quickly turned his thoughts to God in prayer. With his wife laying soundly next to him, he began to pray in earnest all that was in his heart. His pillowcase was moist with tears as he quietly wept hoping that real love for Wanda would consume his heart. As of yet it had not.

He cordially went through the emotions of loving her and for the most part she responded in kind. Wanda, was amazed that he had not responded with hostility or displayed anger as he had before his incarceration when they had heated disagreements. She had some doubt in her own mind if they would ever get back to the point of love that was binding and solid. She wondered if the brokenness that she was feeling every now and then was reflecting onto him. It had been a long time since they actually had a deep heart to heart discussion about the future, mostly because having a future seemed so foreign to them both. And yet a future is exactly what they both secretly wanted and longed for.

John read as many passages about loving his wife as he could fine and picked up some copies of self-help books for couples, and casually left them throughout the house where Wanda was sure to take notice. He was intrigued about the correlation of loving his wife as Christ loved the church. He knew that the protection and unconditional love that Christ has for the church is the kind of love he would have to demonstrate to

Wanda. That would mean becoming more Christ like in both mind and heart. Yes, Tyrone was right, that would mean complete surrender because he lacked the ability to love her under his own understanding. He still was clinging to selfish motives for wanting a divorce or to justify any misdeeds to make himself seem self-righteous. This was not what Christ had in mind. Sooner or later he would have to give up the nonsense, and get on with being the kind of husband, servant and leader of the home that both he and Wanda needed him to be.

It was a very slow but deliberate process of gently guiding her back to Christ, but not as before with his arrogant better than thou attitude, but with a meekness that was far more effective and enticing to Wanda.

On a Friday evening when Wanda opened the door coming home from work, she was greeted by a large bouquet of flowers sitting on the table and a hand written note and a heart that said, "Sweetheart I have missed you, the real you, and I want to get back to being us!"

She peered into the kitchen where John was putting the final touches on a decorated table that had two lit candles. He looked up a bit startled. "Oh wow! You came home early I was thinking you were going to be another 30 minutes or so. Guess my surprise is no longer a surprise." He smiled at her.

"So what are you up to John? Whatever it is I like it so far."

"Well to be honest I was thinking that we have not had a real romantic dinner or outing in a while, and I wanted to do something on my own from start to finish, just to show you I really do love you and that I am in this with you with all of our faults, and that we shall both dance in the sun again."

"OK, I know that, and this is a nice surprise." Her heart was leaping inside her chest as she had not been catered to in such a long time by him.

"Well I hope you will still feel that way after trying my first attempt at baked salmon! I googled everything! So if it does not taste good blame Siri!"

He pulled the salmon out of the oven and placed it sizzling on a platter and put it on the table. After taking off his apron and pouring some wine into the glasses on the table, he walked around to her and pulled her close to him. "The one thing I do not have to google is this."

He kissed her long and hard, and the familiar moan from Wanda began to surge the passion between them.

"Perhaps we should dig into your salmon before we dive in too deep, if you know what I mean." Wanda teased him with a finger across his lips.

About thirty minutes later after the dinner and the effects of the wine began to set in, they embraced again and smiled at each other.

The kiss was long and passionate and with each passing minute the two began to undress each other while looking over their shoulder to make sure Raymond was soundly sleeping.

"We need to do this a lot more often." She said.

"I agree, and you know what else we need to do a lot more often?" He picked her up and slung her over his shoulders and started towards the bedroom and she began to laugh uncontrollably.

"You are crazy, you better put me down or you will hurt your back."

"Oh no, I have seen too many movies. Besides I am going to lay you down gently and then you know what happens from there."

She could barely get the words out from laughing so hard. "No, …what hap…happens next!"

The next morning they both woke up and motherly instincts brought Wanda to her feet, bounding out of bed and into the other room to check on Raymond. After changing him and getting him fed she drifted back to the bedroom to find John on his knees beside the bed, in prayer. She looked at him and thought how caring and loving it was to see him in prayer for them all. She felt the urge to join him even though she did not know what to pray. She moved close and knelt down beside him and gently put her arm across his back. He grabbed her other hand and leaned on her. Over the next ten minutes they both muttered words of hope and total surrender to the will of God and asked for guidance and strength for the unknown future between them. A few tears formed on both of their cheeks, both tears of joy for the renewed love and sorrow for the brokenness of their sin. In the end they both got up off of their knees with a newness in life.

It was refreshing to know that they both wanted a new beginning not only in their marriage but in their commitment to Christ. Although it was a bit awkward at first, they both became more comfortable with the Sunday services and quickly felt the love of the congregation.

Wanda, was grateful to have a family of true believers that never made her feel uncomfortable about her past prolonged absence. John seemed more than eager to have any chance or opportunity to serve.

Over the next year slowly they grew together as a couple and as Christians. Little Raymond was growing and soon would be the next challenge to their relationship. But just as a seasoned captain guiding a ship through an uncertain storm, John would gently guide them both back to the basics of what brought them to their newfound love for each other, Christ.

During a summer vacation a lady at the church decided to help out with Raymond so that John and Wanda could spend some quality time together and alone. John decided to take Wanda to a gorgeous lake for some quiet peaceful relaxation on the water. They packed a light lunch and rented a recreational boat and drove to the lake. A few minutes later John was rowing out into the middle of the lake, as Wanda was taking pictures.

"You are pretty good at this John. I never knew you were such a seaman." She was smiling at him. "I feel very safe with you, as a matter of fact you row like you drive with precision and caution."

He looked at her with disbelief. "Somehow that does not sound like the compliment I thought you were going for."

She laughed while taking her hand splashing water on him. "Shut up! My God, how many times have you made a turn slow and deliberate or waited to get enough space for two tractor trailers to fit in before turning into traffic?"

"Well, which one of us has a million-mile safe driving award, accident free? Enough said." He was gloating and smiling with contentment of his accomplishment.

She rolled her eyes with a grin, and splashed even more water on him. "Whatever!"

THE END

www.ingramcontent.com/pod-product-compliance
Lightning Source LLC
LaVergne TN
LVHW091536060526
838200LV00036B/633